WICKED & WISE

WICKED & WISE

How to Solve the World's Toughest Problems

ALAN WATKINS & KEN WILBER

Complete

First published in Great Britain in 2015
by Urbane Publications Ltd
Suite 3, Brown Europe House, 33/34 Gleamingwood Drive, Chatham,
Kent ME5 8RZ

Second Edition published by Complete Coherence Ltd. in 2021

A CIP catalogue record for this book is available
from the British Library.

Paperback ISBN 13: 978-1-9196014-2-7
ePub eBook ISBN 13: 978-1-9196014-3-4

Design and Typeset by The Invisible Man
Cover design by Julie Martin

We would like to dedicate this book to all those men and women around the world who look beyond their own needs and what they might want in life and serve a greater purpose than themselves. The people who can see that all of the issues we face, even problems within their own family, are our problems not "yours" or "mine". Such a stance reveals a deep understanding of the fact that we are not separate from each other and solving the world's toughest problems will need all of us.

Contents

Acknowledgements

It is a cliché but it's true that a book such as this would never have made it to publication without the hard work of many people and it is those individuals I would like to acknowledge here. First and foremost I would like to thank my co-author Ken Wilber. Ken has been a hero of mine for years since I read his *Brief History of Everything* over twenty years ago. Ken's work has probably made a bigger difference to my understanding of myself, the people around me and reality than just about anything else I have read. When we finally met a couple of years ago it felt to me that I was reconnecting with an older (and wiser) brother. I always had it in mind that I would like to co-author this first book in the series with Ken. But I was not sure whether he had the time or inclination to co-author with me. I was expecting, at best, that Ken might make a few comments that I could incorporate into the manuscript. As it turned out he became a full writing partner and he helped improve the book massively. More than that it was a joy to debate some of the critical points we were making in the text, as well as explore some issues that did not make the final edit. I feel we have become much closer as a result so thanks for that Bro!

In addition to Ken I would also like to acknowledge my editor Karen McCreadie. Karen and I have established a brilliant relationship that has enabled us to land my ideas, which are often a bit vague and sometimes complex in their construction, and she helps do this rapidly without losing intention or tone. I can no longer imagine doing a book without Karen's invaluable support. Not only has she been vital in unravelling some of the concepts that I wrestle with but we are able to laugh about the process too which keeps us both sane. Her ability to find a piece of research that I thought I read years ago is incredible, or better still come up with a more recent example that I had not even noticed. Thank you Karen and buckle up we have plenty more work to do.

Thirdly I would like to thank Matthew at Urbane publishing for having complete faith in the Wicked and Wise book series right from the outset. It was refreshing to find a publisher who understood what I wanted to achieve with the book series and believe in the worthwhile nature of its purpose. Without that commitment of support we would never have got the project off the ground so quickly. Publishing as an industry is currently in a state of transition and Matthew's flexibility and innovative approach to the demands of his market is truly a breath of fresh air. Thank you Mathew let's hope we manage to move the quality of the debate on the issues we will explore forward significantly.

Fourthly, I would like to thank my colleagues in Complete Coherence. Working on the book has taken time away from many other activities I probably should have been attending to within the business. Sometimes it is easy not to notice the small and not so small adjustments that people around you make when you are focused and in the pursuit of a specific goal. I want you all to know that this has not gone unnoticed. So to Carol, Sarah, Louise, Rebecca, Nathalie, Leanne, Maryam, Denise, Alan, Katie, Nick, Chris, Zander and Orowa thank you all so much for the general and very specific help you gave that made this possible.

I would also like to thank all those individuals cited and unnamed who have contributed to the arguments made here through their research and thoughtfulness. Without their efforts there is no evolution in the debate. There is no wisdom to match the wickedness of the problems we face.

Of course I would like to thank my family. My beautiful wife Sarah has, as usual, picked up so much of the work that writing this book has created in other areas of my life. Without that I could never have done this. Thank you for supporting me personally and being prepared to support the purpose of this book and what I hope it can achieve. I am truly blessed to have you alongside me asking, challenging, debating, encouraging, smiling and loving me. You are the centre of my world. Also thanks to my wonderful boys, Jack, Sam Joe and Charlie who make me so proud to be a father and give me hope that it is possible to change the future if we have enough boys to become thoughtful sensitive, compassionate men who are interested in all of us not just some of us.

Finally, thank you the reader. For without readers there are no authors. I hope you can find something in these pages that is of use to you on your journey. I hope it may encourage you to think about our future together amongst the wicked challenges we face and maybe embrace the wisdom we shared so we can all live more effectively together on this beautiful planet we call home.

Alan Watkins 2015

Preface

When Alan first asked me to co-author this book with him, my first inclination (although I truly adore Alan) was to decline—as I have almost always done with dozens of similar offers over several decades. It's not that I'm anti-social or don't play well with others; it's simply that, over some 5 decades of writing, I have ended up, for better or worse, creating a "system"—you can take certified courses, seminars, and trainings in it; there are even graduate degrees in the darn thing, and over 60 disciplines have been reinterpreted using its "Integral Meta-Theory" Framework—and this means there are actually "true" and "false" answers to test questions on it. In other words, although I like to think I am widely open to any and all new views and perspectives, when applying "my" work, there is a fair amount of "kosher" material that—unless you're introducing a new idea—has to be followed "correctly" if it has my name on it.

This makes serious coauthoring a rather narrowly governed (and therefore tricky) endeavor; not only you, but your partner, have to deeply understand the "system" and apply it in a fairly kosher fashion if it's going to pass muster with these requirements. So at first I very politely tended to avoid the issue, and genuinely offered to do a truly sincere Foreword. But Alan and I were happily working together on a major project at the time (still are), in constant contact, and so he would occasionally continue to bring the issue up. I finally explained the necessity to stick to the "kosher system" requirement, and Alan didn't hesitate saying that would not be a problem at all. He knew my stuff very well, and he (and his company, Complete Coherence) was starting a series of books based in part on this Integral Framework as a guiding organizational scaffold (along with, of course, a lot of their own significantly new contributions). He wanted the first book to outline the basic principles of the Integral Framework, and to do so by applying it to a genuine, widespread, and serious problem in today's world—namely, "wicked problems." And his point was that wicked problems haven't really been solved yet because they don't have a model complex enough (yet also elegant and simple enough) to cover all the issues enfolded in wicked problems. He genuinely felt—as do I—that Integral was exactly the model that could do this—as he put it, "Wicked problems require wicked solutions"—and the Integral Framework was about as wicked (complex and comprehensive) as you could get. So with that assurance—keeping whatever we said within the "Integral kosher" requirement—we jumped into the project with much excitement and enthusiasm. I don't want to get pathetically involved in some sort of braggadocio here, but we were both convinced that the Integral Framework really could go farther than any other efforts we had seen to start to alleviate, possibly even solve, the world's major wicked problems. (Of course, Integral has numerous other applications, but this is the one this book would focus on.)

With wonderful help from Karen McCreadie, we jumped into the project with real enthusiasm and I can only say "joy." With Alan's extensive and brilliant career in academic medicine and business consulting, and my working to make sure our contributions were "Integral kosher," the whole project came together with extraordinary ease and brightness. I think I speak for both of us when I say we are delighted with how the book turned out. It does demonstrate, my critics have so far agreed, that the enormously complex nature of wicked problems—a complexity that has prevented any one (or several) models or approaches from thus far being able to get a comprehensive handle on all of the major issues enwrapped in the wicked problem, thus so far failing to adequately address them—but here is fully matched by the comprehensive, inclusive, all-embracing nature of the Integral Meta-Model itself (again, with its enormously increased complexity shaking down into an enormously workable simplicity)—"a wicked problem matched for the first time by an equally wicked Framework," and thus covering all of the crucial bases and hence providing a genuinely possible solution to the complex mess.

If you find this approach usable and effective, you might want to keep an eye out for the rest of the Wicked and Wise book series published by Urbane (which I will be participating in), as well as any of my own books (some 25 books translated into upwards of 30 foreign languages—jut hit google for "Integral Theory" and take it from there.) The hope of both Alan and myself is that by using a more expanded, more inclusive "Integral Coherence" model, a great range of new areas, dimensions, methods, fields, and approaches will be made available to you for a more comprehensive approach to whatever problems you might be facing—from the simplest to the most complex and wicked. We have certainly found this Integral Coherence approach enormously useful and effective, and we can only hope that you find this approach equally compelling. With all good wishes....

Ken Wilber 2015

Part 1

What Makes Wicked Problems Wicked?

By now we are all beginning to realize that one of the most intractable problems is that of defining problems.

- Rittel & Webber

A few years ago I, (AW) was talking to the top 100 executives in one of the UK's largest public sector companies about the nature of change, more specifically cultural change. I was attempting to explain the driving forces that determine success or disable change initiatives. A guy sitting at one of the tables caught my eye with an intense stare, and he clearly had something to share so I invited him to speak. 'I've been with this company for thirty-one years,' he said. 'I have seen five 'cultural transformation' programmes come and go, and I can tell you from first-hand experience that the culture has not changed one inch.'

Many of us could probably tell a similar story. We have certainly seen political leaders sweep into office promising much and delivering little. We may have experienced business leaders describing the nature of the changes they plan to implement, only for things to remain pretty much the same. Of course these occurrences are not just confined to politics or business – they exist in all areas of life. However, they are certainly not a sign of failure or lack of authenticity, and they should not cause us to lose faith or stop trusting others.

But they may cause us to wonder why so many problems we hear about never get fixed and remain stubbornly unresolved. We often listen to the same old issues being talked about, sometimes for years. Occasionally there may be some small improvements, but more often than not, such changes reside in the small hamlet of *Window Dressing* on the outskirts of *Wishful Thinking* and a long way from the metropolis of *Real Change*.

There's an interesting paradox here. While some things never seem to change, we are living at a time of incredible change in the world. In fact it is now widely acknowledged that the world is speeding up at an astonishing rate and the speed of that change has itself changed - the exponential curve has become exponential and knowledge is doubling every 13 months or so.[1] Why is it that given this accelerating pace of change in the world, some things seem completely resistant to change?

Some of these intractable problems are large and seem completely insoluble, such as Middle Eastern conflict, human trafficking, poverty or climate change. These big issues transcend national borders and touch many parts of society. Other problems are more national but exist in many countries: corruption; educational systems that fail too many children; increasingly expensive non-sustainable health care systems; too few women in the C-suite or gender inequality. This suggests that intractable problems are not just defined by scale. Some apparently insoluble problems occur at a company level – after thirty-one years 'the culture hasn't changed one inch'. Some endemic issues occur at an even more personal level: 'Why are there no decent men/women anymore?' or 'Why can't I find a quality date on a Saturday night?'

Despite living at a time of great change, when we are faced with so many important problems that never seem to alter, most of us just shrug our shoulders with an air of resignation, saying 'That's life I suppose'. Or we may proffer the docile sister of resignation—namely, surrender—with a 'That's just the way it is'. But is this true? Is it just the way it is? Could the problems we currently perceive as completely intractable be solved? Are we doomed to suffer the perennial constraints of intractability? Is there any hope of meaningful progress on these problems in our lifetime? The simple answer is 'Yes' and this book will explain why and how.

Which brings us back to my response to that public sector executive – 'You are absolutely right,' I said. 'Most of the time there is no real progress on some of these types of problems – mainly because we don't understand the nature of the problem. And if

[1] Schilling DR (2013) 'Knowledge doubling every 12 months, soon to be every 12 hours', Industry Tap http://www.industrytap.com/knowledge-doubling-every-12-months-soon-to-be-every-12-hours/3950

we don't understand the problem then there can be no progress; how could there be? So if we are stuck in 'cultural confusion' and we really don't understand what culture is, how it changes over time, and how it differs from values, beliefs, attitudes, behaviour, mythology and a whole host of other concepts, then how can we possibly hope to change it?'

So 'the problem' is not really the problem – the real problem is our lack of understanding about the problem. To paraphrase Einstein: We can't solve problems with the same level of thinking that created the problems – we need a new level of thinking. The first step to bringing a new level of understanding to the nature of these complex issues is to dissect the features of extremely complex, difficult, or 'wicked problems'.

A Brief History of Wicked Problems

The term 'wicked problem' was originally used in a social planning context and is attributed to Professor Horst W J Rittel, who discussed the idea in seminars as early as 1967. He would talk of the difference between a 'tame' solvable problem and a 'wicked' intractable problem that was difficult or impossible to solve. The term 'wicked' was used not to suggest that the problem was somehow evil, although the consequences of these challenges can certainly appear evil, but rather because our knowledge and appreciation of the problem is always incomplete; the nature of the problem can appear contradictory and it's constantly changing.

It wasn't until 1973 that Rittel, then Professor of Science of Design at the University of California, Berkley, along with Melvin M Webber, Professor of City Planning at the same University, formalised the concept of wicked problems. Their argument summed up in their paper's Abstract stated, 'The search for scientific bases for confronting problems of social policy is bound to fail, because of the nature of these problems. They are 'wicked' problems, whereas science has developed to deal with 'tame' problems. Policy problems cannot be definitively described. Moreover, in a pluralistic society, there is nothing like the undisputable public good; there is no objective definition of equity; policies that respond to social problems cannot be meaningfully correct or false; and it makes no sense to talk about 'optimal solutions' to social problems unless severe qualifications are imposed first. Even worse, there are no 'solutions' in the sense of definitive and objective answers.' [2]

Rittel and Webber presented a ten point list of 'distinguishing properties of planning-type' wicked problems. In simplified terms the ten properties are:

1. There is no definitive formulation of a wicked problem.
2. Wicked problems have no end point where the problem is considered 'fixed'.
3. It's not possible to identify all the possible solutions to a wicked problem.
4. Wicked problems have no binary right/wrong solution, only better or worse.
5. Every solution is a one-shot operation that can't be undone or redone.
6. There is no absolute test to measure the success of the solution.
7. Every wicked problem is essentially unique.
8. Every wicked problem can be considered to be a symptom of another problem.
9. Wicked problems can be explained in many ways.
10. Due to the consequences of each attempted solution, social planners can't be wrong.

---

[2] Rittel, H W J, M M. Webber (1973). 'Dilemmas in General Theory of Planning', *Policy Sciences, vol* 4: 155–169. http://www.uctc.net/mwebber/Rittel+Webber+Dilemmas+General_Theory_of_Planning.pdf

Rittel and Webber did a phenomenal job at helping us to appreciate and understand wicked problems so that we could begin a dialogue about how best to solve them. Their focus was on the wicked problems that existed in social planning and public policy, such as urban renewal, roadway construction or curriculum design. Of course wicked problems exist outside these thorny areas too. In recognition of this fact Dr Jeff Conklin, Director of CogNexus Institute and specialist in the fields of hypertext and collaborative technology research, sought to simplify and condense these definitions so they would apply to areas inside and outside planning and policy.

Effectively Conklin removed the characteristic that referred directly to planning and expanded the context to make the definitions more meaningful to other types of wicked problems. Conklin also posited that the wickedness of the problems we face was multiplied by social complexity (number and diversity of stakeholders) and fragmentation (the fact that those stakeholders increasingly see themselves as more separate than united) that made finding a genuine solution even harder.[3]

One of the implications that both Rittel *and* Webber and Conklin agree on is that wicked problems are inherently wicked because they deal with societal problems, that is, problems created and exacerbated by people. The former stating, 'As distinguishable from problems in the natural sciences, which are definable and separable and may have solutions that are findable, the problems of governmental planning – especially those of social or policy planning – are ill-defined; and they rely upon elusive political judgement for resolution.' They were adamant that wicked problems could never be solved but only re-solved over and over again.

And frankly if that was true in 1973 when Rittel and Webber wrote their seminal paper, then it is exponentially true today.

[3] Conklin, J. (2005) *Dialogue Mapping: Building Shared Understanding of Wicked Problem,* London: John Wiley & Sons.

Escalating Complexity

If it is people that amplify the wickedness of a problem, either through the sheer numbers involved or the diversity of individuals in terms of culture, opinions, values, beliefs, judgements, and so on, then as the number of people on the planet increases and the complexity of human expression increases, it will become even tougher to find answers to wicked problems.

In 1973, the global population was just under 4 billion; today it's almost double that! The increased challenge of population growth doesn't just come from a simple escalation in the numbers of people on the planet, but from the increase in complexity within our societies that such numbers create. These two factors amplify the effect of each other.

When our grandparents or even our parents were the age many of us are right now, the world they lived in was massively different to the one we experience today.

Back in the early 1980s, futurist and inventor Buckminster Fuller proposed 'the knowledge doubling curve'.[4] Fuller noticed that the more knowledge we accumulated, the faster we created more knowledge. Prior to 1900, the sum total of human knowledge doubled every one hundred years or so. By the end of the Second World War, the complete knowledge of humankind doubled every 25 years. Today knowledge doubles, on average, every 13 months.[5] Such is the rate of social and technological complexity that it's already been predicted that knowledge will eventually double in a matter of hours - 11 to be exact.[6]

---

[4] Fuller, R.B. (1981) *Critical Path*, Gordonville: St Martins Press.

[5] Schilling, D.R. (2013) 'Knowledge doubling every 12 months, soon to be every 12 hours', Industry Tap. http://www.industrytap.com/knowledge-doubling-every-12-months-soon-to-be-every-12-hours/3950

[6] IBM Global Technology Services (2006) 'The Toxic Terabyte: How data dumping threatens business efficiency'.

That's a staggering expansion of knowledge that is changing the world. What's perhaps even more interesting is that when Fuller first hypothesised about the knowledge doubling curve, there was no Internet, no worldwide web, no smart phones, no PCs or laptop computers, no satellite TV, no digital technology, no smart sensors, limited artificial intelligence and no social media. Considering the technological innovations of the last decade alone, it's easy to see how this trend is so transformational, for better or worse. In most modern companies we are already drowning in data. Data is no longer just held as words, numbers or images and archived. It is being digitised and datafied for on-going collection and analysis.

Most business leaders are already acutely aware that this data is valuable and that data is the new currency in a 'Big Data' world; but many have no idea how to use it, harness it, or protect it. It's overwhelming.

The complete and accurate definition of a wicked problem is crucial if we want to find the best solution; and yet the data, information and knowledge that now exist around the various wicked problems we face are vast. We could argue that given the amount and complexity of the data, we will never fully appreciate the parameters of the wicked problems. This is certainly true if we keep applying our current level of thinking to the wicked problems we face. Einstein was right: we need a new level of thinking and a new way of knowing.

Datification and Technological Advance

The data and knowledge explosion described by Fuller has been accelerated by a massive increase in technological capability and storage. For years, even as knowledge was doubling quietly in the background, there was nowhere to put the expanding volumes of data, no way of storing it; and considering the fairly rudimentary and unsophisticated ways of analyzing it, not much point worrying about it anyway.

Today, however, everything we do, say, write, visit or buy is leaving a digital data trail, or soon will, and all that data can now be stored and analysed.

There are now more objects and appliances collecting more types of data than people on the planet, and they are increasingly being connected together by the Internet of Things (IoT). The IoT is best described as a network of connecting and communicating wired or wireless devices, and it is Moore's Law that makes this innovation possible. In 1970s Gordon Moore, one of the inventors of integrated circuits, noticed that it was possible to squeeze twice as many transistors on an integrated circuit every 24 months. Moore's law therefore explains this exponential growth rate in the advance in technology. And it is this exponential growth that has changed just about every aspect of our lives, and it has made the Internet of Things possible.

US inventor and futurist Ray Kurzweil points out that there will be 1000 times more technological change in the 21st century than there was in the 20th century.[7] According to Kurzweil, even Moore's Law will be obsolete by 2019 because the rate of advancement will be even more rapid than the exponential growth it currently describes (Figure 1.1).

In his seminal essay *The Law of Accelerating Returns*, Kurzweil states, 'There's even exponential growth in the rate of exponential growth. Within a few decades, machine intelligence will surpass human intelligence, leading to The Singularity — technological change so rapid and profound it represents a rupture in the fabric of human history.'

Of course this rapid change has far reaching implications for virtually everyone on the planet. Nothing is static. Everything is fluid and dynamic. The speed, size and scope of change is literally creating, collapsing and recreating the playing field faster

---

7 Kurzweil, Ray (2013). *How to create a mind: The secret of human thought revealed,* New York: Penguin Books.

Figure 1.1: The accelerating pace of change

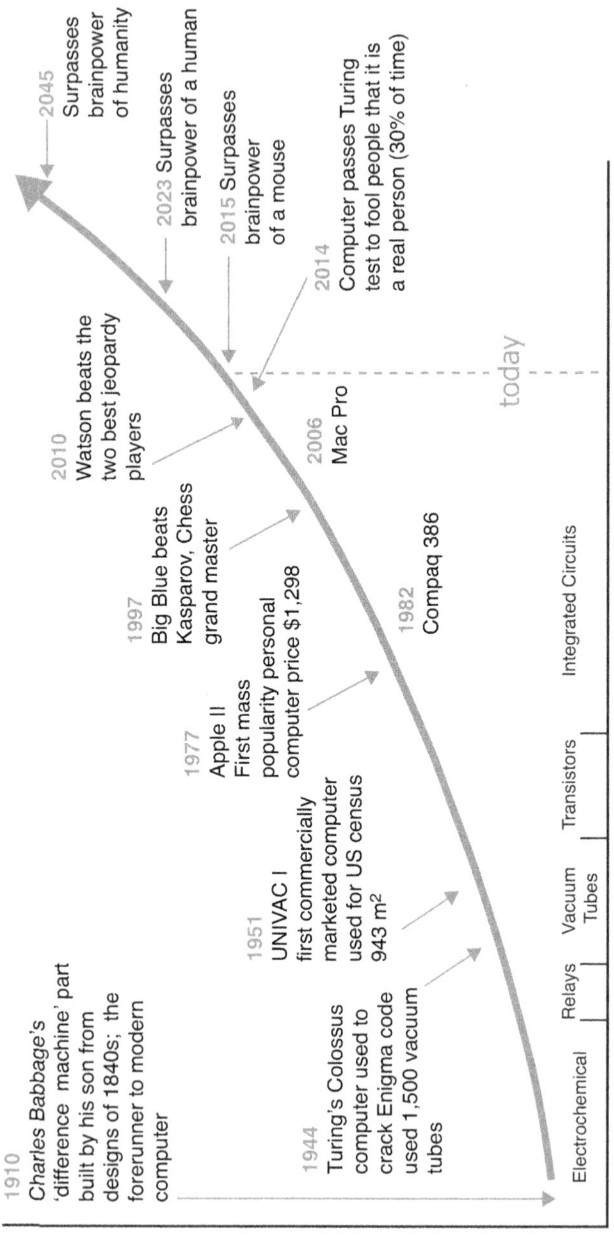

1910
Charles Babbage's
'difference machine' part
built by his son from
designs of 1840s; the
forerunner to modern
computer

1944
Turing's Colossus
computer used to
crack Enigma code
used 1,500 vacuum
tubes

1951
UNIVAC I
first commercially
marketed computer
used for US census
943 m^2

1977
Apple II
First mass
popularity personal
computer price $1,298

1982
Compaq 386

1997
Big Blue beats
Kasparov, Chess
grand master

2006
Mac Pro

2010
Watson beats the
two best jeopardy
players

2014
Computer passes Turing
test to fool people that it is
a real person (30% of time)

2015 Surpasses
brainpower
of a mouse

2023 Surpasses
brainpower of a human

2045
Surpasses
brainpower
of humanity

today

Electrochemical
Relays
Vacuum
Tubes
Transistors
Integrated Circuits

1900
1920
1940
1960
1980
2000
2020
2045

than ever before. Which means that getting a workable stable handle on what the problem is today may render that same definition obsolete tomorrow!

Clearly this rapid rise in complexity is amplifying the wicked problems we already face. This is fuelling the urgent need to find a workable template that we can apply. And the template itself must be able to evolve with the rapid evolution of the problem. If traditionally we have been unable to define the wicked problems, then increasing complexity is going to exacerbate that challenge, not improve it. If wicked problems already have no clear end point, and the rate of change in the environment in which the solutions are implemented becomes even faster than it is now, then the risk is that the solutions we may come up with could be obsolete before they are even implemented!

The truth is in business, leaders are already deeply concerned that they and their people don't have the skills necessary to navigate normal business challenges – never mind turn their attention to the accumulating laundry list of wicked problems the world now faces. The digital revolution is over. There is no going back, so there is no way that we can somehow batten down the hatches and ride out this crazy VUCA phase (volatile, uncertain, complex and ambiguous). Despite how quickly things are changing in business and how volatile and complex the issues we face are now, it may never be this slow again.[8]

Confused Definitions

Rittel, Webber and Conklin and others have certainly helped us to grapple with the serious challenges we need to solve. But if you type 'Wicked Problems' into an online search engine, you will see a range of additional diagrams and definitions that simply

[8] Finkelstein, S. (2004). Why smart executives fail: And what you can learn from their mistakes. New York: Portfolio Trade, an imprint of Penguin Group.

appear to suit the author's purpose at the time. This confusion is not helpful. In fact, poor definition may be the single biggest obstacle we face in tackling wicked problems effectively.

In their paper Rittel and Webber stated, 'By now we are all beginning to realise that one of the most intractable problems is that of defining problems (of knowing what distinguishes an observed condition from a desired condition) and of locating problems (finding where in the complex causal networks the trouble really lies). In turn, and equally intractable, is the problem of identifying the actions that might effectively narrow the gap between what is and what ought to be. The formulation of a wicked problem is the problem.' [9] Conklin too appreciated this fact when he said, 'Part of the pain is a misunderstanding of the nature of the problems at hand.'[10]

Figuring out how to actually define the wicked problems we must address is actually the active ingredient in the wickedness. While this point may seem pedantic or nothing more than a semantic issue, it is not. Figuring out how to accurately define wicked problems is actually the central issue and where most of the initial work is required in solving them.

The key question is, 'Do any of these definitions get us closer to a definitive way that we could solve or perhaps re-solve wicked problems?'

Considering how many wicked problems we now face, we can only assume that any progress we may have already made is simply not enough. The reality is that the definition of a wicked problem is itself a wicked problem!

Which brings us back to the point we were making at the start

---

[9] Rittel, H. W. J., Webber, M. M. (1973). 'Dilemmas in General Theory of Planning' *Policy Sciences*, vol 4, pp. 55–169. http://www.uctc.net/mwebber/Rittel+Webber+Dilemmas+General_Theory_of_Planning.pdf

[10] Conklin, J. (2005) *Dialogue Mapping: Building Shared Understanding of Wicked Problem,* London: John Wiley & Sons.

of this chapter – the reason we can't fix wicked problems is largely because we don't understand the problem in the first place. Sure wicked problems have a set of characteristics that can help us to identify them; there may be dispute over what those characteristics are and they may change depending on the problem being discussed, but the fact remains that if we can't map all the contributing, interconnected factors that make the wicked problem wicked, then what we *don't* know, or are unaware of, will always derail the solution process.

Although Rittel and Webber recognised this fact, the majority of commentary ever since has missed it – the wicked problem isn't really the problem; the real problem is that we don't understand the wicked problems well enough to affect real solutions. The wicked problem isn't climate change; it's that we don't understand climate change or enough people don't understand climate change well enough – if they did we would collectively be taking very different actions than we are to rectify the potentially fatal damage we are doing right now.

The problem isn't gender diversity or a lack of women in business; the problem is we don't understand gender diversity and why that creates a lack of women in business. The problem isn't culture; it's that we don't understand culture. Too often the solutions put forward for dealing with wicked problems, or any problems for that matter, are much too simplistic. In one online diagram on wicked problems, for example, the authors have stated that a wicked problem requires 'behavioural change'. But everything requires behavioural change. Most solutions to most problems require some form of behavioural change. Solving wicked problems requires significantly more than behavioural change, both on an individual and collective level. It requires a change of mind or attitude that underlies behaviour, otherwise the change won't stick and those involved will go back to what they were doing originally. It also requires a change to beliefs – both individually and culturally. Not to mention institutional changes, political changes, social changes – which are all part of the very problem of definition.

So while those who have sought to define a wicked problem have all pointed to the fact that wicked problems are difficult to define, their own attempts to do so have then fallen short. This is one of the reasons that we have failed to move forward, which in fairness is hardly surprising because wicked problems are so difficult to define! The definition of a wicked problem has therefore got an inherent fault line in it that will cause the definition to fail, or often make matters worse and exacerbate the existing failure, or at best keep us trapped in the town of *No Progress*.

What we have therefore sought to do in this book is to stand on the shoulders of those who have gone before us in an effort to make the definition – and therefore the solution – more comprehensive. Our definition is an attempt to be more complete for the simple reason that unless we can adequately define the wicked problems to begin with, our chances of actually solving them are significantly diminished.

Often the definitions used simply reinforce the wickedness. In many cases, this is a direct result of the context the definition is offered in. For example, the original definition was created with planning problems in mind. Clearly some of those definitions do not hold true when they are used to explain wicked problems outside that context. Rittel and Webber talk about a solution being a one-shot operation. In other words, any attempt to solve the problem will have significant consequences that can't be completely undone. So when a new, alternative solution is attempted, it is difficult to know what caused what because the consequences of the previous solution can't be removed. You can't 'reset' the problem back to a starting point and therefore test various solutions in a process of trial and error to find the best one, because each attempt changes the problem and therefore changes the solution and the outcome. Rittel and Webber believed that you can't build a bridge, test its impact and then unbuild the bridge and try something else. But in some cases, outside that planning context, some degree of resetting is possible.

What we've done in this chapter therefore is to fold in the best bits of Rittel and Webber's original definition and take a more comprehensive, more inclusive, hopefully more enlightened view which takes the best of their insights – and indeed all the available perspectives, because they all have some value to offer.

At the heart of the 'Integral' mindset, which we will explore in more detail in Chapter Two, is the notion that no one person can be completely right all the time and no one can be completely wrong all the time. If we are to genuinely find workable long lasting solutions to the wicked problems we face then, we must step back to identify the elements that stand up to rigorous scrutiny and everyone agrees on, and then fold those common threads into something Rittel and Webber thought impossible – a definitive criteria that can help us to really understand wicked problems and find appropriate, more inclusive and holistic solutions.

Definition of a Wicked Problem for the Twenty-first Century

In order to really find a way to solve these intractable issues, we need a definition that can direct our thinking while also being sufficiently structured to provide a framework for exploration that takes all important considerations into account. And that is part of the claim that we are making, and part of how our approach should be judged: does our framework for exploration really 'take all important considerations into account?' Only an approach that truly does can be expected to help us. Only then can we really start to make headway with these issues.

We suggest therefore that a wicked problem has six key properties (Figure 1.2) that must be understood before real progress can be made:

1. A wicked problem is multi-dimensional
2. A wicked problem has multiple stakeholders
3. A wicked problem has multiple causes
4. A wicked problem has multiple symptoms
5. A wicked problem has multiple solutions
6. A wicked problem is constantly evolving

Figure 1.2: Definition of wicked problems

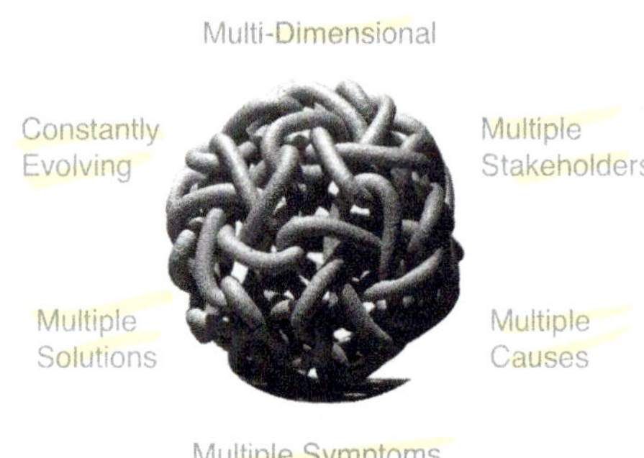

Too often the definition of a wicked problem is just too narrow. And a narrow definition will never solve a challenge that is as wide as an ocean. Equally if the definition becomes too broad or too abstract, it's equally useless. Something Rittel and Webber were clearly aware of when they stated, 'Of course the higher the level of a problem's formulation, the broader and more general it becomes: and the more difficult it becomes to do something about it.'

Seen from this context, it's easier to see why the various solutions to wicked problems have so often failed. When the definition is too narrow, we miss too much of the puzzle; and worse, we don't even realise we missed it because we aren't looking for it. On the other hand, if it's too abstract, it becomes too general and no headway is achieved.

To that end we have sought to simplify the definition, while also ensuring it is comprehensive enough to make a genuine difference.

Multi-Dimensional

In truth all problems – wicked and non-wicked alike – are multi-dimensional. The reason it's included here and is the first property of wicked problems is because it is almost exclusively ignored.

Every aspect of human experience and every second of that experience exist or are occurring in more than one dimension (see figure 1.3).

Just take a moment to consider this… As you are reading these words you are having an individual interior experience. Additional thoughts and feeling may be bubbling up to your conscious awareness. For example, you may be thinking, 'What on earth are they on about?' or 'Oh I've got to remember to pick up the dry cleaning tonight, otherwise I'll have no clean shirt for tomorrow.' You may feel confusion or irritated – whatever you

Figure 1.3: Original AQAL model

I (individual interior) Self and consciousness – invisible (i.e. thinking, feeling, emotions & awareness)	IT (individual exterior) Action and System (visible behaviour)
WE (collective interior) Culture and worldview	ITS (collective exterior) Social system and environment

are thinking or feeling as a result of the words on this page – it's a purely individual, interior experience. No one else is privy to what's happening inside you. As such you are experiencing that moment from the subjective interior dimension of 'I' or 'being'.

If you put the book down and go for a run, you move into exterior action. It's still you going for the run, but the experience is now also an exterior experience. Other people can witness you visibly running. In that moment, your experience is probably both individual interior and individual exterior. So you are probably thinking about stuff as you run and you are certainly feeling stuff as your physiology changes with the increased effort of running; plus you can be witnessed by others running around the harbour. Individual exterior is the 'IT' dimension of 'doing'.

If you happen to join up with your running group, you move into the 'WE' dimension of 'relating'. You may talk to your running buddies and share experiences or ask questions, but in that experience you are relating to other individuals. And that is a separate dimension too. As you all stop to rest, you may take in your environment and notice that a huge cruise liner is coming into the harbour. This experience is happening externally whether you are witnessing it or not, but you are also collectively witnessing it and discussing how the ship is going to manage to make the necessary turns, and you are also individually having an internal thought about the ship as it reminds you of one you went on with your family two years ago.

In the same way as the individual can be experienced from within ('I') or from without ('IT'), the group can be experienced from within (as a cultural 'WE') or from without (as a systems 'ITS'). The 'WE' experience is different for each of your running friends; but you all know exactly who is in that circle of friends and who is not in it; who belongs and who doesn't belong. You can't see this 'WE' circle of friendship 'out there' in the exterior world; just as your interior 'I' experience can't be seen running around 'out there' in the objective world. But nobody in the group doubts its existence, or the dimension that it makes up, which we might call 'relating'. Each 'I' in the 'WE group' feels directly related – some stronger, some weaker – to every other 'I' in the group.

And likewise that group can be looked at from its outside. You could actually videotape the entire group as it runs around the harbour. The 'borders' to this group tend to shift, just as the borders to a 'forest' or a 'town' can shift over time. For example, individual members of the running group may come and go, some may run on certain days, others may stop and play golf in the winter. But the group looked at from without – in a dimension we might call 'interacting' – does exactly that: the members interact, in this case, following the rules of the running group. In the forest's case, ecological principles govern its interaction; in the town, political and legal systems, among others, govern the behaviour – the interaction – of the town's members.

So every moment is occurring simultaneously in all three or four dimensions; 'I', 'WE', 'IT', and 'ITS'. And yet for the most part we don't realise that; and frankly, even if we do, we don't really see what the big deal is. Only it is a big deal because this deceptively simple frame, which we'll unpack in more detail in the next chapter, allows us to understand a good deal of the complexity of the modern world, and allows us to see why some of the most intractable wicked problems have become so intractable.

Someone experiencing poverty first-hand in a township in Africa is having a very different internal subjective experience of poverty than someone living in relative luxury in an office in Florida who is seeking to find objective solutions to poverty. The different and often disparate groups involved in coming up with collective interventions have a very different experience again, and much of that difference lies in the multi-dimensional nature of everyday life that we are not really conscious of. So naturally they will offer very different perspectives on what to do about poverty and what the important factors are that need addressing.

All problems, wicked and otherwise, can be viewed from these dimensions – doing, being, subjectively relating, or objectively interacting. When it comes to wicked problems, the common tendency is to almost exclusively focus on the exterior objective dimensions or 'Right-Hand' quadrants. In other words, we exclusively look at behaviours ('IT') or systems, processes ('ITS') in the world of 'doing' and objectively interacting. What are people doing about the problem? What systems and structures do we need to put in place? What do people or the planet need to 'do'? We completely ignore the interior subjective 'being' and 'relating' dimensions and any changes that will be required in those 'Left-Hand' quadrants. This is despite the fact that we already know that very often human relationships and social transactions are at the epicentre of all wicked problems. Wicked problems are social problems. Global warming requires individuals to change what they are 'doing' in enough numbers to reverse the damage. But they won't do that unless their 'being' can be changed and they can be connected with enough like-minded individuals through 'relating' to push through the change that alters the 'doing' and the actual interacting.

Wicked problems exist in a number of very important dimensions. At the very least they exist in the 'I,' 'WE,' 'IT,' and 'ITS' dimension – each with its own truths, its own values, its own perspectives, yet all of them incredibly significant. And as we'll see in this book if we don't recognise the multi-dimensional nature of wicked problems from the very start, then our attempts to solve them will continue to fail.

We see this happen in business all the time – the leader or executive team will fix the 'ITS' (i.e. a business process) but the business still doesn't work because the 'WE' of culture is still broken. Or a business consultant may advocate redundancies to cut costs in the business so that might make the business look better on paper, but if there is then no one to do the actual work then the business will still fail – it will just fail in a slightly different way or on a different dimension. So removing cost may be right for profitability, but because it is a solution that doesn't take the other dimensions of 'I' and 'WE' into account, then we simply create a problem that is potentially even more fatal than the problem the redundancies were designed to solve.

The multi-dimensionality of wicked problems is easier to see if we explore larger scale wicked problems. Take the Ukraine, for example. The country is deeply divided with the west of the country leaning towards the European Union and the east of the country leaning more towards Russia. The current instability and safety issues in the east could be addressed by flooding the eastern Ukrainian cities with pro-Europe security forces from the west. But a dramatic increase in gates, guards and guns will do very little to address the feelings of insecurity and fear of the people in those cities. Viewing security and safety as a purely external problem without addressing the multi-dimensional nature of security and safety means that it may not actually matter how many gates, guards and guns are employed – the people still won't feel secure and safe. You can't solve an interior problem (feeling unsafe and insecure) by employing an exterior solution (gates, guards and guns). And conversely you can't solve an exterior problem by employing an interior solution. If the entire population of Ukraine decided to just ignore the problem and hope it goes away, then nothing gets done and the problem becomes more deeply entrenched.

And here's the kicker – you can't deal with the dimensionality of a problem if you don't even realise the problem has a number of different dimensions to begin with. Plus each one of these four dimensions is affected by global megatrends often described using the PESTLE acronym.

PESTLE

These global megatrends actually affect 'I', 'WE', 'IT' and 'ITS' and yet they are only normally considered in terms of how they impact the latter two exterior dimensions. As we explore the PESTLE elements we've sought to redress this imbalance and point out some of the interior dimensions to these issues to widen the perspective and counter the typical 'reductionistic' approach. The PESTLE elements are:

P = Political
E = Economic
S = Sociological
T = Technological
L = Legal
E = Environmental

This widely used assessment acronym serves two very important purposes. It illustrates the 'multi-dimensional' aspect of wicked problems *and* it highlights the fundamental lack of awareness of anything other than the external dimension. It is this one-dimensional view which is holding us back. Virtually every one of the PESTLE issues is conventionally defined in almost nothing but objective, interactive, systems in the world of 'ITS.' Thus 'sociological' is specifically not 'psychological.' 'Technology' deals with the objective, material world of information transfer and communication device – and not with people's awareness or insights or feelings about information transfer. 'Legal' refers to the exterior rules and regulations that have automatic applications to individuals and organisations and nations – and does not explicitly include the topic of morals and ethics per se, or the interior thoughts and considerations that go into particular laws. 'Economics' is constantly criticised for only dealing with the exterior material exchanges of goods and services and their representation by items such as money or finance – and leaving out items such as 'values' or 'happiness' or 'caring' or similar interior feelings (leaving them out of, say, how to calculate the GDP, and there are already many economic approaches that explicitly include these interior factors).

If business, politicians, economists, even human rights organisations are using the PESTLE framework to assess their challenges, believing that this framework gives them the whole story, then it's small wonder we make such little progress! The point is that while each of these major areas – political, economic, sociological, technological, legal, and environmental – are important considerations, they can each be looked at through all four quadrants, and each time we do so we get another, very important perspective on the topic. Part of the problem with wicked problems is that they tend to be approached solely through the Lower-Right quadrant ('ITS'), looking at the collective issue through an objective, materialistic, scientistic, systems view. But if we take a problem such as climate change, the conclusion of the vast majority of the scientific community – those who approach all problems almost entirely from the 'ITS', objective, materialistic quadrants – is well over 90 per cent of them believe that climate change is caused by humans and that immediate reduction in CO_2 is recommended.

But nothing gets done, because the change requires that human beings change their hearts and minds – in the 'I' and 'WE' spaces. The multi-dimensionality of the problem – the fact that it exists in several different dimensions – means that all of the significant dimensions need to be addressed simultaneously. We know everything we need to know in the Lower-Right, objective, materialistic quadrant, the 'ITS' systems quadrant – but we are not yet treating 'I' and 'WE' effectively enough to get enough individuals to believe differently enough (in their Upper-Left 'I' dimension) to behave differently (in their Upper-Right 'IT' dimension) and thus, for example, make their opinions known to their political representatives and the companies that they buy their goods and services from. This problem is a wicked problem right at the start – it does not include how it appears and manifests in all four quadrants, and thus no truly comprehensive or inclusive approaches to it have yet been taken – and thus, virtually nothing is being done about it. PESTLE approaches are taken, but only in the Lower-Right quadrant, dealing with the objective, material, systems and structure aspects of the issue, and almost entirely missing the 'I' and 'WE' dimensions that are ultimately responsible for any changes actually happening. And the fact is, we already know a great deal about the growth and development – and actual stages – that humans go through in both the 'I' and 'WE' dimensions, information that could be put directly to use in this area – if leaders were simply aware of it. We'll return to this important topic in the next chapter.

Poverty: A case in point

Nowhere can the importance of a multi-dimensional approach be seen more clearly than with poverty – and how the PESTLE approach actually will not work effectively – and often just makes matters worse – unless all of its components are applied in all four quadrants.

So if we consider poverty, there are obviously political factors ('P') involved with different political parties believing the root causes lie in different directions. And different parties will often place the major blame for the cause of a problem in different quadrants, instead of seeing that all four quadrants are always involved. Thus, for example, a Conservative or Republican tends to view the cause of poverty as lying in the individual—he or she just doesn't work hard enough, or doesn't have a strong enough work ethic, or expects the government to do everything for them. Labour or Democratic believers, on the other hand, tend to see the problem as 'society's fault' – the individual is not to blame – it's the way they were raised, or poor parenting, or an oppressive society that represses their gender or race or belief or sexual preference. But it's certainly not the individual's fault. (So is the fault on the interior or the exterior?)

Likewise, because a Conservative or Republican government tends to believe in the power of the individual, they believe that everyone should stand on their own two feet and government should get out of the way so they can make their own way in the world through enterprise. The inference from this political perspective is that poverty is a choice because the individuals simply don't want to work hard enough to make their situation better. Conversely a Labour or Democrat government believes in the power of the collective and that we are stronger together helping each other. The implication from this political view is that poverty is something we all need to tackle together and some people are poor through absolutely no fault of their own. Of course both are correct to some extent or another (because all of these quadrants actually exist and are having a real impact), and the reality is that a combination of both of those perspectives and more is required to really eradicate poverty. Having all of these dimensions – 'I', 'WE', 'IT' and 'ITS' – involved, means that all of them need to be addressed. This is part of the reason why poverty has never been eradicated because political parties can't agree on the root causes or the solutions. This is often exacerbated by the nature of democracy itself. As the balance of power flips from one view to the other, many of the actions taken by one ruling party end up being undone when the opposition party comes to power and the new government then sets off in search of a solution in the opposite direction. Such political lurching can itself become the problem. Rather than politicians helping, they often inadvertently worsen the issues that some of them went into politics to resolve, largely because they aren't taking a comprehensive or inclusive enough perspective to begin with.

Poverty also has macroeconomic dimensions ('E'), and this is usually closely linked to political perspective. For example, more left-wing political parties may increase the welfare state and taxes on the working population or on business to pay for increased social provision, while the more right-wing parties usually seek to reduce the welfare state and taxes on business so that there is more incentive to make more money. Of course, neither of these solutions works alone because the problem is more complicated – and at either end of the political spectrum people are gaming the system. So at one end we have people who don't want to work or choose not to work because they can make more money on social benefits than they can going out to work, and at the other end we have huge corporate giants spending millions in shell companies and off-shore accounting creativity to avoid paying any tax at all if they can.

Of course poverty also has a sociological impact ('S') as the rich get richer and the poor get poorer; divisions emerge in society and a 'them' versus 'us' culture makes any real collaboration even harder.

The challenge of poverty is also intimately linked with low educational attainment. This is where 'I' and 'WE' dimensions can really swing into play. Many developed countries like to hold themselves up as examples of equal opportunity, but if you can buy a better education many parents will. In a world that is becoming increasingly digital, the better schools have better technology and better technology training, so the risk is that the impoverished communities become increasingly left behind and the poverty gap widens still further. And this is not solved simply by providing more computers for poor neighbourhoods, although that undoubtedly can help. The ability to access technology and take advantage of the new digital world requires great teaching resources. Fortunately, the trend for more and more teaching to be provided for free over the Internet can itself start to make a real impact. The Khan Academy is one such shining example of the democratisation of high quality education around the world. [11]

Technology ('T') has dramatically increased the degree of social connectivity in society. At last count, for example, Facebook had 1.2 billion users; and that does not include anyone in China where Renren reports that it currently has 250 million users. File sharing, social connectivity and the provision of free teaching on the web is also having an impact on legal systems globally. When we are increasingly connected, the very nature of defendable 'intellectual property' becomes increasingly problematic. Aggressive IP protectionism used to be the way that many rich multinational giants generated profits and kept others out of the market and in relative poverty. Simply by flexing their greater economic muscle, they could effectively shut out any new competitors through

[11] https://www.khanacademy.org/

litigious attacks and the defence of their 'property'. Today, the world is changing so quickly, first mover advantage is marginal at best because competitors can catch up or even leapfrog your product offering very rapidly. Others will simply innovate around your 'intellectual property' and by the time you get to court the relevance of your position may have diminished anyway.

This type of strategic legal IP defence (the 'L' in PESTLE) that we witnessed in the music industry and are still seeing in the publishing industry is increasingly pointless and a waste of resources, because the market that's being so vigorously defended is moving underfoot, or in some cases disappearing all together.

In this brave new world, brand and reputation is increasingly the only thing that can genuinely keep you ahead of your competitors. When the world is changing so quickly, it simply doesn't make sense to defend a 'set' position for too long. In the movie *Pirates of Silicon Valley* (1999), there is a scene where Jobs and Bill Gates are arguing and Gates gets the better of the discussion. As Gates walks out, Jobs whispers, 'But we still have a better product,' and Gates stops, turns around, and says, 'You still don't get it. That doesn't matter.' In other words, it's not just the degree of quality in the Right Hand material artefacts being sold, but the perception and desire in the Left Hand 'WE' market that determines the final outcome. All of the quadrants are important – and that's the major issue.

And finally some have argued persuasively that a great deal of the poverty trap is down to national environmental conditions ('E')[12]—both the natural environment and the institutional social environment. Climatic conditions and national culture can often impair all attempts to lift developing nations out of poverty.

No wonder wicked problems are so difficult to define – the

[12] Harrison P (1993) *Inside the Third World: An Anatomy of Poverty,* London: Penguin Books.

definition will change depending on each dimension and the perspective of every single stakeholder. Plus, there are actually 24 real and significant dimensions at play – the six PESTLE elements as experienced in each of the four quadrants! Tragically most approaches focus on three or four dimensions which at most leaves the remaining 'active' but unappreciated dimensions to blindside progress. The really 'wicked' part of these issues is our almost complete ignorance of their total and real causative elements

There is also absolutely no way to definitively formulate the problem or the solution because the answer, as typically given, is probably only going to address a quite small number of favoured dimensions with little regard to the repercussions of that solution in other areas or other dimensions. On that basis, no solution is ever 'right'; rather it is simply the 'most workable' or 'best at this time', because nothing more concrete is even possible when you bring a group of disparate interests together to hit a moving target. But one thing is certain: the more perspectives you take into account, which certainly includes 'I,' 'WE,' 'IT,' and 'ITS', then the better your 'best at this time' solution is likely to be because it gives you access to different views, different truths, different values, and different motivations that all need to be fully addressed. Conversely, the more perspectives you ignore or leave out, the worse your 'best at this time' solution is likely to be.

Taking a multi-dimensional approach can profoundly affect wicked problems. For example this approach is used by Foundation Paraguay – consistently voted as one of the top two or three organisations in the world for ending poverty most effectively.[13] Founder Martin Burt, former Chief of Staff to the President of Paraguay, started looking at poverty; and the first thing he noticed in all of the existing programs around the world was how poorly – how narrowly – they defined poverty. Most of them, again,

[13] http://www.fundacionparaguaya.org.py/?lang=en

were focused almost exclusively on the 'ITS' quadrant in some version of PESTLE. So Burt, explicitly following the model we will present in the next chapter, very carefully gathered evidence of what poverty looks like *in all four quadrants*. This gave him, not just the standard half-dozen to a dozen PESTLE type items, but 50 elements; each of these was then further explored from all four views. The result was 200 'characteristics' of poverty. He then searched extensively for programs and systems that showed some capacity to handle all 200 characteristics to create a total interwoven approach. By employing this more inclusive and comprehensive approach Burt almost immediately started gaining the success that has led to Foundation Paraguay's recognition in the field. This approach to the wicked problem of poverty worked where so many failed precisely because a more integral, multi-dimensional approach was taken.

Multiple Stakeholders

Not only are wicked problems multi-dimensional, but they involve multiple stakeholders – each of which are multi-dimensional in their own right.

Wicked problems are wicked mainly because they involve people – usually a lot of people. Clearly there are a lot of people affected by global warming, poor education or poverty, and there are a lot of people trying to find solutions to these intractable challenges. And people are notoriously difficult to manage or direct. Everyone is different. Each person sees the world in their own unique way based on where they were brought up, who brought them up, what culture they live in, what language they speak, their religious and political convictions, and so forth. People have different values, they have different cognitive capabilities, different levels of emotional intelligence, different levels of maturity, different belief systems – and therefore different ideas about the problems we face and how to tackle them..

Each stakeholder group therefore views the problem differently;

they have different motives, opinions and objectives and will invariably stand behind a version of 'the truth' that suits their purpose, while simultaneously dismissing all others

Making real headway in tackling wicked problems is especially thorny because the responsibility for finding a workable solution to wicked problems always cuts across many groups of people who will not all be aligned on the problem, the cause or the solution.

The solutions therefore come down to a matter of judgement about what is 'better', 'worse', 'good enough' or 'not good enough'. If we can't define the problem or the definition varies depending on the stakeholder we ask, then there can't be an accepted objective determination of the problem or the quality of the solution.

Take climate change, for example. There are stakeholders involved in this problem that don't even believe it's a problem! They believe that global warming is a cyclical phenomenon that has been occurring on the planet for millennia – often citing the Ice Age as evidence of this position. There are others who feel so passionately about solving this problem they will risk their lives in front line protests. Each believes the other is an idiot and that they are 100 per cent correct, and that their actions or inaction is fully justified.

Of course when you have multiple stakeholders, each of them takes a different perspective, which can make finding a collective, mutually agreed understanding of the problem hard enough, never mind a collective, mutually agreed solution.

Perspective taking – who's on first

At the heart of the problem of multiple stakeholders is the fact that most get stuck in a singular perspective and will often defend their view to 'the death'. Thus most people are totally immersed in their own perspective on the world and believe themselves to be 'right' and therefore all others must be 'wrong'. They are wedded to their 'I' perspective with unshakable certainty (they are stuck in their Upper-Left and don't know they're stuck). Such a binary right/wrong duality combined with the lack of awareness of which perspective they are taking is the real problem here. In other words it's not that we have different views on things; the problem is we are intransigently stuck in one view with no awareness that we are stuck.

Let us unpack this a little more. Most people when arguing about anything, a tame or a wicked problem, take one of three perspectives. These are called the first , second or third person perspective. For those a little rusty on their grammar, first person perspective is the person speaking; second person perspective is the person being spoken to; and third person perspective is the person or thing being spoken about.

First-person perspective is the personal subjective perspective. Stakeholders operating from the first person are focused on 'Me, My, I'. They enter discussions about how to grapple with and solve the problem believing they are right and everyone else is wrong. Their priority is to deliver on their own agenda and protect their own interests. When stakeholders communicate in the first person perspective, they are putting a stake in the ground about what they want, think or believe. As a result they tend to be very attached to what they communicate in the first person. The first person perspective is very passionate, it's powerful and engaging, but it can also be dogmatic and unyielding. It is based on personal experiences in the world, things the stakeholder has witnessed and 'knows' to be true because they have seen them with their own eyes. This is often the approach of religion or faith, as well as certain die-hard political positions.

If the stakeholders don't get stuck in first person perspective, then most likely they are stuck in the third-person rational, objective perspective. Stakeholders operating from the third person will helicopter up above the issue and present facts, figures and data to support their case. They believe the 'evidence' reveals 'the truth' and the answer must be evidence based. This is the approach of science (or more specifically, 'scientism'). These stakeholders will say things like, 'the evidence states' or 'the data doesn't lie'. This perspective is very common in business. It is often claimed that the answer is 'nothing personal'. As such people taking the third person perspective can inadvertently abdicate any personal responsibility for the outcome – a sort of 'it's not my fault... I was simply doing what the evidence suggested I should do' approach.

If stakeholders are not stuck in first or third then they may flip flop between both. At times they will hold firm to the direct, passionate first person perspective, stating their case and hanging on to that position come hell or high water. If such passionate advocacy doesn't work they may then flip into an objective rational third person perspective in an attempt to win the argument through meritocracy.

To add to the complexity, these two perspectives (first and third) are often deeply intertwined. For example, stakeholders will often use the objective data to validate their own first person perspective while disguising themselves as dispassionate rational observers. Alternatively they may delude themselves that they are taking an evidence-based approach when they are selectively choosing only those pieces of evidence that they happen to believe are correct based on their first person values.[14]

The great irony is that progress only ever tends to be made when stakeholders can access the gap between first and third and get into second person perspective taking. We have to be careful here, because there are degrees of second person perspective, which can run from the very narrow to the very broad. A narrow-view second person perspective might be a fundamentalist believer in a particular religion – their religion and their religion alone is true and real, and all others are false or even demonic. They have expanded their identity from a narrow first person 'me'

[14] Wilber K (1998) *The Marriage of Sense and Soul: Integrating Science and Religion,* New York: Random House.

to a wider 'us' (that includes second person), but that 'us' is a 'chosen people,' more special and select than any other group or any other 'us' in existence, and even selected by God to rule the world. It is this type of narrow second person perspective taking that celebrates the execution of French cartoonists for poking fun at their version of God, even though the cartoonists poke fun at every version of God.

But the more open version of second person is simply the perspective where a person can drop or expand their own narrow first person viewpoints and collaborate with others in making a larger 'we' or 'us.' Real collaboration occurs in the second-person perspective. Unfortunately very few people operate from this perspective, or have any real world experience of the difference it can make to successful collaboration; or they stop at a narrow, fundamentalist or extremely limited version of it.

Many of us have a nagging suspicion that we're not great at communication. If we are honest with ourselves, misunderstanding and miscommunication is not that rare in our lives. This is in part because we don't listen very effectively and partly because we just don't understand the anatomy of successful relationships. For most people, listening is simply 'waiting to speak'. So when we bring multiple stakeholders together in a room, they often don't really connect effectively with each other in a way that would solve problems. Instead they tend to transmit their own perspectives and hope that others agree with them. They are not really listening; they are waiting to get their point across so they can hopefully persuade everyone that they are right and everyone else is wrong. The whole gathering is not a real dialogue but a series of parallel monologues. In that process, they will flip into passionate advocacy of their view from the first-person perspective and may back it up with dispassionate data from the third person perspective. What they don't do is proactively build a shared commitment to find a workable solution that works for everyone. And that's because we don't really understand the secret to great relationship – second person perspectives.

When a first-person 'I' and a second-person 'you' come together, the result is a 'We.' So 'We' is sometimes counted as part of a successful second-person perspective. So what we have is that the 'I', 'WE' and 'IT' perspectives are first-, second-, and third-person viewpoints. Every major language in the world has these three major pronouns – further showing the ubiquitous and widespread recognised existence of the quadrants.

The second person perspective is the *shared* perspective (the Lower-Left 'WE' or relationship dimension). It's where the stakeholders give up their 'Me, My, I' first person perspective (or Upper-Left 'I') and surrender the desire to helicopter up to the third person observer perspective (the Right Hand 'IT/S'). Rather they set aside both first and third and build second – that which is common, shared, mutual. People who are skilled at creating second-person space will often go into increased detail or pull back to higher principles until they find some common ground that both parties can agree on. They will then build from there until they have a more solid basis for agreement and deeper connection. This is a very subtle and skilled process that some can do more naturally than others, but very few are conscious of these perspectives and even fewer are proactively moving between the perspectives in order to clarify the misunderstanding with the intent of creating a shared view that honours all parties.

Most non-wicked, albeit complex, problems have a few stakeholders and usually they all have different opinions about the problem, but the limited number of stakeholders means that resolution is often likely – eventually – especially if those stakeholders can move into the shared space of the second person perspective. For wicked problems, there are multiple stakeholders. Often they are all pulling in opposite directions and so no real headway is ever really made. And it is often this endless bickering and infighting that fuels the sense of futility around wicked problems, which makes them feel inevitable and unsolvable. But when stakeholders learn about the second person perspective –and actually take it to heart – the endless rounds of futile positioning can be transcended and some real connection and progress can be made.

Multiple Causes

Not only are wicked problems multi-dimensional and involve multiple stakeholders, but they have multiple causes. And of course the multiple stakeholders never agree about the multiple causes!

What causes poverty for example? You could argue that political unrest and the consequent leadership vacuum causes poverty, and certainly there is evidence to back that up. Countries that are in turmoil tend to have more people living in poverty than those that are stable. But political unrest is not the only cause of poverty. There is a very strong case that low educational attainment contributes to poverty. After all, if someone doesn't even have the basics in reading, writing and arithmetic it's very unlikely they are going to be able to land a job that pays more than a pittance. Lack of job opportunity also promotes poverty. Poverty can be caused following a natural disaster, or geographically if a large local employer closes down and there are few alternative employment prospects. Remember Foundation Paraguay identified 200 characteristics of poverty which point in a number of different causal directions.

When there are multiple causes, it becomes very difficult to separate those causes and identify those that are having the biggest impact. Plus they are often so intertwined and interdependent it's impossible to know for certain what is causing the wicked problem.

With regard to climate change, for example, some people believe that it's being caused largely by the burning of fossil fuel, others believe it's caused by normal cyclical patterns that occur on the planet every generation, and some still believe that climate change is caused by the explosion in global population – there are simply too many people on the planet. And others don't believe it's occurring at all.

Of course, whatever the agreed upon cause then determines the proposed solution. For example, a stakeholder group who is adamant that climate change is brought on by too many people on the planet is going to propose a radically different solution to the stakeholder group that believes that climate change is caused by the burning of fossil fuels. One is going to lobby the Pope to recommend birth control and the other is going to propose the investment in carbon capture green technology.

Ironically it's often only when we've implemented a solution, at great expense in terms of effort, time and cost, do we more fully appreciate the real causes. Perhaps nothing changes or perhaps the situation is made worse because we only start to understand the real causes, the degree of multi-dimensionality and stakeholder interdependency of a wicked problem, once we've failed to solve it. But seeing an implementation failure as part of the solution to the wicked problem runs contrary to the way we've been taught to solve problems. Traditionally we've been told that in order to solve a problem we need to gather all the relevant information, analyse that information and decide on the best course of action to solve the problem. Such an approach doesn't work with wicked problems because we can't understand the problem without knowing its context and we can't meaningfully search for all the information we need without first having some idea about what we think the cause is and therefore what we think the solution might be. In other words for wicked problems, everything is back to front. Only when we have implemented solutions based on judgement and assumption around cause do we fully appreciate the far-reaching interdependent complexity of the problem in the first place.

Plus we are encouraged to avoid failure at all costs from an early age. And yet when it comes to solving wicked problems, we absolutely must be comfortable with failure so that we can get closer to success. It's actually through the failure that we learn what we really need to learn as we tend to learn much less when we succeed with an answer.

Paradoxically when it comes to wicked problems, failure can cause success, which may itself be one of the reasons we can't seem to solve them because we are so obsessed with success that the very notion of failure has become so unpalatable that we have simply stopped trying.

It is however only through our repeated attempts to understand the causes and interdependencies between those causes that we begin to appreciate how inadequate our approach is, or how our proposed solution may have knock-on effects elsewhere that were not previously considered. These new insights require on-going adjustment to the definition of the problem and the proposed solution. Ultimately when we can't identify what is really causing the problem, we can't fully appreciate the interdependencies of these causes and that certainly amplifies the wickedness.

The 'way forward' we are proposing in the next chapter therefore allows us to systematically identify all the deeply significant causal factors – virtually all of which are completely ignored in any typical approach to difficult problems. Once understood, you will probably be as flabbergasted as we are at their almost universal exclusion or absence which will in turn give you a newfound appreciation for why most wicked problems remain wicked indeed.

Multiple Symptoms

Not only are wicked problems multi-dimensional, involve multiple stakeholders, and have multiple causes that no one can agree on, but they also have multiple symptoms. It is often these multiple symptoms which muddy the water when it comes to the various causes of the problem in the first place. Plus many of the symptoms of one wicked problem are wicked problems in their own right.

If you think about poverty and poor education for example, both are wicked problems and each is a symptom of the other. Poverty can be a symptom of poor education because unless an individual can gain at least a basic education where they can read, write and count, then it becomes much harder to secure a well-paying job.

Conversely poor education can also be a symptom of poverty because if a child is continuously sent to school without food because the parents can't afford breakfast, then that child will probably not have the concentration necessary to attain a good education that could help lift them out of poverty. Plus in many developing countries there may not be a school nearby, or the children may be removed from school and sent out to work so as to supplement the family income because the family is so poor. Of course those children then never get the education that could help them to break the poverty cycle.

Wicked problems are incredibly challenging to handle because of the interdependencies between causes, symptoms and potential solutions. If your overall approach, from the beginning, is geared to multiple dimensions and interdependencies in virtually all realms, then you are much more likely to be able to spot – and address – these multiple complexities from the start.

Complex inter-dependencies

Although 'six degrees of separation' is considered an urban myth, the idea that we live in an increasingly small world is not. We are incredibly interconnected and interdependent on things we may not even consider. Globalisation is a product of our escalating interdependency. The economic collapse of 2007 is a living example of that interdependence. Someone in a room in the US said, 'Hey, I have an idea: instead of trying to sell mortgages to our existing market that is increasingly saturated, we could effectively create a new market by lending to people we would normally reject. Let's call them sub-prime.' The logic was that it would be okay because the value of the underlying asset was increasing anyway, so if things did go wrong then the asset could be sold to recoup the investment. Except the assets stopped increasing. By which time other people in other rooms had come up with increasingly complicated ways to carve up the toxic debt and on-sell it in the market. And the collective decisions of, by some estimates as few as 50 individuals, ended up affecting everyone on the planet. What happens in the UK economy or the Japanese economy or US economy affects all the other economies because we are so interdependent.

And this interdependence is increasing. For example, one study looked at 43,060 transnational corporations and suggested that there were, in reality, only 147 companies that actually determine global outcomes across the planet.[15] Due to their share ownership, these companies, many of which are banks or financial institutions, control what happens in most of the other companies. For example, a few pension funds, insurance companies, mutual funds and sovereign wealth funds hold $65 trillion, or 35 per cent of all the world's financial assets.[16] So in effect 500 individuals, mainly men, pull the ownership strings of 147 companies which indirectly control the other 43,060 companies which in turn drive the global economy and determine the destiny of over 7 billion people.[17]

We are profoundly linked to each other – even though we may wish we were not. Of course when we don't understand the phenomena of interdependency, it's either your fault and your problem or my fault and my problem. We either ignore it or wash our hands of the situation because it's nothing to do with us, or we storm in from our singular first-perspective believing ours is the only right definition or solution. Either way the problem

---

15 Vitali S, Glattfelder JB, Battiston S. (2011) *The network of global corporate control*, PLoS One. 2011; vol 6, no.10, Epub 26 Oct 2011.

16 Barton, D (2011) 'Capitalism for the long term', *Harvard Business Review* March 2011.

17 Rothkopf D (2009) *Superclass: The Global Power Elite and the World They Are Making,* New York Farrar, Straus and Giroux.

persists because we don't fully appreciate these interconnections between causes, symptoms and how the proposed solutions will have a knock on effect and create unintended consequences in areas far removed from the original problem.

We may want to believe that we can turn our back on wicked problems, ignore the causes and pretend the symptoms don't exist, but the escalating interdependencies inherent in these issues means that they are not your problems or my problems – they are universally our problems, and pretending otherwise is utterly futile.

Unfortunately we don't fully understand these interdependencies, and this misunderstanding has us scurrying back to our own positions and holding fast. Instead of reaching out into the world to embrace this interdependence, we retreat back into our respective tribes, cultures or intellectual silos. We withdraw from the challenge by telling ourselves, 'That's got nothing to do with me, it's not my problem.' We turn our back on the issues we need to face because they seem so far removed from us and our everyday lives, and yet the nature of interdependency means that we will be affected by them one way or another. We simply can't afford to stick our head in the sand indefinitely.

The wicked problems we face as a species are now so significant and so pressing that we often feel overwhelmed by them and have no faith in our individual or collective ability to address them. So we ignore them – but, of course, we will not be able to ignore them forever.

The life model that states that I will just look after my little tribe here because my life is not affected by everybody else is no longer fit for purpose. Even if you go deep into the Amazon Rainforest, those tribes are now deeply affected by the outside world. The tribal elders can pretend that they aren't, even though they can hear the chainsaws, but the chainsaws will still come. We can pretend that the trouble in the Ukraine, global warming or the actions of the group calling themselves Islamic State are not our problem, either, but they are. In the same way that, 'Evil prospers when good men do nothing'; wicked problems prosper when good men and women fail to appreciate just how much our actions, decisions and inactions affect everyone else.

At this stage in our evolution, as a species there are simply not enough people who are sufficiently mature or evolved in their thinking to really appreciate this dynamic. Wicked problems are therefore fundamentally developmental problems, and if we really want to find a constructive way forward we need to adapt and take a quantum leap in our level of thinking so we can address the issues instead of just pretending that they don't exist or that they don't concern us because the nasty unpleasant symptoms are occurring on a different continent to a different 'tribe'. And this means very specifically, as we will see, that part of the solution to wicked problems will involve the actual growth and development of the consciousness of the change agents themselves.

Multiple Solutions

Clearly if a wicked problem is multi-dimensional, involves multiple stakeholders, has multiple causes that no one can agree on, and displays multiple symptoms, then there will inevitably be multiple potential solutions.

If, for example, a stakeholder group believes that poverty is caused by low educational attainment, then their conviction in that cause will influence their choice of potential solution. When sourcing a solution they will only look at education and how they can 'fix' education from their perspective. Many different stakeholders have proposed many different solutions for 'fixing' education. For example school league tables were introduced in the UK to rank all schools against each other based on student results. The idea was that if performance was measured and ranked it would improve education, but as a 'solution' it's fraught with problems. School league tables don't improve student performance in the same way that health care waiting lists don't improve the performance of the health care professional. What waiting lists and league tables really do is allow those within the various systems to take their eye off the real objective so as to effectively manipulate the outward appearance of performance. This drift towards the 'gamification' of any metric has become a huge, time- consuming activity in its own right. But just because we can manipulate the data to look like performance is improving, either by refusing to add people to waiting lists until the very last minute or by lowering the level at which an exam or assessment pass is granted, does not mean that performance is actually improving. It just means it looks like it's improving.

Initiatives designed to improve performance have in many cases achieved the exact opposite, as people spend their time fixing or fudging the results rather than improving them. In education, the introduction of 'continual assessment' in schools is another 'solution' to raise educational attainment. And yet like so many so-called solutions to wicked problems, those who implemented it didn't consider the consequences and didn't appreciate the interconnectivity between the various causes and symptoms, and so they just made matters worse. Clearly the idea was to ensure that children who didn't cope well with the intense stress of single tests or examinations were not unduly penalised. To some extent it was a valid idea, but a wicked problem is complex and interdependent, which means that any attempts to solve it often result in negative unintended consequences elsewhere. As a result, now all children are often stressed all the time, not just once at the end of the term or the end of the year.

Another stakeholder group determined to reduce poverty may believe that the solution simply lies in increasing the income that enters a household. Pretty logical – poverty is after all a lack of money. In an effort to alleviate child poverty, for example, many countries pay child benefit and ensure additional support is available to families with children. The unintended consequence of this well-intentioned initiative is that there is now a financial and social incentive to have children. As well as receiving government money per child, social housing is prioritised to parents, especially single parents. This seems logical in order to protect the children, but it also means that people game the system. Instead of using the money as it was intended, people are simply having more children than they really want, so they receive an income and have a place to live. Of course, if someone's primary purpose for having children is to get extra money and have their rent paid, then the money paid out to prevent child poverty is almost certainly not being spent on the children!

Wicked problems don't exist in a vacuum. Because the causes, parameters and objectives vary, often the so-called solutions end up exacerbating the problem or creating new additional problems. If we look again at education, is the objective to prove that something useful is taking place in school? Or, is it to cultivate our children's innate curiosity and work with what they know to develop a lifelong passion for learning? Is it to impart information about the world or equip children with transferable life skills that will grow and develop as *they* grow and develop? A lot of what happens in modern educational systems seems to be more focused on pouring information into children's heads and then rewarding them for regurgitating that information rather than genuinely educating them and preparing them for the world we live in today or the world they will live in tomorrow.

There are a myriad of possible solutions to every wicked problem; which one is decided upon will depend on the stakeholders, their level of development, their agenda, their conviction in the root causes of the problem, and which symptoms they are seeking to alleviate first. There are also possible solutions that are never even considered.

Ultimately whether a solution is 'good enough' or not will largely depend on the social context and who is making the assessment and the stakeholder's interdependent values and objectives. The interconnected nature of the causes and symptoms also means that binary 'right' and 'wrong' assessments are impossible. When it comes to wicked problems, 'most workable for now' is often the best we can hope for. But that also leaves us an enormous range of variance – from 'most workable' to 'most disastrous' – there are still much better, and much worse, ways to approach wicked problems – as we hope to demonstrate.

Constantly Evolving

Of course, all this means that the problem itself is constantly evolving. The stakeholders involved in solving the wicked problem are constantly changing, as some leave departments or when there is political regime change. The stakeholders themselves are also personally evolving as their understanding, views and opinions morph over time. The causes are also constantly evolving, new causes are identified and new symptoms manifest.

Plus each solution usually highlights a new, different and often conflicting aspect of the nature of the problem, so there is no end point. We will never reach a point where we can, for example, tick off 'poverty' as a task that has been completed and a wicked problem that has been eradicated. The problem solving process as well as the problem itself is constantly shifting and evolving, so it only ends when we run out of resources, be that time, money or the desire to solve it. Successive governments, for example, may shift their focus from one area to another because of their political persuasion, but the problems themselves are still there.

Trying to solve a wicked problem is often like trying to hit a moving target. Paradoxically solving wicked problems requires us to appreciate that we really can't but try anyway. We are only able to get a handle on a challenge at a given point in time. Any solution therefore will probably be out of date or even obsolete by the time it's evaluated and implemented. And yet instead of attempting, failing and turning away from the problem, we need to attempt, fail and turn back to the problem armed with fresh insights and a new, better understanding of what we face.

There is no end, or as Rittel and Webber called it, 'no stopping rule,' because the landscape is evolving so quickly that it's impossible to know when we've 'finished' or been successful. The fact that there is no end is itself not a bad thing. Evolution has no end yet we still consider it to be a powerfully positive phenomena. And just because there is no end does not mean we can't engage now in useful activity that is constructive and beneficial to many.

Even if we reach a point where we think we've nailed it because the symptoms of the wicked problem have abated and we hubristically think we've solved it, all that's usually happened is the problem has become dormant (or simply shifted elsewhere). The mistake is that often we think we've solved it but we haven't really. Or it simply pops up somewhere else in a different form. In most cases there is no definitive test to determine if the solution has been successful anyway because the consequences of each implemented solution can be far reaching. And these solutions – whether successful or not – can't easily be undone, so trial and error is not really possible with wicked problems. Again this is due to the complex interdependencies – known and unknown – that are the hallmark of wicked problems. Tackling wicked problems is like playing that 'whack a mole' game at a funfair. As soon as you whack one mole, another two pop up somewhere else!

Plus how can we ever really nail anything if the environment in which we are implementing the solution is changing all the time? And that's the ultimate paradox if we are ever to really solve wicked problems: we need to accept that we will never solve wicked problems! We will only ever be able to solve and re-solve over and over again. This constant evolution is part of the very fabric of life. We don't need to be scared of it; we just need to embrace it – with, of course, a wider understanding.

Embracing evolutionary complexity

So far there have been four great ages of humans (from the view, in this case, of the Lower-Right quadrant). The age of the hunter-gatherer lasted about 200 000 years. Life was pretty straightforward at this point – hunt, gather, stay alive and breed.

Our hunter-gatherer ancestors didn't have wicked problems to solve. There were not enough humans on the planet to create complexity. Tribes even a few hundred miles from each other could live in relative isolation. What one tribe did probably didn't have any impact on what another tribe did. The interdependencies and complexities simply were not significantly present at that point.

As human beings evolved, we became more sophisticated at manipulating our environment. The nomadic hunter-gatherers moved more into being farmers during the Agrarian age (AD 500 – AD 1500) they developed tools, cultivated crops, and raised animals for food, a state of affairs that lasted about 10 000 years. Of course there were pockets of more highly evolved cultures, such as the Mayan, Aztecs, Greeks and Romans during this period, but the vast majority of the population were still in farming mode.

Clearly the reality of knowledge doubling was already in motion as the duration of the first age of humans to the duration of the second was significantly shorter. As a species it took us 200 000 years to evolve to the second age and only 10 000 years to reach the third age of humans. In the third great age, people became more creative and cooperative. There were many more people on the planet, and we began to trade with each other. Business emerged, and as commerce grew, more and more workers were required. Towns and cities developed to house the workforce, and industry followed. This Industrial age, which lasted 200 – 300 years, was a period of immense creativity and invention made possible by the Age of Enlightenment. This heralded the widespread emergence of Reason itself that allowed the hypothetico-deductive approach of genuine 'science,' and inspired the world's smartest minds to turn their attention to scientific understanding and innovation. On a physical dimension at least, we began to really understand what caused things to happen like why apples fell from trees. We made huge strides in science and medicine; and we came to appreciate the interconnected nature of reality (what the

Enlightenment called 'the great interlocking order of nature'). [18] Today we are in the post-industrial age (also called 'postmodern') which is marked by service-oriented work and the 'knowledge worker,' and is characterised by an increase in the service sector, outsourcing or increase in mechanised manufacture, technology and information. For that reason it is also sometimes known as the Information Age, and it's only due to last for another 70 years.

The speed of development from stage to stage is significant – 200 000 years of hunting and gathering to just 100 years or so in the information Age and this evolution is likely to quicken. The faster the knowledge doubling, the faster the change and the quicker we evolve – or at least the quicker we must adapt.

The more sophisticated we get, the more elaborate we become; and therefore the danger is the more complicated our lives become. But complexity is not something we need to fear – it's actually a positive sign of evolution. There are three stages to the evolution of anything, whether that's a new product, a new idea or a new species.

1. Emergence
2. Differentiation
3. Integration

Emergence is pretty straightforward and everything starts with emergence. When human beings first emerged is open to debate; but we obviously did. Over the course of many thousands of years, we needed to evolve and adapt to the changing environment. Differentiation follows where we need to establish difference. As human beings, the very nature of our own consciousness and identity is based in part around differentiation. As children we must define 'me' and 'not me' in order to even recognise that we exist as a physical entity separate from our mother. This ability to separate one thing from another is right at the core of who

[18] Taylor, C. (1992), *Sources of the Self* , Harvard: Boston University Press.

we are. It doesn't just happen at the 'I' level, it also happens at the 'WE' level; and in hunter-gatherers it become crucial to differentiate who was in our tribe and how we differed from the other tribes. This was often a matter of life and death. We still differentiate tribes today though nationality, religion, gender, culture and sport, and so on.

Differentiation is an incredibly important evolutionary step in the world of 'IT' as well as the world of 'I' and 'WE'. In an effort to understand the world around us, we still often break it down to its smallest parts so we can understand 'IT'. Science as a field of study is the result of our drive toward differentiation. A lack of differentiation will often lead to an imprecise solution and certainly this is true for wicked problems. As evidenced by the knowledge-doubling curve, we now live in a highly differentiated world.

But in order for that differentiated knowledge to be really useful we need to integrate it and understand it as a whole. It may be entirely possible to break a problem down into very clearly defined smaller issues, but unless there is integration, the danger is that this leads to fragmentation or even disintegration. It is this fragmentation and disintegration that is often at the heart of wicked problems.

We can see this phenomenon at work in modern scientific medicine. Our understanding of the human body has advanced significantly over the last 150 years. For most of that time, scientists and physicians have been unravelling the complexity of the human body by systematically reducing it to ever smaller parts for study and analysis. And it's been incredibly successful. Reductionism has shed new light on how the human body works. It has generated an enormous amount of new information, spawned whole new areas of medical research and created new languages to capture the myriad of discoveries being made.

A by-product of this reductionist approach is that it's become impossible to keep pace with all the new data and discoveries on health or human anatomy. As a result, each part of the human body developed its own expert and each is a separate 'ologist'. These 'ologists' now publish their new insights in their own journals, speak in their own unique language, and attend specialist conferences to share increasingly finer details about their specialism. Physicians often become not just specialists but super-specialists.

Like the so-called solutions to wicked problems, this reductionist approach has many unintended consequences. In medicine, for example, we have largely mastered the emergence part of the evolutionary process, we are pretty skilled at the differentiation element, but we have a long, *long* way to go to master integration. In fact 'integrated care' and 'interdisciplinary research' has only really emerged in the last 20-30 years as a concept, let alone matured as a practice. The human organism is an example of a complex system, and complex systems cannot be understood simply by understanding each differentiated part of that system, because the whole is *always* greater than the sum of the parts.

A modern example of the influence of differentiation can be seen through the Global Financial Crisis (GFC). During a visit to the London School of Economics in November 2008, Queen Elizabeth, capturing the mood of public exasperation, broke with protocol of such visits and asked an economist why his profession had not seen the crisis coming. A group of top British economists then wrote to the Queen to answer her question. The letter signed by London School of Economics professor Tim Besley, a member of the Bank of England monetary policy committee, and eminent historian of government Peter Hennessy, stressed that although everyone had been doing their individual jobs correctly, as a group the economists had missed the big picture of a 'series of interconnected imbalances'.

In summary they wrote, 'The failure to foresee the timing, extent and severity of the crisis and to head it off, while it had many causes, was principally a failure of the collective imagination of many bright people, both in this country and internationally, to understand the risks to the system as a whole.'[19] Differentiation is extremely important in understanding the parts, but it absolutely must be integrated back into the whole.

Integration is the real challenge we face today. The knowledge available to all of us now is staggering, so staggering in fact that it has pushed many individuals in all walks of life into specialist subjects and intellectual silos. In times of confusion we can often feel threatened and so this drive to differentiate often pushes us back to the safe harbour of our own culture, religion or way of life, further creating this 'them' and 'us' mentality. We just need to look at the escalating problems in the Middle East to see this in action. Scotland nearly chose to break away from the United Kingdom and the minority party UKIP is making political progress in Britain as it encourages more people to rail against 'them' – whoever 'them' may be. More people are considering a retreat back to an 'us' of tribalism, mythic simplicity and polarised opinion in a mistaken belief that this will be progress and yield a brighter future.

Such a desire for increased tribalism in a complex world, whilst understandable, is not the solution. It's time to integrate all the really insightful and important 'parts' of all the myriad of complex systems to create a more complete understanding of the pressing issues we face, so that the whole is once again greater than the sum of the parts.

When we don't appreciate the three-step process of evolution and we don't therefore understand or manage the complexity of the world, then this wonderful, beautiful awe-inspiring elaboration of humanity can very quickly become a knotted congealed mess. If this complexity is mismanaged, it morphs into a whole series of stuck wicked issues that seem to defy solution. In a very real way, wicked problems are simply the product of our evolution – they are a product of our escalating complexity. Our ability to

[19] Stewart, H. (2009) This is how we let the credit crunch happen, Ma'am... *The Guardian* www.theguardian.com/uk/2009/jul/26/monarchy-credit-crunch

understand that escalating complexity and find a framework to untangle and comprehend that complexity is the part we've not yet mastered. The good news is wicked problems do not defy solution, they just need a more sophisticated approach and a far greater understanding of how to effectively navigate human interactions and find common ground from which to orchestrate workable solutions in real time. If we can understand the complexity and reach a new level of integration, then new and beautiful things emerge and the whole magnificent evolutionary process begins again.

Correct Diagnosis

So how do we know if we are up against a wicked problem or just a complex problem? We can get a pretty good idea by the number of properties the problem we face has from the list above (see Figure 1.4).

This is not a hard and fast rule, but it will help us to better diagnose the problems we face so we can use the right tools to solve the right problems.

Figure 1.4: Problem type by complexity

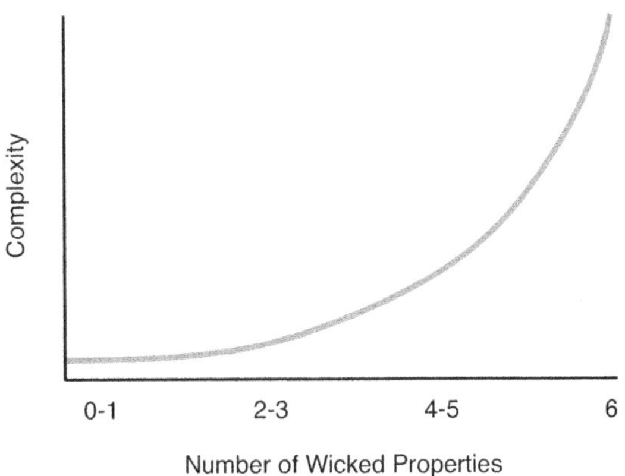

A simple problem will usually have none or perhaps one of the properties of a wicked problem. For example, winning a game of chess is a simple problem. Chess may have multiple solutions but it isn't multi-dimensional. A chess game has two stakeholders, not multiple stakeholders, and there are no causes or symptoms of the problem, and the game of chess is not constantly evolving.

A difficult problem will usually have two or three of the properties of a wicked problem. For example, employee engagement is a difficult problem. There is multi-dimensionality to employee engagement because engagement is affected by the employees' internal subjective world, the external objective world and the interpersonal world of colleague relationships. There are also multiple causes and multiple symptoms, but probably only a few viable solutions. Although there may be multiple employees with mixed engagement, there are only two stakeholders – the employee and the employer. And finally it's not constantly evolving either – employee engagement may make the occasional evolutionary leap forward or back when, say, there is a companywide pay rise, change in management or pay freeze, but engagement as a phenomena is not constantly evolving.

A complex problem will usually have four or five of the properties of a wicked problem. For example, strategic failure is a complex problem. If a business has sought to launch a new product in a new market and the strategy has failed, then the only properties that are unlikely to be present is constant evolution. The strategy has either succeeded or failed. Strategy failure is multi-dimensional. It will have multiple stakeholders, including the executive team, researchers in the new market, customers in the new market, product designers, employees, and so on. The failure will be multicausal – it could be down to the product design, lack of marketing, lack of understanding of the new market and the new customer base, poor implementation, product defects, the economy in the new territory, global economy, political regime change or uncertainty, competitors, and so forth. There is also likely to be multiple symptoms to the strategic failure, including a drop in employee morale, senior executive unrest, loss of revenue, resignations, heightened absenteeism, increased negative media and PR, among others. Because there are so many causes and symptoms there will invariably be multiple potential solutions, each formulated based on a judgement as to which of the causes or symptoms the solution is designed to address.

A wicked problem however will exhibit all of the six properties.

When faced with a problem, we can use this framework to ask ourselves what are then six obvious questions:

1. Is the problem multi-dimensional?
2. Does the problem involve multiple stakeholders?
3. Are there multiple causes for the problem?
4. Does the problem exhibit multiple symptoms?
5. Does the problem have multiple potential solutions?
6. Is the problem constantly evolving?

Having answered these questions, we can then get a better sense of the type of problem we are facing in terms of complexity. We need to appreciate that the traditional methods of solving problems will only really work for simple and difficult problems. The truth is we are not even making enough progress with the many complex problems we face, never mind the escalating number of wicked ones. And considering that wicked problems are considerably more complex than even the most complex problems, then we are in trouble. At least we are unless we find a new way of tackling these complex and wicked problems.

Wicked Problems Require Wicked Solutions

If we are serious about solving and re-solving wicked problems, we must recognise that the solution needs to be every bit as wicked as the problem it is designed to solve.

It's been suggested that there is no obvious answer to wicked problems. We are proposing there is – that the solution must match the nature of the problem. If we are facing a wicked problem that is multi-dimensional, then the solution must be multi-dimensional and address all dimensions. If the wicked problem involves multiple stakeholders, then the solution must involve and collaborate with all those multiple stakeholders. If the wicked problem has multiple causes, then the solution must take those multiple causes into account and expect and seek to anticipate multiple far-reaching repercussions. If the wicked problem has multiple symptoms, then the solution must address all those symptoms so as to ensure that at the very least the solution doesn't exacerbate those symptoms or create new, potentially worse symptoms! If the wicked problem has multiple potential solutions, then we must accept that we will need to implement multiple solutions before we can make any real progress. And finally if the wicked problem is constantly evolving, then the solutions we implement must also constantly evolve.

The solution has to be complicated because the problem is complicated. So it's not a simple answer; it's a complex answer. How do you reverse global warming? How you do stop child trafficking? These are wicked problems that can't even be explained easily, never mind solved easily. Too often we seem more interested in the sound bites about a problem, the headlines or the Tweet-able facts, than actually really unpacking the problem and getting to grips with it properly. And that's another item that needs to change.

First we need to appreciate that the only way to solve a wicked problem is with an equally wicked solution. When it comes to wicked problems, the wise solution is the solution that is as wicked as the problem.

And second, we need to appreciate that contrary to popular opinion, wicked problems are not impossible to solve. It is this helplessness that often feels so overwhelming – especially for those charged with finding real solutions to these intractable challenges. The chaos and futility of wicked problems can leave us beaten before we've even begun – sure that what we face is inevitable and we'd better just accept it.

Those searching for solutions must feel their way through the challenge and discover new emergent 'better' solutions as they go. Of course this ability requires complex judgement, high levels of intelligence and maturity so as to dynamically steer the evolving solution to the evolving problem and manage the issue in real time.

Wicked problems can be solved – and we need to start solving them and keep solving them today (and tomorrow and a hundred years from now). We need a framework that will allow us to appreciate the characteristics of the wicked problems we face in enough detail and with enough sophistication that we can successfully fail our way forward.

And that framework is called Integral Coherence.

Part 2

Wicked Problems Need Wise Answers

A wise woman once found a very precious stone in a stream. Realising its value, she put it in her bag. The next day she was accosted by another traveller who asked her for some food. When the wise woman opened her bag, the traveller saw the precious stone and he demanded the wise woman give it to him. The wise woman did so without hesitation. The traveller left deeply satisfied as the stone was worth enough to give him a lifetime of security. But, a few days later, he returned and gave the woman the stone back.

"I've been thinking," he said. "I know how valuable this stone is, but I give it back to you in the hope that you will give me the thing that enabled you to give away this stone in the first place."

Anon

For most people wisdom is an aspirational concept rather than a daily practice. This is partly because wisdom is not well understood, and it is certainly not common in the modern information age and knowledge economy. The idea of wisdom is often imbued with religious overtones. People talk about the 'wisdom traditions' that come from Buddhism, Christianity, Gnosticism, the Vedanta, Daoism, Sufism and many other religious disciplines. But there is also a wisdom tradition in philosophy and rationalism dating back to the writings of Plato and Aristotle. Clearly wisdom does not require a denominational adherence or commitment to any specific doctrine or institutionalised religion.

The cultivation of wisdom in this sense refers to a means of personal transformation, an expansion of our individual and collective consciousness, more constructive and positive relationships, and a more complete understanding of the way we relate to our world. In essence there are three dimensions to wisdom; subjective ('I'), interpersonal ('WE'), and objective ('IT').

The wisdom traditions have most to say about subjective personal transformation and the expansion of our consciousness (the 'I' dimension). Through wise practise of techniques that have been tested and honed over centuries, we can rediscover universal truths about our own identity, our potential for goodness, the nature of genuine happiness, and the causal nature of our own consciousness. These evolving truths about who we are have been, at least partially, revealed throughout history by the great wisdom traditions of human civilization, including religion, philosophy, and more recently science. These traditions have to a lesser extent illuminated the secrets of relationship; our relationship to ourselves, to each other (the 'WE') and to all things including the objective world (the 'IT').

And boy do we need some wisdom in the world right now. Why? Because we stand at the greatest inflection point in human history, where very likely the decisions we make in the next 35 years will determine the future of mankind for the next 500 years. If we are wise, we might very well have the opportunity to experience the greatest renaissance the world has ever seen. We can, for the first time ever, integrate the ancient insights and modern knowledge of the East and West, North and South and launch ourselves into a much brighter tomorrow. Alternatively we could simply annihilate each other.

The time is ripe for humanity to take the next step in our evolution. We believe such a developmental leap forward is required if we are to have any hope of resolving the *wicked* problems, not to mention all the complex and tough issues we face in all walks of life. This developmental leap is absolutely critical if we are to successfully rise to the challenges of today's world and flourish well into the future.

In this chapter we will offer a framework for wisdom that is non-denominational, not focused on any particular God but rather focused on the wicked problems that abound. We call this frame 'Integral Theory' – and this particular application of it, 'Integral Coherence' – and we'll explain both essential ingredients ('Integral' and 'Coherence') in a moment.

The Integral Frame offers a virtually complete theoretical vantage point from which to view wicked problems and how to set about solving them. But to do so requires a specific type of application of the Framework. At the epicentre of every wicked problem are human relationships and social interactions. And unfortunately human beings are usually not very good at either. And that's where the Coherence comes in.

The *Integral Frame* defines the specific pieces of the puzzle that need to be in place to ensure we can solve wicked problems. Coherence defines the quality of interaction between those pieces. It matters deeply what pieces are in play AND how they interact with each other. In a healthy circumstance the pieces of the Frame naturally arise in a harmonious and coherent fashion because it is in their evolutionary nature to do so. But not every circumstance is healthy and functional. Many, for reasons we will go into, are dysfunctional and incoherent – pretty much the opposite of wisdom. Think of this marriage between 'Integral' and 'Coherence' like a star-studded soccer team. The team can be full of star players but if they don't gel and become a coherent, harmonious team, then they will never unlock their full collective potential and become a star team.

The *Integral Frame* allows us to know what ingredients are required, and *Coherence* reminds us of the inherently functional and harmonious nature of these ingredients. Coherence within the Integral Frame therefore enables, among other items, the quality of the dialogue among a set of diverse stakeholders to produce a positive and wise outcome. We need both theory and practice if we are to generate wise answers to wicked problems. We need both Integral AND Coherence.

What is an Integral Frame?

Integral Theory is a *meta*-theory or a theory that is created by studying *other* theories. The more other theories are studied, the more inclusive, comprehensive and embracing the meta-theory becomes. In other words, the more areas, disciplines, dimensions, or aspects of life to which the meta-theory will apply. Meta-theories are one of our surest routes to truth. If we look at business, for example, we find that there are four or five major different theories of business management and leadership in terms of what it is, how it operates, why it works, what activities it involves, and how to become better at it.

Given these four or five major theories, we have two fundamental choices when we approach business management: first, we can maintain that just one of these four or five approaches is true, and the others are incorrect or inadequate. How we arrive at this distinction may be chance, it may be that we conduct some research into the four or five approaches, seek recommendations from people we trust, or we may simply decide to throw all our eggs in one business management basket and 'go with it'.

However we arrive at our chosen approach, we invariably gather all the evidence and data that we can to support our chosen theory and attempt to prove that it is right, and all the others are wrong. In effect we seek to validate our choice and discredit the rest. This approach is by far the most widely used approach in virtually all areas of human life, academic study, and pragmatic actions. We select one view as being true, and we dismiss all the other options as being wrong, untrue, incomplete or mistaken.

But we do have another choice. The other major approach open to us takes a completely different stance. Instead of maintaining that there is just one true view and the other contenders are all various degrees of wrong, this 'Integral' or 'integrated' approach maintains that *all* of the several major approaches to the topic each presents some important piece of the truth. Not that one is right and true and all the others are wrong and false, but that *all* of them are true but partially true, all of them have some piece of the puzzle, all of them have some aspect of the overall truth, and thus all of them need to be included in any truly comprehensive, inclusive or all-embracing '*Integral*' truth. As a result, the fundamental question switches from, 'Which of these approaches is completely right and which are completely wrong?' to, 'How can all of these approaches be partially true with each of them containing an important piece of the complete puzzle? The fundamental question becomes, 'How is the universe constructed such that each of these major theories all have something important to tell us, all have some slice of actual reality? What view of the situation allows them *all* to be partially right?'

When we ask that kind of question, and we succeed in answering it well, we get a meta-theory, a theory that covers much more of reality than any single, partial, individual, limited theory, each of which tends to take just one perspective, or looks at only a particular dimension of reality and ignores all the others, or uses just one method for discovering truth and denies reality to all the others, or otherwise takes a limited, narrow, partial view of an issue or problem and thus produces limited, narrow, partial results. When we unilaterally choose to follow one theory over another, major areas of reality always get left out. And if major areas get left out, the outcome always suffers.

The premise behind an inclusive or integral view is that the human mind is incapable of producing 100 per cent error; or, as we say, nobody is smart enough to be wrong all the time. Each of the major schools of thought in virtually every discipline has thousands or millions of rational adults believing in their partial perspective, and many spend their entire lives studying just that one particular approach.

We just don't believe that so many individuals would devote their lives to studying something that was totally false and wrong. The human mind just wouldn't be motivated to do so. At the very least, every major approach or theory has some degree of truth; it holds some piece of the overall puzzle, and some aspect of the approach therefore needs to be included if we are to have a fully rounded, complete, and inclusive view of overall reality itself – a meta-view or meta-theory that takes all of the true but partial facts and weaves them together into a fuller account. When we do this, we get a much richer, truer, fuller, more effective view of everything from government to business, from security to foreign policy, from science to art, from morals to history, from economics to law, from growth to therapy, from philosophy to psychology to spirituality. All of those topics – in fact, virtually any topic whatsoever – can be approached in an integral, inclusive, comprehensive fashion, and when we do so, the results are much, much more satisfying.

As an example, let's look more closely at four of the major theories of business management – how to manage employees, what management is, how it operates, and how to succeed in doing it best. These major, general theories have already been identified and named. They are Theory X, Theory Y, culture management, and systems theory. Theory X largely focuses on the individual worker and the individual product in an objective, scientific, exterior, analytic fashion. It focuses on individual reward and punishment – the so-called 'carrot and stick' motivation – and it also gives attention to the individual product and quality control measures. There are of course other behavioural theories in this quadrant such as High Performance Management Competencies (Harry Schroder and Tony Cockerill),[1] The Competent Manager (Richard Boyatzis) [2] or the Managerial Grid (Robert Blake and Jane Mouton) [3] but Douglas McGregor's Theory X captures the essence of the focus on the individual and the objective exteriors and behaviours.

McGregor's Theory Y, on the other hand, looks at the *interiors* of the individual worker – at what makes employees (and leaders) happy; how they can find meaning in their work; how their jobs can provide value and purpose in their lives; how the workplace can become a source of joyful engagement.[4] Authors such as Frederick Herzberg,[5] Rensis Likert,[6] Elton Mayo[7] and more recently Daniel Pink[8] have also explored different aspects of

---

1 Cockerill, A.P., Schroder, H.M., and Hunt J.W. (1993) 'Validation Study into the High Performance Managerial Competencies', London Business School. Unpublished report – sponsored by National Westminster Bank, Prudential Corporation, Leeds Permanent Building Society, the Automobile Association, the UK Employment Department and the UK Civil Aviation Authority.

2 Boyatzis, R. E. (1982) *The Competent Manager: A Model for Effective Performance*, London: John Wiley & Sons.

3 Blake, R. R. and Mouton, J. S. (1964) *The Managerial Grid*, Houston: Gulf Publishing.

4 McGregor, D. (1960) *The Human Side of Enterprise*, New York: McGraw Hill.

5 Herzberg, F., Mausner, B. and Snyderman, B. B. (1959) *Motivation to Work*, New York: John Wiley & Sons.

6 Likert, R. (1961) *New Patterns of Management*, New York: McGraw Hill.

7 Wood, J. C. and Wood, M. C. (eds) (2004) *George Elton Mayo: Critical Evaluations in Business and Management*, London: Routledge.

8 Pink, D. H. (2011) *Drive: The Surprising Truth About What Motivates Us*, New York: Penguin.

internal motivation. Abraham Maslow's needs hierarchy is also often pointed to in this regard.[9] For example, Maslow found that individuals grow and develop through a nested hierarchy of needs. In sequence, from the lowest to the highest, they are physiological needs, safety needs, belongingness needs, self-esteem needs, self-actualisation needs, and self-transcendence needs. As a lower need emerges and is satisfied, then the next higher need can emerge; if that is adequately satisfied, then the next higher emerges, and so on in a phenomenon he called 'prepotence'. The point is that individuals have different needs and motivations at different stages of growth and development, and individuals at different levels of needs will be motivated to work for very different reasons, and hence *they need to be managed in very different ways*.

For example, individuals at the self-actualisation level find that the meaning of their work is more important than what they are paid – and so meaning and value, not salary, become most important for them. A year ago, the famous polling company Gallup did a worldwide survey in 155 countries asking people what was most important for their happiness.[10] They found the most often given answer was not money, was not family or marriage, was not fame – rather, it was 'a good job' – work that is meaningful, purpose-driven, and valuable. The CEO of Gallup stated, 'What the whole world wants is a good job. This is one of the most important discoveries Gallup has ever made.' And yet, studies consistently show that in the West, less than a third of all employees are engaged in, or happy with, their jobs – that's a horrible statistic.[11] And that's what Theory Y is about – the interior of individuals is

---

[9] Maslow, A. H. (1943) A Theory of Human Motivation *Psychology Review* 50, pp. 370-396 http://psychclassics.yorku.ca/Maslow/motivation.htm

[10] Gallup's Word Poll, www.gallup.com/businessjournal/101680/Global-Migration-Patterns-Job-Creation.aspx

[11] Macke, J. and Sisodia, R. (2013) *Conscious Capitalism: Liberating the Heroic Spirit of Business,* Boston: Harvard Business Review Press.

the most important ingredient in excellent business management. Satisfy an individual employee's interior, intrinsic needs and drives, and you will have a successful company.

About a decade or two ago, an entirely new approach to business management and leadership came on the scene – it was referred to as 'culture management.' What is culture? Culture is, in a sense, the interior of a group – it's the group's shared values, meanings, purpose, ethics and morals, mutual understanding, shared habits and worldviews. It's what holds a group together from the inside. All individuals exist in various groups – family, friends, colleagues, sometimes religious or political affiliations, tribes, states, nations, a collective humanity. And every business, as a particular group of individuals, has a specific culture, an interior set of values, meanings, rules and roles that hold the group together from within. As management experts began studying what matters most in business management, they soon hit upon the company's culture itself. As James Heskett of Harvard Business school says, 'A strong culture can help or hurt performance. Culture can account for up to *half* of the difference in operating *profit* between two organisations in the same business. Shaping culture is one of a leader's most important jobs.'[12] Peter Drucker, world famous leadership guru, put it bluntly: 'Culture eats strategy for breakfast.'[13] In other words, guiding culture is more important than business strategy and mission itself! Conscious culture is sometimes summarised with the acronym t-a-c-t-i-l-e, which stands for trust, accountability, caring, transparency, integrity, loyalty, and equality. In short, culture management is managing the *interiors* of the *group*.

The fourth and final major theory is the ever-present school of

---

[12] Heskett, J. (2011) *The Culture Cycle: How to Shape the Unseen Force That Transforms Performance*, New Jersey: FT Press.

[13] Mackey, J. and Sisodia, R. (2013) *Conscious Capitalism: Liberating the Heroic Spirit of Business*, Boston: Harvard Business Review Press.

systems theory. Where culture management looks at the *interiors* of the *group* and finds interwoven networks of mutual meaning and values, systems theory examines the *exteriors* of the group, and finds interwoven networks of interrelated systems and structures. Systems theory is the opposite of atomism. Atomism suggests that the ultimate reality is the single individual object, and usually the smallest possible, such as atoms, and claims they alone are real. Systems theory maintains, on the contrary, that every individual is set in networks and systems of mutually interdependent and interwoven processes –and it is these systems or networks that are ultimately real. System theory suggests that it is only by studying the whole system, and not its parts, that a true understanding of the situation can be attained. And so business management and leadership that are focused on systems theory focus on managing the overall system of the company as a single unified web (which itself is part of a larger market web, which is part of a larger national corporate system, international commercial system and ultimately global planetary system) – and *not* a collection of separate divisions, regions or parts.

Now although systems theory is holistic in that sense – the whole must be studied, not just its parts – it still focuses almost entirely on exteriors, on systems looked at from the outside, in an objective fashion. So if we look in any textbook on systems theory, we will find an emphasis on looking at whole systems and holistic networks, but these are all looked at from the exterior, from the outside, in an objective stance – so subjective consciousness is looked at as a flow of objective information data bits, and we won't find anything on art, aesthetics, morals, ethics, individual growth and development, beauty, meaning, value, and so on. Where culture looks at the *interior* networks of groups, systems theory looks at the *exterior* networks of groups – what holds the group together from the outside. This holistic *exterior* approach is often described by the acronym PESTLE, which as we explained in chapter one stands for: political, economic, social, technological, legal, and environmental aspects. These are all group or collective activities approached in an exterior, outer, objective fashion.

So which one of the four major business management theories is correct? According to Integral Theory, all of them are. Instead of asking which one of those four is right and which are wrong, the Integral approach instead asks, what view of reality would allow ALL of them to explain an important piece of the overall truth of business management?

Quadrants

After studying hundreds of different theories from pre-modern, modern, and postmodern times, Integral Meta-Theory suggests that every phenomenon can be looked at through at least four major vantage points – the interior and the exterior of the individual and the group. This gives us four major perspectives or dimensions, which we call the 'four quadrants' – the interior individual, exterior individual, interior collective and exterior collective.

One version of these four quadrants is given in Figure 2.1, which shows the *interior* of an *individual* in the Upper-Left quadrant (the 'I' space); the *interior* of the *group* or network is shown in the Lower-Left quadrant (a communal 'WE' space, the culture); the *exterior* or objective view of an *individual* is in the Upper-Right quadrant (an objective, outer, or 'IT'; the it space); and the *exterior* of the *group* or communal is shown in the Lower-Right quadrant (an 'ITS' space, a space of exterior collective systems or networks).

These four quadrants – 'I', 'WE', 'IT', and 'ITS' dimensions – are sometimes reduced to three major areas, combining the two objective or exterior quadrants ('IT' and 'ITS') into a single 'IT' or objective space. These dimensions show up in virtually all societies, pre-modern, modern, and postmodern. All major languages, for example, have first-, second-, and third-person pronouns:

first person is the person speaking (or I, me, mine) – the 'I' space of the Upper-Left quadrant;

second person is the person being spoken to (or you; and a 'you' plus an 'I' is a 'WE') – the 'WE' space of the Lower-Left quadrant;

third-person is the person or thing being spoken about (he, she, they, or simply it or its) – the objective 'IT' or 'ITS' space of the Upper-Right and Lower-Right quadrants.

Figure 2.1: Some details of the four quadrants

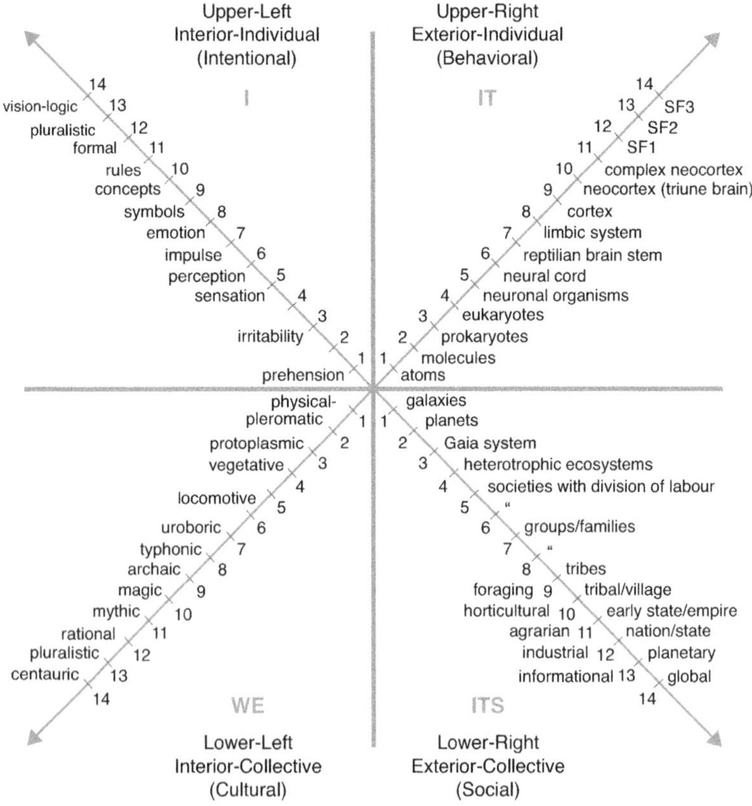

These are the basis of items such as the Good, the True, and the Beautiful – the *Good*, ethics, or how 'WE' treat each other (the Lower-Left); the *True* – or what is objectively true, individually or collectively (the objective Upper-Right and Lower-Right quadrants); and the *Beautiful*, or the Beauty that is in the 'eye' – and the capital 'I' – of the beholder (or the Upper-Left quadrant – the interior consciousness of an individual being).

As we saw with the four major business management theories, those four quadrants each have a different view or perspective on things, they have different values and meanings, they have different types of truth, they have different types of methodologies. And clearly, *all* of them are important.

Figure 2.2: Some quadrant differences

	Interior Left-Hand Paths	Exterior Right-Hand Paths
Individual	Subjective *Truthfulness* sincerity integrity trustworthiness	Objective *Truth* correspondence representation propositional
Collective	Intersubjective *Justness* cultural fit mutual understanding goodness	Interobjective *Functional Fit* systems theory web structural-functionalism social systems mesh

Several of these differences are shown in Figure 2.2, including 'validity claims' – or how the different truths are judged and determined in each quadrant. In the Upper-Right, for example, the validity claim is representational 'truth' – such as, 'Is it raining outside or not?' To find out, we go to the window and look, and if we all see rain, we decide that 'It is true that it is raining outside' – a correct *representation* of reality. We can actually *measure* the amount of rain and quantitative, measurable means are often hallmarks of the Right-Hand approaches.

But in the Upper-Left quadrant, the question is not so much 'Is it raining outside?,' but 'When I tell you it is raining outside, am I telling you the truth or am I lying?' Not so much truth, but *truthfulness* becomes the measure of the true in this quadrant, including how truthful I am about my own self; if I lie to me about myself, I produce 'unconscious' or 'shadow' elements where I hide the truth from myself, producing neurotic symptoms in its place. Since nobody can directly see what is going on inside me, the only way for anybody to know is if I tell them, and that depends upon my truthfulness with them; most human interaction rests on the degree of truthfulness between the people interacting. When numerous untruthful humans gather together, the result is *cultural lies*, cultures dedicated to hiding, distorting, corrupting, and oppressing the truth, thus actually teaching their members to lie about what is really going on; the domination and distortion of the truth is the purpose of *propaganda*.

In the Lower-Left, what especially matters is how all of our individual roles fit together in an appropriate and just fashion – *justness, appropriateness or doing the 'right' thing*; this will become the foundation of ethics or how 'we' decide the best or most appropriate way that we *should* treat each other. This is not objective truth and it's not truthfulness; it's *justness or goodness*.

In the Lower-Right, it's not how the *interiors* fit together in cultural mesh, but how the *exteriors* fit together in systems mesh or *functional fit*. If the Lower-Left is the experience of ethical awareness, the Lower-Right is the actual structure or form of the law (or systemic legal codes).

So overall we have *subjective* truth (in the UL); *objective* truth (in the UR); *intersubjective truth* (in the LL); and *interobjective* truth (in the LR) – all are incredibly important validity claims and types of truth, and all of them need to be honoured and included. Plus, these can of course be subdivided in any number of ways, including their own 'subjective' and 'objective' versions, or 'zones'. These are the very foundations of *art* (subjective), *morals* (intersubjective), and *science* (objective and interobjective), for example.

So when trying to determine whether an answer to a wicked problem is 'true' or not, it depends which quadrant you are standing in and which version of the 'truth' you are placing your faith in.

And in the same fashion, different major theorists have focused on a different quadrant when advancing their central ideas. For example see Figure 2.3, which is an extremely short list of some very famous theorists in each quadrant.

Nowhere is the 'true but partial' nature of the truth in each quadrant more obvious than in looking at the list of theorists

Figure 2.3: Some famous theorists in each quadrant

	Left-Hand Paths • Interpretive • Hermeneutic • Consciousnes	Right-Hand Paths • Monological • Empirical, positivistic • Form
Individual	Freud C.G. Jung Piaget Aurobindo Plotinus Guatama Buddha	B.F. Skinner John Watson John Locke Empiricism Behaviourism Physics, biology, neurology etc
Collective	Thomas Kuhn Wihelm Dilthey Jean Gebser Max Weber Hans-Georg Gadamer	Systems Theory Talcott Parsons Auguste Comte Karl Marx Gerhard Lenski

that have become famous with their theories that focused on a particular quadrant. How on earth could we claim that the ideas from an entire list in any quadrant are 'totally wrong'? Look at those theorists! They are gorgeously ingenious, brilliant pioneers. Entire schools of study are still based on each of their breakthrough ideas. And either we will have room for at least some of their pioneering ideas or we will have a badly broken theory. It's all a matter of how truth-*inclusive* we really want to be....

So all of these different quadrants, with their different truths, different motivations, different needs and values and meanings and methods are all equally important. All of them need to be included if we want to re-solve wicked problems – whether in medicine, business, law, politics, art interpretation, values, academic studies, and so on. An Integral approach to business management, for example, can be shown in Figure 2.4.

All of these quadrants are equally important and they absolutely must be included if we are serious about taming wicked problems.

Figure 2.4: Integral business

Theory Y Focuses on psychological understanding I	Theory X Emphasises individual behaviour IT
WE Culture Management Emphasises organisational culture	ITS Systems Management Emphasises the social system and its environment

All of reality, in any domain or area, can be looked at from these four major vantage points, and each of them tells us something very important, as we saw with the major theories of business management. Realising that all four of those perspectives are real and are a genuine part of reality itself, means that we would expect there to be at least these four major views (or aspects) of business management, since each one focuses on one of those real perspectives. Including all of them gives us a truly Integral, inclusive or comprehensive view of business management, and leaving out any of them will give us a limited, partial, fragmented, broken view.

And yet, of course, that is what most approaches do; they ignore or leave out one or more of the four quadrants, with very unfortunate results. Most approaches commit *quadrant absolutism*, or the belief that one quadrant, and one quadrant alone, is actually real. In order to make real progress with the numerous wicked problems, we must address each problem from all four quadrants. It is only such an approach that will ensure the most complete, most accurate, most truthful account of both the nature of the problem and the potential solutions.

And, in one sense, this is just the beginning. We will find the same thing with the rest of the elements of the Integral Meta-Map or Framework – which include, in addition to quadrants, 'levels', 'lines', 'states' and 'types' (all of which we will explore below). And since most typical approaches usually leave out several of these elements, the Integral approach to wicked problems is a very novel, new, and often unexpected way to approach intractable complex wicked issues. As such, an Integral approach ensures a much more embracing, inclusive, comprehensive, accurate and truthful account. When we emphasise the dynamics of coherence, we believe we now have an approach that offers the possibility of genuine breakthrough on the world's toughest, most wicked problems.

Levels

Another dimension of reality that is, oddly, often overlooked is vertical developmental. We say 'oddly' because 'developmental' is very closely related to 'evolutionary,' and evolution is probably the single most influential idea in the modern world. Despite this fact this view is rarely applied to the growth of individuals or cultures, with the occasional exceptions.[14] And yet the evidence is overwhelming that virtually all human beings have somewhere around a dozen major *levels of interior growth* available to them. Moreover, these levels have been extensively studied by developmental psychology and sociology in extraordinary detail, and virtually all of the various schools – although often focusing on different quadrants – are almost always in general agreement as to the overall nature of these levels themselves. In fact, *Integral Psychology*, includes charts from over *100 different schools* of developmental studies from around the world.[15] What was so amazing is the general agreement among virtually all of them as to the nature of these major levels. The various schools all maintain a general consensus as to the major interior levels of human development which are, to date, detailed as follows.

Level 1

The human being, at birth, cannot yet distinguish itself – its body – from the environment. It exists in a state of 'fusion,' although numerous other terms have been applied. The infant can't tell where its body stops and the chair begins. This is often called the 'archaic stage,' or the basic sensorimotor stage.

At somewhere around nine months, the infant begins to make the fundamental distinction of 'me' and 'not me'. This is best seen if you watch a baby look at themselves in the mirror. It is absolutely

[14] Habermas, J. (1991) *Communication and the Evolution of Society*, Oxford: Polity Press.

[15] Wilber, K. (2000) *Integral Psychology: Consciousness, Spirit, Psychology, Therapy*, Boston: Shambhala Publications

beautiful to witness the dawning realisation that the strange object looking back at them is, in fact, themselves. Infants at this level start to conduct experiments with their body parts. They will put their foot in their mouth and bite. They can feel the pain in their foot and their mouth as a result. They realise that the painful thing is 'me'. In contrast when they bite the table they can feel their gums but not the table. It starts to dawn on them 'I am the thing that hurts when I bite it'. Of course they don't think in those terms but on some level they realise they are physically separate from their mother and everyone else. So the first step of self-awareness is rooted right there in their physiology.

Level 2

At around 18-24 months the baby starts to increasingly differentiate not only simple physiological data that defines their physical body but a more nuanced integrated set of physiological data streams, namely their emotions. Emotions are really just composite physiological signals from all the bodily systems. Looking at these 'I' events in terms of their 'IT' correlations, they are composed of all the pressure waves, electrical waves, sound waves, chemical signals, electromagnetic waves, heat waves, etc., from every single bodily system. All of this energy-in-motion is integrated and interpreted in the brainstem. As these complex data streams are integrated and reach conscious awareness, they are perceived and become feelings in the mind of the infant. Basically the baby starts to become aware of its feelings. Prior to this awareness developing, they do not realise that their feelings are separate from others. So if a one-year-old is hungry, then they assume the world is also hungry, so why aren't we eating? This phase often opens on to what is referred to by parents as the 'terrible twos'. Infants can become incredibly demanding simply because they have no understanding that their feelings may be different from their parents. Again, it is beautiful to witness the moment when children start to realise that there is more than one feeling present in the world. Picture the infant screaming in frustration in the aisle of the supermarket because they can't get their own way. At the same time they look at their mother through their screams and tears, completely baffled as to why their mother isn't also screaming and crying!

This is the moment of emotional separation or differentiation. At this stage the infant is primarily driven by impulse and immediate gratification of their emotional needs; it has a magical or fantasy mode of thinking; and it is focused on the immediate now moment. This stage, level 2, is often called 'impulsive'.

Level 3

As the self continues to grow and differentiate itself from its surroundings, and moves from level 2 to level 3, it becomes more and more aware of its tenuous separate existence, and starts to worry about its own safety and security and self-protection; as recourse, it develops a strong set of power drives. This stage is often called the 'safety', 'self-protective', 'power' or 'opportunistic' stage. If this stage sustains into adulthood in an unhealthy fashion, it is often the source of criminal behaviour and significant corruption. The person's power drives control their behaviour, and they haven't evolved yet to the next higher stage – the conformist law and order stage – and so they set their own standards and create their own laws, driven by their need for security and power. Whatever they want is what is right, and they set about to simply take it, society be damned. You can, for example, see a child steal a pencil because 'they wanted it'. When asked whether they took their sister's pencil they will flatly deny doing so. In their own mind there was no theft because the pencil was theirs in the first place!

The unhealthy version of this power-level is found in abundance in criminal institutions, Mafioso type organisations, corrupt governments, and so on. It sees the world as a survival of the fittest; the biggest and strongest win; do it to somebody before they do it to you; it's a law of the jungle, a dog-eat-dog world, tooth and claw are needed, and individuals operating from this level are capable of some truly vicious acts.

These first three major levels or stages are all 'narcissistic' or 'egocentric,' which means the self is stuck in a first-person, 'me/mine' perspective. Individuals stuck at these stages are not yet adept at taking the role of other. They are poor at putting themselves in somebody else's shoes and find it difficult to take any other perspective than their own. So the self is everything, the self rules, the self and what it wants is supreme – 'give me, me and mine' is the rule.

Level 4

As an individual enters the next major stage of development, level 4, a new dramatic capability comes online. This stage is often called the 'conformist', 'mythic-membership' or 'belongingness' stage. The self starts to be much more able to take the role of other, and thus its identity can expand from its own self to belongingness in various groups. Individuals at this stage start to prize family, clan, tribe, nation, religion, political party, and so on, much more highly. This is the switch from an '*egocentric*' to an '*ethnocentric'* identity – 'me-focused' to 'group-focused' or 'us-focused.' This is a very important switch, without which stakeholders will never really be able to solve wicked problems.

As one of its names implies, the early stages of this fourth level can be very conformist. The self can take the role of other, but it is often caught in that role, a view often called 'my country, right or wrong', or 'my religion, right or wrong', or 'law and order', and so forth. Strict adherence to rules becomes very important here, and historically, some of these rules were barbarically enforced – cutting off a thief's hands, for example, or stoning a woman to death for adultery.

When egocentric-level individuals come together into criminal, corrupt conformist networks, these criminal networks also often have very strict and rigid rules and codes of behaviour – such as the Mafia's 'code of silence', the demand not to reveal or talk about the criminal network ('la cosa nostra' – which is how Mafia members refer to each other – literally means 'this thing of ours'), and breaking this 'code of ours' is also usually met with swift and severe punishment, often death, and often in a signature fashion that lets people know this was specifically done in retaliation, such as two neat bullets to the forehead.

Thinking is very concrete here, and thus often has what is called a 'mythic-literal' view – myths, such as those in the Bible (Moses parted the Red Sea, God killed the first-born of all Egyptians, Elijah rose straight to Heaven in his chariot while still alive, and so on) are taken to be concretely, literally, absolutely true. Clare Graves referred to this level as 'absolutistic'. Mafioso types, strange as it sounds, often see themselves as good Catholics. *Fundamentalist religion* stems primarily from this level – although fundamentalism can apply to any fervently-held belief, which is believed to be absolutely and literally true with or without any real evidence, but simply because a significant authority says it's true. So this could apply to fundamentalist Christianity, or fundamentalist Marxism, or fundamentalist feminism, or fundamentalist science (so-called 'scientism'), or fundamentalist criminal families, and so on. As we have noted, in its unhealthy forms, it is often populated by individuals with major residual power-drive components, and so these power/conformist networks are often at the core of criminal power networks, networks of oligarchic corruption, la cosa nostra criminal families, whole branches of corrupt governments, street gangs, imperialistic and colonialist self-serving rulers (who always claim they're doing it 'for their people'), and so on. Governments with this ethnocentric identity and underbelly are deeply imperialistic and colonialist, always looking to expand their empires with any means possible, from economic forces to actual warfare and physical invasion.

This level often sees truth as embodied in a single book, which is taken to be absolutely and ultimately true—whether the Bible, the Koran, a Pure Land sutra, Mao's Little Red Book, and so on. Similarly, governments with this structure often place power in a single all-powerful person or omnipotent dictator or occasionally a small group of select individuals holding all power and who rule with a totalitarian authority. This was true of the Nazis, many communist-dominated countries during the Cold War, the USSR for most of its history, Iran and China, among others today. Although China is making moves toward more modern economic and political systems, power is still concentrated in the hands of a select few. 'Power corrupts, and absolute power corrupts absolutely' applies to these structures.

Ethnocentric cultures infused with egocentric power is the major form of systematic corruption in today's world. The individual is still driven primarily by power needs and self-promotion, but he or she is also part of a network of cronies and corrupt partners or oligarchs, who conform to their own corrupt rules, codes, and ethics, and, as noted, anybody violating the network's rules is simply murdered or otherwise quickly and efficiently disposed of. The network is driven by fear and even terror, nobody really trusts anybody, you always have to be watching your back, and rigid hierarchies are often in place, with the more powerful and dominating bosses at the higher levels. This is the source of *dominator* hierarchies, instead of the healthy *growth* hierarchies.

In the natural growth hierarchy from atoms to molecules to cells to organisms, each higher level is more and more inclusive and embracing. Molecules don't hate atoms or dominate atoms or oppress atoms or exclude them, they embrace and include them, if anything they love them. And each higher level becomes more and more inclusive and capable of more and more love and compassion. But corrupt dominator hierarchies are the opposite – the higher someone moves in those hierarchies, the more corrupt power they have, the more they can terrorise, oppress, dominate and control more people. All driven by their own pathological power drives.

We can't simply outlaw corruption, that is, apply laws to make such behaviour illegal. This would be an exterior, objective, Right-Hand-quadrant move. While laws are extremely important, especially if enforced, corruption has its primary origins in the Left-Hand interiors of consciousness and culture. It relies on networks of power-driven individuals setting their own laws, so corruption must ultimately be dealt with by working with consciousness (including shadow work), and particularly by developing people and culture to the next level up, which is called '*worldcentric*'. Unlike the majority of *ethnocentric* individuals who identify with a limited, specific group of individuals, based on race, ethnicity, religion, corrupt power networks or any manner of us versus them dimensions, *worldcentric* individuals identify with all humans, and treat them all fairly regardless of race, colour, sex, or creed.

As consciousness continues to evolve from *egocentric* to *ethnocentric* to *worldcentric,* we begin to glimpse the emergence, for the first time, of the possibility of more true, democratic, free, open, and transparent individuals, cultures, and governments.

Level 5

So, when the conformists at level 4, with their second-person perspective and the beginning capacity to take the role of other, further develop to the next level up, the emergence of a *third-person perspective*, or the capacity to take an objective, scientific, universal 'IT' perspective emerges.

This enables the switch in identity from a local ethnocentric identity to a universal or global *worldcentric* identity – a switch from 'us' to 'all of us,' which, as we'll see, marks organisations such as the European Union. This more universal, global, expansive awareness occurs because thought can operate not just on the concrete material world (as with level 4), but thought can now operate on thought itself (with level 5). Literally we develop the ability to think about our own thinking. Thus introspection, self-esteem, conscientious, self-reflection, universal identity – a Cosmopolitan identity – becomes possible.

Immanuel Kant defined 'cosmopolitan' awareness as one where, paraphrasing, 'if a person anywhere suffers, I suffer.' In other words, there is a deeply felt identity or solidarity with all of humanity, and the issue of the Universal Rights of Men and Women comes to the fore for the first time. Not just a particular clan, tribe, club, religion, nation, or group of individuals – but all groups, all humans, all nations.

Because this stage, level 5, is marked by the ability of thought operating on thought, it is often referred to with names such as reason, rationality, formal operational, conscientious, achievement, excellence, self-esteem. Self-esteem needs emerge at this level because a third-person perspective means the individual can stand outside of themselves, so to speak, and objectify their own existence. They can form an opinion about themselves and naturally they want it to be as positive an opinion as possible, hence the self-esteem needs.

Thus, Maslow's needs hierarchy runs from physiological needs (levels 1 and 2), to safety and self-protective and power needs (level 3), to belongingness and conformist needs, healthy or corrupt (level 4), to self-esteem needs (level 5, with a few higher levels we'll look at in a moment). At level 5, one's identity expands to a global or worldcentric view, and we also see the emergence of a real *individuality*. So this stage is also marked by the emergence of the drive toward excellence, accomplishment, merit, achievement, progress. A third-person perspective allows individuals to stand outside of the present moment and be aware of historical time, and hence compare the present with the past and an imagined future – and thus wish to improve the present as much as possible in comparison, hence the drive toward excellence, achievement, merit, and progress. This is a very noticeable drive in individuals in various cultures, and is easily spotted.

This level 5 evolutionary leap to a higher level of consciousness and culture marked the Western Enlightenment, or what has been called 'The Age of Reason and Revolution'.[16] Reason, which allows 'as if' and 'what if' thinking, allowed alternative realities

---

[16] Durant, W. and Durant, A. (1961) *The Story of Civilization : The Age of Reason Begins*, New York: Simon & Schuster.

to be conceived; alternatives to slavery (what if we abolished it?), to monarchy (what if we had representative democracy?), to patriarchy (what if women had equality?), to fundamentalist mythic religion (what if science offered more truth?). And revolutions brought them into existence, whether politically with the French and American revolutions; or the revolutionary legal outlawing of slavery in every major industrial-rational country the world over (the first time that had ever happened in all of history); or the truly revolutionary modern sciences from physics to chemistry to evolutionary biology to sociology – all of these are the result of this monumental shift to level-5 consciousness.

The emergence of a third-person perspective, and the ability to objectify anything, including perspective taking itself, provided a true three-dimensional depth to life.[17] This was reflected in the art of the Renaissance which started to take on a three-dimensional perspective for the first time. Human faces took on real contours, peaks and valleys all jump out in nature, portraiture becomes extremely popular, and all of a sudden we are in a very, very different world – the modern world, the world of reason, depth, and third-person, three-dimensional features. As we said, every vertical level of growth actually brings with it a new and different world in many ways, and virtually every adolescent today goes through a similar internal turmoil of 'reason and revolution' as they hit the teen years and rationality and self-esteem needs begin to emerge.

The main problem right now, globally, is in moving enough people to worldcentric levels. But unfortunately the world political order is currently undergoing something of a shift, not to a new worldcentric order, as hoped, but to a profusion of the previous ethnocentric regimes; in some cases, an actual *regression* from worldcentric to ethnocentric modes.

The central elements are less ideas, economic systems, universal

[17] Watkins, A. (2015) *Four Dimensional Leadership*, London: Kogan Page.

values, and international agreements, but ethnic ties, blood and soil, geopolitical territories, imperialist drives, and moves that benefit only their own race, clan, blood, soil or territory.

For example, there are many ethnic Russians in Eastern and Southern Ukraine, threatening to split the country. Similarly, the Arab Spring didn't produce a series of new democracies, as was hoped, but an explosion of ethnocentric segments: religious war in Syria; chaos in Libya and bedlam in Yemen; renewed dictatorship in Egypt; and Tunisia, viewed by some as the sole success of the Arab Spring, can't control its southern borders with Algeria and Libya. Tripoli is now the central switchboard for warring ethnic tribes, gangs, and militias, all fighting for territory. Damascus is the centre, not of Syria, but only of Syria's strongest warlord, Bashar Assad. Baghdad is the capital of a tribalised Shi'ite domain dominated largely by abutting Iran, with a virtually independent Kurdish northern region and a jihadist Sunnistan on its west, home of literally hundreds of war clans extending to the Mediterranean. Iran is a medieval ethnocentric Sunni monarchy occupying much of the Arabian Peninsula, in an ongoing series of proxy wars with Saudi Arabia. In short, the Middle East has largely devolved into innumerable anarchic, ethnocentric, warlord fragments.

In the Pacific, Cold-War desolated states of China, Singapore, Vietnam, Malaysia, South Korea and Japan have virtually all benefited from many years of economically productive capitalism, but the net result has been an increase in ethnocentric territorialism. In addition to the modernisation of their economies and militaries, Asia's share of military imports of the world total has risen from 15 per cent in the 1990s to a staggering 40 per cent of today's total, most of it going to territorial disputes among all of them in the South China and East China seas. Ethnocentric nationalism – based on race and ethnicity, fuelled by imperialistic territorialism – is flourishing in Asia. India and China, long kept peacefully separate by the Himalayas, have increasingly come into conflict as technology has collapsed distance. Middle classes have significantly grown across sub-Saharan Africa, but geopolitical realities have led to many ethnocentric, tribal, and religious conflicts, as between the Central African Republic and South Sudan.

The European Union, on the other hand, is largely an encouraging example of individuals moving from an ethnocentric country – just me and my nation *versus* all those other nations – to a more worldcentric union – me, my nation, *and* many other nations as well, all brought together under a unifying and integrating umbrella. This is the result of a genuine evolution to a higher level of consciousness and culture itself. There is a real change in the interior quadrants of 'I' and 'WE' and a move from an ethnocentric to a more worldcentric perspective. These changes are accompanied by changes in the exterior quadrants, meaning changes in the actual form and structure of governments and society – 'IT' and 'ITS' system changes such as representative democracy, free and open elections, fair and transparent laws, open economic markets, transparent governments and politicians, financially responsible actions, and so forth. That said, not everyone in Europe holds to such ideals or is even in favour or seeing the benefits of European societal evolution. Far from it, there are many politicians, who seek to leverage the adolescent growing pains of the new emerging *worldcentric* perspective in Europe to opportunistically try and grab power for themselves and their own tribe.

These leaders are advocating a retrograde step back to ethnocentricity but are dressing it up as greater 'self-determination'. Scotland got all the way to the 'divorce courts' before sufficient number of Scots realised that a 300-year-old union that delivered economic stability and continuity for everyone was preferable to a potentially acrimonious separation with far reaching consequences. But the divisive forces of ethnocentricity still loom large in Scotland and in England. The UK Independence Party (UKIP) seeks to fan security fears, obfuscate the facts on economic migration, and when mixed with a strong dose of disillusionment with the political establishment, is providing a very potent cocktail that has the other parties running scared. Their success at the ballot box is emboldening a whole host of other ethnocentric voices across Europe, from the Basque separatists to the more right-wing factions such as Front National, lead by Marine Le Penn in France.

But if the *worldcentric* order emerging in Europe is going to actually work and take root, change has to occur in all four quadrants. There has to be a change in personal consciousness, group culture, individual behaviour and institutional systems change. The four quadrants arise together, change together, and evolve together, and if one of them gets left out, the change won't get sufficient traction and will eventually fail. If all the Integral elements do not emerge coherently, they are almost inevitably doomed to dysfunction or even extinction. This is why wicked problems are considered so intractable – the solutions only ever focus on one or two quadrants. For change in any area to deliver positive outcomes the change must address all four quadrants or none at all.

Level 6

Of course there are reasons to be hopeful – level 5 is not the final evolutionary step in the drama of humanity's evolution. A major stage or level of consciousness and culture, level 6, started to emerge and was noticeable in the student revolutions of the 1960s, eventually bringing in the civil rights movement in America, the massive environmental movement worldwide, feminism on a personal and professional level, and multiculturalism in general—in other words, the emergence of *postmodernism*. The 'post' in 'postmodernism' means that this next higher level, like all higher levels, brought a new and higher perspective into being. Where rational modernity introduced a third-person perspective, this new stage—known variously as pluralistic, postmodern, relativistic, multicultural – came with the emergence of a *fourth-person perspective* — the capacity to reflect on, and criticise, third-person perspectives, including science.

This led to the whole movement called deconstruction, where a higher perspective – not always with the healthiest of motives – reflected on previous levels and began criticising and 'deconstructing' them, pointing out their major limitations and partialities. In many cases there was a fair amount of truth in their criticisms; but postmodernism in general tended to be taken to extreme forms, where it contradicted itself. It maintained that all truths are culturally constructed; there are no universal truths; there are no Big Pictures or meta-narratives (such as we are giving now); that all knowledge is context-bound, and contexts are boundless. The problem is, postmodernism (whose central claim is that all knowledge is culturally constructed) claims that all of those items we just listed are not mere cultural constructions, but are true for all people, in all cultures, in all places, at all times. In short, they claim that it is universally true that there are no universal truths; they claim that theirs is a superior view, but they also claim that there are no superior views anywhere. So this tendency to self-contradiction has to be watched in any postmodern movement or idea.

Most human rights organisations in the West are at this pluralistic multicultural stage, or level 6. They believe that all people are absolutely equal – a view known as egalitarianism – and that no culture is superior to another culture. The majority of non-governmental organisations ('NGOs') are at this stage of values as well. This is where the common postmodern self-contradiction can come into play with unfortunate results. The standard NGO, with its postmodern relativistic values, believes that no culture is superior or better than another; and yet it goes into countries, where it is working, and assumes that its own values are in some ways better than or superior to those of the culture it is helping. Otherwise, why would it consider what it is doing as being 'help,' if it didn't have something more valuable to offer than what those receiving the 'help' presently have? So many NGOs (with their level 6 values) go to work in a developing country whose major values are at tribal power (level 3) or traditional mythic network (level 4) and attempt to impose their level 6 values on the culture and population, and the whole endeavour backfires badly.

Again, one of the important discoveries of developmental research is that level/stages of development can be accelerated but not skipped or bypassed, and so it is literally impossible for a level 3 or 4 entity to move directly to a level 6 entity. The same holds true for any changes to a group or culture. Change will only stick if it is a result of a well-thought-out series of social and cultural systems, growing out of the organic background of the group or culture itself and not imposed from the outside. With few exceptions, the 'layer cake' of a culture needs to be organically grown layer by layer by layer – in all four quadrants – in order to take root at all.

Level 7

Hope floats even higher when we realise that the postmodern level of consciousness, or level 6, is not the last major level to emerge in human evolution. A few decades ago, developmentalists began noticing the rare emergence of an entirely different type of stage or level, one that was fundamentally and significantly different from anything that had emerged to date in all of history. All of the previous levels – up to and including postmodern pluralism – believe that their truth and values are the only truth and values in the world; that all the others are misguided, confused, infantile, or just plain wrong. But this newly emerging level believed that there was some significance in every single previous level, no exceptions. If nothing else, they are all steps to one's own higher perspective, and without those steps, there would be no higher perspective in the first place. Clare Graves, a pioneering developmentalist, called the emergence of this level a 'monumental leap in meaning'.

To emphasise this difference between the new level and the previous levels, the first six levels were all called 'first tier,' and these new levels were called 'second tier' Some early evidence suggested that there might be two sub-levels in this 'Integral' stage, which we refer to as levels 7 and 8. But, since their similarities are much greater than their differences, we often refer to them as 'the' Integral level, or level 7/8, or simply level 8 – and several models just treat them as one level. But none of this should detract from the central fact that the emergence of 'the' Integral level was a profound, utterly unprecedented 'monumental leap in meaning'. All the first-tier levels tend to take a partial, narrower, exclusive view driven by a mind-set of insufficiency. In contrast second-tier levels are inclusive, embracing, comprehensive, integral, and driven by a mind-set of abundance. This is the first time in human history that any sort of level of consciousness like this had ever emerged to a significant degree. It was still fairly rare – today, only around 3-5 per cent of the worldwide population is at Integral levels of development. But they are game changers – they literally change our views of virtually everything they approach. It is these levels of thinking and being that we will need in order to be able to truly resolve the wicked issues we face.

The emergence of second tier value systems offers hope that we can overcome the current global 'Culture Wars.' The Culture Wars are an ongoing battle between the predominant upper levels of first tier – namely, traditional fundamentalist religious values (level 4); modern rational scientific values (level 5); and postmodern pluralistic multicultural values (level 6). Entire segments of the population are identified with these different values; political parties embrace one or another of them; various individuals identify themselves with one or another. These values run like hidden strata through the very seams of culture itself, defining how individuals think, what they value and desire, what motivates them, what they are willing to work for. Most religions operate from mythic-belongingness, level 4; most businesses are rational-achievement, level 5; most human rights organisations are pluralistic, level 6. They are everywhere, and yet few people embracing them realise that they are being driven by a specific stage of actual human development, whose deep structures are the same the world over (although their surface structures vary from culture to culture and even individual to individual, depending on variables in all four quadrants).

The patterns of these 7 or 8 major levels of values development are not usually seen or recognised by the typical individual because they are not something that can be easily seen by introspecting or looking within. The reason is that they are more like the rules of grammar governing how words fit together, rather than any specific words themselves. Everybody born in a particular language-speaking culture will grow up speaking that language more-or-less quite correctly; they form their sentences correctly, they fit the words together correctly, they natively follow the rules of grammar correctly. But if you ask any of them to actually write down on a sheet of paper a list of all the rules of grammar that they are following, almost nobody can. You only know the actual rules of grammar if you specifically study them. The same is true of the patterns and values at each of the main levels of consciousness – people can't see these levels, they can't see that they are following a particular set of values because those values are like the rules of grammar. Each of these major levels of consciousness is something you look *through*, not something you look *at*. It is a lens through which you interpret and thus experience the world, without ever being aware that you are actually doing so, even though you follow them quite correctly. The only way to know about the patterns, rules, and values of each of these levels is to study them, as we are briefly doing now. Without any awareness of the levels from which we operate, it's easy to see why the various stakeholders involved in a wicked problem never agree! They are operating from different quadrants and from varying levels. Not to mention lines, states and types!

Lines

The unifying levels of second tier also recognise that human beings don't just develop in one way, there are multiple 'lines' to individual development. These lines embrace the multiple intelligences popularised by Howard Gardner of the Harvard Graduate School of Education.[18] Depending on which author you read, numerous different intelligences have been suggested. So in addition to a cognitive intelligence, there is emotional intelligence, moral intelligence, aesthetic intelligence, a values intelligence, an introspective intelligence, a mathematical intelligence, a musical intelligence, a self intelligence, and a spiritual intelligence, among several others. And although these multiple intelligences, or *lines of development*, are each quite different from each other, they all develop through those 8 or so major *levels of development* that we outlined above. Different lines, same levels.

These different intelligences are relatively independent. This means that you can be highly developed in some lines, moderately developed in others, and poorly developed in yet others. This is important because different intelligences tend to be required for success in different areas and fields. A doctor requires different intelligences than a politician, who requires different intelligences than a priest, which are different than an educator's. And what research has demonstrated is that there are different exercises and practices that can assist and help with the growth and development of each intelligence. And, in order to make real progress it is absolutely vital that 'vertical' development is differentiated from 'horizontal' learning.[19]

Studies repeatedly show that vertical development, or increasing *altitude*, is one of the single most important factors in success in virtually any field that has been tested; education, business management, political leadership, even military and strategic thinking. And this *altitude development* is dramatically different from *aptitude training* or horizontally learning a specific skill,

---

[18] Gardner, H. (2011) *Frames of Mind: The Theory of Multiple Intelligences* New York: Basic Books.

[19] Watkins, A. (2014) 'Learning is not development', ChangeBoard.com www.changeboard.com/content/4747/leadership-and-management/learning-is-not-development/

acquiring more knowledge or simply gaining more experience. That's not to say that 'horizontal learning' isn't of great value – it is – but it does not step change capability. 'Horizontal development' simply 'adds more apps' whereas 'vertical development' upgrades the human operating system.

And if we stand any chance of solving the serious problems we face, including wicked problems, we absolutely must upgrade the human operating system. We need to massively expand our capability by increasing our altitude across each of the three dimensions of 'I', 'WE' and 'IT'. This expansion allows us to see further, understand more, become significantly more sophisticated and flexible in the way we approach people and situations.

Vertical development draws on very rich scientific literature on adult 'development', and it is really crucial to enabling us to successfully resolve wicked problems now and in the future. And genuine 'game changing' vertical development is not some utopian, unobtainable fantasy – it is absolutely obtainable and remarkably doable. Working with large multinational organisations for 20 years, there are for example eight lines of adult development (see Figure 2.5) that are instrumental to progress and performance improvement. These eight lines of development can be accurately measured and significantly improved; and it is development up these key lines that significantly determine an individual's ability to resolve complex or wicked problems.

Clearly there are other important lines that we all need to develop in order to evolve to our highest potential. Moral and spiritual intelligence, for example, are critical lines of development for the human race, but these eight are the lines that resonate most with senior leaders and therefore, consistently add the most value. The reality of modern business is that there are very few people at senior levels of business or government that are even willing to discuss issues such as morality or spirituality – regardless of their importance or potential impact on overall performance. We've therefore found time and again that the eight lines of development

Figure 2.5: Key lines of development

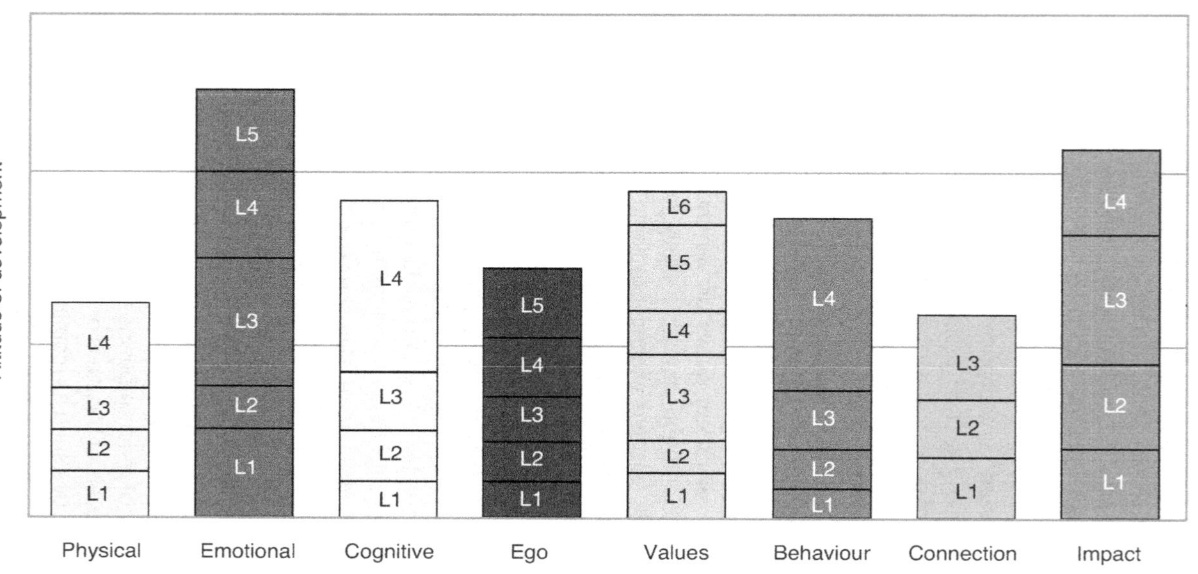

above are the most useful in stimulating transformational growth and development in senior leaders. The discussions that occur during the development of these eight lines do however often open doors into new conversations into morality, spirituality and other important lines. Remember these lines, while independently measurable, can and do affect each other. Thus an individual's development up the cognitive, emotion or values line may also facilitate a shift in morality and raise awareness of spiritual issues.

Keeping different lines in mind as we approach wicked problems is a crucial and extremely useful aspect of any truly Integral approach. Although different lines of development (other than the eight we highlight) may be more relevant in different contexts the ones we have identified are especially relevant for leadership. Clearly if we are to solve wicked and other highly complex challenges we need strong and effective leadership. Our findings and real world experience of wicked business and leadership problems has demonstrated that a successful approach *requires* addressing not only all quadrants and all levels, but these very specific lines as well.

As a species, we stand at a critical juncture. The world is changing very quickly; it is increasingly complex and interconnected, and we are faced with bigger, more complicated, and intractable challenges on an almost daily basis. We have two choices. We can crash and burn under that weight and pressure, or we can rise to the challenge and take a quantum developmental leap forward. In virtually all cases, that leap requires *vertical development*.

Obviously skills, knowledge, and experience are very important in business, in government, and in the solving of these big issues; but they are simply not enough. Regarding many of these intractable issues, we have already reached a point where more knowledge and experience of the problem is not going to change the outcome. That is not what is holding us back. We've all met really gifted, highly intelligent or hugely experienced individuals who are in a position to do something about these issues, but there is still little progress.

Whether we learn how to manage these wicked problems or not will largely depend on whether the people involved in solving them are vertically developed or not. Furthermore, that development has to occur across many lines, in all quadrants and in states and structures of human consciousness – and it must be coherent. This is the whole meaning of 'Integral Coherence' – it's very inclusive, very specific, very measurable, and very doable.

Development is not linear and these lines are not equal. Nor is development constant and sequential. Development up the ego maturity line for example, is relatively straight forward as we grow from a child into an adult, but the *real* transformation – particularly at the leading-edges of our own development and evolution – occurs when we mature as adult human beings and expand our perceptual awareness. The conscious and active development of the ego maturity line of development along with the emotional line (to mention just two prominent examples) can have profound implications on the internal subjective world of 'I' and the interpersonal world of 'WE', which in turn has significant impact on the external world of 'IT'.

For example, lack of vertical development up the emotion and maturity line can fundamentally stall progress in virtually any area. The fact is that even if you get a bunch of experienced, highly intelligent experts in one room, they often can't work together effectively. Because they are human beings before they are experts, and human beings are notoriously poor at building and maintaining relationships. Right now in the world we have countless separate government bodies, NGOs or other national and international organisations who are dedicated to everything from the eradication of cancer to the understanding of autism to climate change to social capitalism. Most are doing great work, but there is still very little integration. The wisdom, knowledge and expertise in each silo are almost always sealed within that silo, leading to duplication of effort and often colossal waste of resources. There is also insufficient, if any, collaboration or sharing of information because each operates like its own little empire.

The people inside these organisations, whilst well-meaning, are frequently operating from an ego-centric perspective (at least within their own siloed area).

So while we may understand the first-person perspective of 'Me, My, I' and we can objectify and pop out to the third-person perspective really well, we are collectively very bad at moving into the higher stages of the shared second-person 'WE' space. If we want to break down the countless silos all seeking to solve some pressing issue from their own often conflicting perspective, we need a frame that allows those disparate groups to interact at a human being level. We need to enable and facilitate the relationships so that all that expertise and knowledge and all the potential solutions can be shared and discussed in a spirit of collaboration, so we can actually solve these things. At the moment, there is rarely enough vertical development among the key players to allow that to happen. Instead they all have a slightly different view, they don't share easily, and they can't or won't reconcile and integrate their views because they are all stuck in first person 'my approach is best' ('Me, My, I') or third person 'this is what the data says'. They can't play nice. They don't have a frame to help them move forward together; and even if they did, at a human being level they just can't bring themselves to do it!

The reason is simple and solvable. The development from adult human being to mature adult human being is not an automatic process that will occur if you just wait long enough. In the passage of 18–20 years, a baby will virtually always develop physically into a child and eventually an adult, but the transition from adult to mature adult requires conscious effort and attention. This is a simple and in some ways obvious point; but the fact is, the failure to really grasp this point is an inherent part of our consistent failure to solve complex – and certainly wicked – problems. This transition is critical if we are to solve the serious issues we face. This starts with a simple acknowledgment of the vertical developmental levels through which our various developmental lines grow and unfold.

States

Today, for the first time in history, we have access to virtually all of the world's great cultures, extending back tens of thousands of years, and we can put them all on the table, compare and contrast them, and create out of that a composite map of all human possibilities. This is what we've done to get the four main quadrants, the 8–12 major levels of development, the eight key lines of development that are crucial in most organisations (and we have only discussed levels and lines in the Upper-Left quadrant; all four quadrants have various levels and lines – and states and types – all equally important). States are also relevant to the resolution of wicked problems; and not only states of consciousness in the Upper-Left or 'I' quadrant – but also cultural 'WE' states in the Lower-Left, brain states in the Upper-Right ('IT'), and everything from weather states to political states in the Lower-Right ('ITS').

For example, the states of consciousness in the Upper-Left quadrant can completely change an individual's ability to be effectively present for the debate. We do not intend to unpack in any detail all the different states of consciousness, as this has been done very effectively elsewhere,[20] [21] but in essence, more than 50 000 years of experiential evidence state that there are four or five major *natural states of consciousness*. Listed by many of the world's great meditative and contemplative systems they are:

1. Waking state
2. Dream state
3. Deep dreamless state
4. Pure witnessing or pure awareness state
5. Non-dual unity state

---

[20] Wilber, K. *The Religion of Tomorrow*, in press, Boston: Shambhala.

[21] Wilber, K. et al (1985) *The Transformations of Consciousness*, Boston: Shambhala.

Further, most of the great traditions give maps of the development of awareness within every one of these states. Most people are only conscious or aware during the waking state, and when they pass into dream or deep dreamless states, they tend to pass out or lose awareness, and so, according to the great traditions, they miss the incredible secret treasures lying in these deeper states of consciousness. The current Western enchantment with 'mindfulness'[22] really only cultivates navigational capability in the awake state.

It is important to realise that the levels and lines of development discussed earlier are really *'structures of consciousness'*, and track the process of 'Growing Up', whereas levels of awareness in this second major axis of development concern *'states of consciousness'* and track the process of 'Waking Up'. States, unlike structures, are first-person, direct, immediate experiences, and thus individuals having them are definitely aware that they are doing so, unlike structures, which – like grammar – they follow without knowing that they are doing so but can be objectively described in the third person.

Thus, if you are meditating and you have an experience of universal love, or radiant bliss, or universal care and compassion, you will definitely be aware of those often overwhelming experiences, and you can keep track of their unfolding, growth and development if you wish, which is why human knowledge of states goes back at least 50 000 years to the earliest shamans.

So states can be clearly experienced by any who traverse them. Structures, precisely because they cannot be seen by introspecting, cannot easily be seen and thus were not discovered until around 100 years ago, but now make up virtually all Western development models, while states make up virtually all Eastern

[22] Schatz, C. (2011) 'Mindfulness meditations improves connections in the brain', Harvard Health Publications. www.health.harvard.edu/blog/mindfulness-meditation-improves-connections-in-the-brain-201104082253

models. But nowhere, East or West, premodern or modern, are *both* of these extraordinary developmental sequences included except in the Integral Model.

So what this composite or Integral Meta-Map shows us is that humans have at least these two very different types of developmental sequences available to them – *structure* development resulting in 'Growing Up', and *state* development resulting in 'Waking Up'. Both are absolutely crucial in human development and the ability to address wicked problems.[23]

Types

Organisations have in recent times been fairly obsessed by typologies. The thinking has been if we can define what type of leaders we want, we can build them and then we will succeed. This is a strange view to take because if you were to summarise the entire leadership literature, you would say that the one thing that all authors agree on is to be a great leader you have to 'be yourself', i.e. there is not a 'cookie-cutter' type of leader. Everyone leads in a different way. That is not to say that typologies are not fascinating or useful; they are. Typologies can be very helpful in raising awareness. But the problem is that there are dozens of typologies – in fact, in the various quadrants, there are hundreds of different types of things, events, processes, phenomena, societies, cultures, organisms, and on and on. There are many different types of religion, types of governments, psychological types, types of species, types of electromagnetic radiation, types of physical forces, types of values, and motivations, and emotions, and plant types, and organic systems, and so on and so forth.

---

[23] For more information on states of consciousness and Waking Up, see Wilber, K. (2015) *Integral Meditation*, Boston: Shambhala, or Wilber, K. (2006) *Integral Spirituality* Boston: Shambhala.

Perhaps the most important reason to understand typologies is that they can reveal something useful about the diversity of perspective, and if we wish to create a fully inclusive Integral Frame we must use the fewest number of items to explain the most amount of reality. Since most things come in various types, if we actually listed all the types, we would almost be listing all things in the known universe, which is an enormously complex map hardly worth using for anything. But the point of the approach we are suggesting here is that the Integral Frame can be adapted to virtually any human endeavour – even the solving of wicked problems. As we apply the Framework to any particular area, we will often want to use various typologies that apply to that area itself, and so we include 'types' as a generic item reminding us to look for any typologies that might be beneficial in any particular approach that we take.

The Application of an Integral Approach to Wicked Problems

The Integral Framework is a meta-map which helps shed light on wicked problems so that we can finally have a way of defining them properly. Only when we can fully appreciate the challenge we face can we ever really come up with better solutions. Looking at wicked problems through the Integral Frame begins to disclose several absolutely stunning insights. It includes *quadrants* – or first-, second- and third-person perspectives on every issue (as well as divisions within quadrants, called 'zones'); it includes *levels*, or the degrees of vertical development unfolded through evolution, with each of at least 8–12 major levels having dramatically different values, drives, needs, morals, and worldviews; it includes *lines*, or specific areas of development, including at least eight very different lines required for success in any modern organisation, all moving through the same basic 8–12 levels of development in the process of 'Growing Up'; it includes *states*, including the various natural states of consciousness that lead to a profound Waking Up; and it include *types*, or any number of useful classifications of the various kinds of items available – including negative translation or 'shadow work' and positive translation or 'flourishing.' When any problem, issue, or area is looked at using all of these elements, profoundly new, novel, and creative solutions become possible, touching on all the major bases, an approach that is itself truly revolutionary.

In effect, the Integral Frame is the first genuinely overall or comprehensive map of the human being that has been made, including major discoveries made in the pre-modern, the modern, and the postmodern world. All of the world's great cultures were literally put on the table to create a map that included the true but partial insights of all of them. Something like this had never been done before, simply because, before this, nobody had had access to all the world's cultures to begin with. So these insights include not only today's leading-edge big discoveries – from quarks to brain neuroplasticity to psychological growth techniques – but discoveries going all the way back to the earliest shamans, some 50 000 years ago. By comparing and contrasting all of the major maps left by the great human cultures around the world, this approach would let us decide which components of them were indeed global and universal – and therefore still valid – and which aspects were only culturally local and relative – and therefore belonged in the museum.

What we are proposing is that we use this newly uncovered meta-map to find better, longer lasting solutions to the world's escalating number of wicked problems. Some of it is obvious; some of it is staggeringly novel; all of it has an overwhelming amount of evidence supporting it.

One of the biggest challenges of wicked problems is that they are essentially novel and unique. We can gain some experience about the approach to wicked problems, but we are always essentially starting from scratch. The Integral Frame means that we don't have to. Using this meta-map – a comprehensive distillation of the best and brightest from the major cultures around the world over the past 50 000 years – we can see the challenge from a number of stable perspectives that can bring everyone up to speed quickly and make sure everyone is at least on the same page when it comes to defining the problem. That alone can save valuable time, money and energy in the formulation of the best solution. When we add the second ingredient – Coherence – the Integral Frame becomes immensely powerful.

Coherence

While there is an inherent tendency in all elements of the Integral Framework to arise in a harmonious, balanced, and constructively interconnected fashion, evidence shows that doesn't always occur in practice. There are healthy and unhealthy, functional and dysfunctional, coherent and incoherent versions of every single one of the elements found in the Integral Meta-Theory.

So while the Integral Framework is crucial in helping us find genuine solutions to the wicked problems we face, we also need to ensure that the healthy, functional and coherent versions show up and not the unhealthy, dysfunctional and incoherent! That is where 'coherence' comes in.

When we strip back the complexity and interdependency of any wicked problem, human beings are at the epicentre. Wicked problems are human problems. They may be very large, very complex and highly interconnected human problems, but they are human problems none the less. Climate change is a wicked problem exacerbated by too many human beings on the planet and our love affair with fossil fuel. Solving climate change will require widespread human change. Poverty is a wicked problem exacerbated by over-population and exploitation of resources from the hands of the many into the hands of the few. It is also further amplified by other human issues such as poor education and socio-economic problems. Solving poverty will also require widespread human change.

The Integral Frame is the most comprehensive map of the human being ever created, but human beings still need to actually use the map. The people charged with finding and implementing solutions actually have to use it, apply it and put it into practice using the best, healthy version of their capabilities whatever developmental level they are at, otherwise the dysfunction they can bring can create an even more complex mess instead of the Integral wisdom we so desperately need.

Plus as Alfred Korzybski reminds us, 'The map is not the territory'.[24] A map of New York is not New York but a representation of New York, and in order to really experience New York we must take our map and visit the 'Big Apple' itself. Most of the current maps on how to solve wicked problems provide, at best, a fragmented, limited, partial or broken view. As a result they are misleading and ineffective maps of the real territories that we inhabit.

And if the Integral Frame is the most accurate map we have, coherence ensures we can actually use the map in practice to achieve the best possible results in the territory. One of the biggest challenges with some of the most brilliant, potentially revolutionary theories on the planet right now is that they rarely, if ever, make their way into mainstream discussion. They are almost never reported in newspapers; and if they are, they are 'dumbed down' or diluted to a Tweet-able sound-bite. They are rarely discussed in business schools, boardrooms or government white papers, so they rarely reach the people who could actually use them to change the world. And even if they do, unless all those people are sufficiently developed across all quadrants, lines, levels and states AND are able to express that development healthily and functionally (at whatever level they are at) then little will actually change. Part of the truly difficult nature of wicked problems is that the difficulty lies not just in the problem but in

[24] Korzybski, A. (1994) *Science and Sanity: An Introduction to Non-Aristotelian Systems and General Semantics*, 5th edition, New Jersey: Institute of General Semantics.

the change agents themselves – which is the last place usually looked.

Coherence therefore facilitates practical, 'in-the-heat-of-battle' application of the Integral Frame in the real world territory of wicked problems while also ensuring that the healthy, functional and coherent versions arise from every single one of the elements found in the Integral Meta-Theory.

Integral Coherence is therefore an attempt to solve wicked problems in the *real* territory by starting with the most accurate and comprehensive map. By ensuring effective *practice* of highly effective *theory* we are able to uncover *and implement* genuine, long lasting solutions – made workable, practical and successful by real people, knee deep in serious, often overwhelming real world wicked problems.

Coherence: The Big Picture

Coherence is paradoxically both simple and extremely complex. When we are in a coherent state we experience (in the first person) a sense of harmony, balance, optimal functioning and flow. It can be visualised (in the third person) as a stable dynamic pattern of change or variability. It is this stable dynamic pattern of variability that facilitates change and evolution in the complex system we call life.

Unfortunately we rarely think about the nature of change so we miss the relevance of coherence – or this stable dynamism – as a facilitator for ongoing change and evolution. In the same way that we rarely think about our own thinking, we rarely think about the nature of change, even though both thinking and change are constantly present and constantly defining our lives. We live in a rapidly changing VUCA world, full of wicked problems – but we never really stop to consider the deep nature of the changes happening to us and all around us all the time. As a result we often feel at the mercy of those changes. It is hardly surprising therefore that so many people are afraid of change; they find it unsettling and will often resist it.

And yet change is actually a sign of health in all complex systems, whether we are talking about the human body, society, business or government. Systems that are static and never change, that demonstrate no variability or dynamism, are either dead or dying.

If we look at coherence objectively (from the third-person perspective, although the same notions of change apply fully and equally to first- and second-person dimensions of coherence as well), there are two aspects of variability that are critical to the optimum functioning of the system, namely the *amount* of variability and the *pattern* of the variability. When a system exhibits a consistent pattern of stable variability it is a vibrant, healthy, living system. A lack of variability indicates a lack of health, brittleness, rigidity and an inability to adapt to changing conditions.

To help put this idea in context, consider the Burj Khalifa in Dubai. When it was designed, the architects needed to create a design with the right amount of variability so the building, currently the tallest in the world, would bend in the wind, as it were. Too much variability or flexibility and it would be unstable and the people inside the building would feel seasick. Too little variability or adaptability and the building would be rigid, making it vulnerable in high winds or a major sand storm.

This dynamic can also be seen in business. Too little variability or adaptability and the business is vulnerable. When a leader refuses to budge from an evidently failing strategy the business will eventually fail. This was witnessed in the music industry when record companies focused their attention on suing illegal music download websites rather than appreciating that their market was changing and they needed to change along with it. Had they demonstrated greater variability, the fact that a significant proportion of their customers no longer wanted a physical product could have been a major cost saving and an opportunity to evolve to a more profitable business model (which the successful companies eventually did).

Conversely, too much variability can also make the business unstable; it becomes too changeable, jumping from one new idea or new strategy to the next. Struggling businesses with their backs against the wall will often become excessively flexible – diversifying into new untested markets or new untested products or services in a desperate bid to find a solution to falling revenue or diminishing market share. It rarely works. Such businesses are basically descending into increasing chaos and ultimately collapse.

A sign of health in ALL systems from buildings to business to biology is therefore the right *amount* and *pattern* of variability. When we achieve that balance we achieve coherence and healthy, functional progress is more likely.

In practice coherence allows us to *consciously* access and manage our highest capability at whatever level of development we are at. Vertical development (or altitude) is absolutely essential in solving wicked problems, but we also need sustained and consistent access to those increased capabilities (heightened aptitude). Often, even when vertically developed we can be brilliant one day and mediocre the next. This inconsistency is confusing because we never quite know why some days we are able to bring our very best thinking or huge reserves of energy to a problem and the next we can barely appreciate the problem. Coherence (at whatever level) is the missing link that allows us to consciously and consistently access those elevated levels and optimal performance so we don't have to rely on good fortune, circumstance, or whether we are wearing our lucky socks or not!

Physiological Coherence Unpacked

Often the easiest way to really grasp the importance of coherence as a concept is to unpack coherence in a particular line of development. The easiest is the physiological line because we all have a body: we are all impacted by what is happening in our physiology and by the nuanced physiological signals that are being sent from one organ to another inside the extremely complex system that is our whole body – whether we are aware of that impact or not.

Most people don't realise the significant influence that our physiology has on our ability to think clearly, make good decisions and deliver high quality, consistent results. Although not the same as actual vertical development, coherent physiology creates a stable biological platform that can help facilitate vertical growth across other lines of development. Being brilliant or being able to solve wicked problems is, after all, extremely difficult if you are exhausted and in need of several stiff drinks or a pack of cigarettes just to get through the day. The importance of physiological coherence is explained in more detail in *Coherence: the Secret Science of Brilliant Leadership,* but for the record physiological coherence is not fitness, health or even muscular strength. It is simply stable, dynamic variability in the human body – something that is made possible by consciously controlling our heart rate through correct breathing.[25] (We'll give a brief example of this breathing technique as soon as we explore the general concept.)

The impact of physiological coherence can be seen when examining the electrical patterns created by the human heart. This also serves to demonstrate the role of variability and its impact on the health of a system – in this case the health of the human biological system or human body.

Our heart rate is never constant. It changes every single beat because the distance between every heartbeat is constantly changing (see Figure 2.6). This is known as 'heart rate variability' or HRV for short. The amount of this change defines how much variability we have. A loss of HRV has been repeatedly shown to

[25] Watkins, A. (2015) *4D Leadership* London: Kogan Page.

predict 'all-cause mortality' or death from anything.[26] It is also known to predict illness before any physical symptoms emerge, which means it can also be used to quantify risk of ill-health.[27] Plus HRV can be used to quantify ageing, because as we get older we lose HRV at a rate of approximately 3 per cent per annum.[28] This is why increasing physiological coherence can literally turn back the clock and give us access to the levels of energy we had ten years ago.

Figure 2.6: Changes in the inter-beat interval

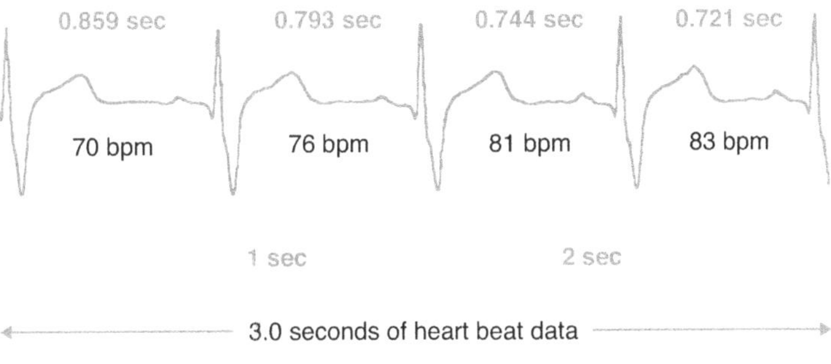

[26] Dekker, J. M., Schouten, E. G., Klootwijk, P., Pool, J., Swenne, C. A. and Kromhout, D. (1997) 'Heart rate variability from short electrocardiographic recordings predicts mortality from all causes in middle-aged and elderly men. The Zutphen Study' American Journal of Epidemiology, vol. 145, no. 10.

[27] Gerritsen, J., Dekker, J. M., TenVoorde, B. J., Kostense, P. J., Heine, R. J., Bouter, L. M., Heethaar, R. M., and Stehouwer, C. D. (2001) 'Impaired autonomic function is associated with increased mortality, especially in subjects with diabetes, hypertension, or a history of cardiovascular disease: the Hoorn Study', Diabetes Care, vol. 24, no. 10.

[28] Umetani, K., Singer, D. H., McCraty, R., and Atkinson, M. (1998) 'Twenty-four hour time domain heart rate variability and heart rate: relations to age and gender over nine decades', Journal of the American College of Cardiology, vol. 31, no. 3.

Human health, as in all complex systems, requires change or variability. The amount of variability in general predicts longevity. But as we have said, it is not only the *amount* of variability that matters but the *pattern* of variability or change. Figure 2.7 shows various heart rates similar to those you might see on a TV medical drama.

Figure 2.7: The relationship between HRV chaos and coherence on heart performance

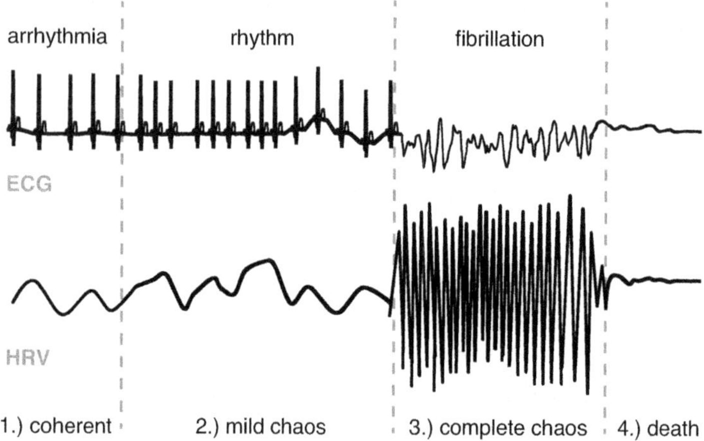

If we look at Figure 2.7 the top ECG trace shows how an ECG might change in a patient in the Emergency Room. Sections 1 and 2 are both normal; section 3 illustrates a loss of the normal ECG signal typical of someone having a heart attack; section 4 is seen in someone whose heart has stopped and there is no ECG signal. But when we look at the HRV trace generated by the ECG we can see the effect of ECG changes on both the pattern of variability and the amount of variability.

In the first section the ECG is normal; the corresponding HRV trace is coherent. This means that the pattern of change or variability is stable, sinusoidal and predictable. Such a pattern is often driven by breathing and the ECG is said to be demonstrating 'sinus arrhythmia' which simply means the distance between the heart beats is varying predictably. In the second section the ECG is still normal, the heart is beating properly but the variability of the HRV is mildly chaotic and less predictable. The ECG is said to be in sinus rhythm. In section three, the heart stops beating properly and starts 'fibrillating'. This is a pre-death state and there are no visible heart beats. The amount of HRV increases to an alarming degree and the pattern is completely chaotic. If the patient does not receive urgent debilitation then they will 'flat-line' shown in the last section. There are no detectable heart beats or ECG signal because the heart is no longer generating any electrical activity. This is called 'asystole' (no contractions) and death follows pretty quickly thereafter.

Little or no variability, as well as excessive variability, suggests a system that is unstable and close to collapse.

If the heart rhythm is restored so that the amount and pattern of variability returns to create a coherent heart rhythm (Figure 2.7: 1.) then health and recovery are at least possible. This greater coherence creates greater stability, greater flexibility and adaptability which in turn can significantly increase the physical energy in the system and help to optimise performance. This is the 'horizontal' benefits of coherence. But we both also believe that coherence can facilitate vertical development in virtually all the major lines of development via healthy 'prepotency' if nothing else.

Prepotency is one of Maslow's central findings from his needs hierarchy. It is simply the idea that each higher level will fully emerge only if its immediately preceding lower level has first been satisfied. Somebody who is starving (survival needs) will not be very interested in finding their higher potentials in self-actualisation because they will be too busy looking for food. Since all of the basic levels of development remain in a human even after the period during which they emerged, this 'prepotent' necessity for handling all of our levels becomes a crucial component of any truly comprehensive or Integral approach.

For 'Integral Coherence,' prepotency tells us one crucial item: lack of coherence on a previous level prevents the emergence of the next-higher level. Evidence found in almost 20 years in this field[29] is that significant developmental strides and performance improvement become possible once individuals cultivate coherence within and across multiple lines of development (in a prepotency that includes physical, emotional, and mental). The starting point for many leaders is to develop physiological coherence in the physiology line of development so that they can significantly increase energy reserves and their ability to drive performance. Furthermore, this level of Coherence facilitates the emergence of a yet higher level, the general emotional line itself. Likewise, training that level for its greatest possible capacities and functionality – in general, an emotional coherence (including emotional literacy) – directly facilitates the emergence of the next yet higher dimension of consciousness, that of cognitive intelligence. This becomes immediately obvious in that leaders will often be unable to access their best, most creative thinking, or get the most out of others, if they don't first develop some degree of emotional coherence. More advanced levels of emotional coherence facilitate more constructive and powerful working relationships and more refined cognitive intelligence. Thus, one's cognitive intelligence is facilitated by emotional coherence, which is facilitated by physiological coherence – an example of 'vertical coherence' being enhanced by 'horizontal coherence'. Twenty years of working with leaders – as well as the entire field of developmental studies relating to 'prepotency' – has strongly suggested the value of coherence both within and across multiple lines. The idea that 'book smarts' alone is all you need to succeed has long been discredited.

[29] Watkins, A. (2014) *Coherence: The Secret Science of Brilliant Leadership,* London: Kogan Page.

The consequences of physiological chaos and coherence

When the heart rate fluctuates in a random, unpredictable way, it creates a 'chaotic' HRV trace (see Figure 2.8). In contrast, when the heart rate varies in a more stable dynamic way, the pattern is completely different even though the average heart rate has not changed.

In Figure 2.8, the amount of variability when the trace is chaotic is roughly the same as when the trace is coherent. In addition, the average heart rate remains roughly the same during the period of chaos and coherence. The coherent period is, however, characterised by a much greater level of efficiency and minimal wasted energy.

Figure 2.8: HRV chaos to coherence

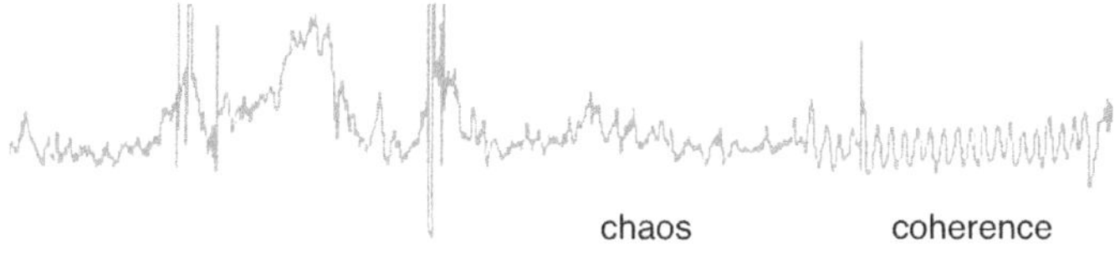

It is similar to driving a car in very unpredictable city traffic. The driving conditions mean that you may have to stop, start, accelerate and break frequently as you navigate traffic lights and tailbacks. This type of chaotic driving uses more fuel, even though you may only be travelling a few miles and it leads to more wear and tear of the car. Driving on a motorway is completely different. Even if the traffic compresses from time to time you don't have to stamp on the brakes or suddenly accelerate to the same extent. You may end up travelling the same distance in both cases but the motorway driving has more stable dynamic variability and therefore consumes less fuel than city driving and is kinder on your car. The human body is remarkably similar – physiological coherence enables us to operate more efficiently and conserve much more energy which can help us to 'go further' and maintain high performance for longer.

Whether chaotic or coherent the heart's electrical signal travels to the brain every second of every day and alters brain function.[30] In short, as we just noted, our ability to think clearly can be radically impaired when the electrical input from our heart to our brain is chaotic (the external objectively visible chaos, and Upper-Right Hand quadrant phenomena altering the Upper-Left Hand quadrant thought process). Such physiological chaos often results in a 'DIY Lobotomy' which is designed to shut our brain down, and this mechanism has been saving our life for over 200 000 years. When we are in danger we do not need in-depth analysis and extensive reflection – we need action. For example, if you met a grizzly bear in the wild you don't need to ponder what type of bear it might be or whether it looks hungry or upset, you need to run or hide!

When we are in danger or under pressure, our physiology will naturally go into chaos, our thinking becomes binary – fight/flight or play dead – so that we increase our chances of survival. However, we very rarely encounter grizzly bears when trying to solve wicked problems, and yet the same mechanism is often triggered. We experience the same frontal lobe shut down and find ourselves blurting out stupid answers, or 'going dumb' – neither of which will help us to solve problems, let alone wicked problems.

In contrast, when we input our brain with a coherent electrical signal, the frontal lobes can turn back on and we get full and consistent access to the best, most perceptive and insightful thinking we are capable of at whatever level we are at. Of course this is not an all or nothing phenomenon. But having worked

[30] Watkins, A. (2014) *Coherence: The secret science of brilliant leadership*, London: Kogan Page.

with leaders all over the world for more than 20 years we have repeatedly seen that it is possible to significantly improve clarity, creativity and the quality of decision making with increasing levels of physiological coherence. This increased access to capability does not necessarily mean that the individual has definitely developed vertically, they may just be functioning at a more optimal degree within their existing developmental level; but increasing coherence, as we previously stressed, can certainly facilitate a leap forward in a leader's development.

One of the reasons that physiological coherence unlocks a new level of capability is because it drives something called 'entrainment'. Entrainment is now a widely understood physiological phenomenon where different bodily systems literally synchronise with each other and create a state of heightened efficiency and performance. The heart is the body's main 'pacemaker' or generator creating a total of 3.5 watts of energy (enough to power your mobile phone[31]) – that's 50 times more electrical power output than the brain and 5000 times more electromagnetic power than the brain. This power causes other body pacemakers, or biological oscillators, to synchronise with it. These other biological oscillators are clusters of cells that have automatic and spontaneous electrical activity. For example, in the brain stem there is a cluster of cells, called the respiratory centre, which determines the rate at which we breathe. Thus our breathing rate is set and adjusted automatically by these cells without the need for any conscious thought. Similarly the vasomotor centre controls and adjusts our blood pressure. Clusters of cells in our gut control the speed of passage of food

[31] Nelson, D. (2009) 'Heartbeat converted into electric current to recharge mobile phones', *The Telegraph* www.telegraph.co.uk/news/newstopics/howaboutthat/6339171/Heartbeat-converted-into-electric-current-to-recharge-mobile-phones.html

through our bowel by altering peristalsis.[32] The brain has a very large number of biological oscillators transmitting information on four different wavelengths.

Each one of these biological oscillators sets its own rhythm largely independent from the other pacemakers. This independence enables a certain degree of flexibility in responsiveness, but it can also disable effectiveness. Coherence generated by the heart entrains – harmonises and coordinates – these disparate oscillators to enable us to access a state of optimal performance.

When present, coherence at any level facilitates the growth or development of the system on the whole. Vertical coherence directly expands capability; horizontal coherence ensures maximum functionality (at its level) and facilitates the growth and development of the next-higher level in the overall system.

Obviously if an individual is a self-serving narcissistic egomaniac then little progress is possible, even with coherence! This is why we need coherence AND vertical development across the various elements in the Integral Meta-Theory. This potent combination ensures that we have consistent access to the healthy iteration of our increasingly elevated development and not consistent access to increasing dysfunction.

Unfortunately, although coherence is an entirely natural state for most people, it is not very common. For most of us we rarely experience a coherent state, and even if we occasionally do, we have no idea how we got there. And if we don't know how we got there, we can't replicate it and produce that optimum state more of the time. Coherence needs to be cultivated.

By mastering some simple, practical techniques it is possible for example to increase the amount of energy available to you. One of the main ways we lose energy is through an erratic HRV which

[32] Gershon, M. D. (1998) *The Second Brain*, New York: HarperCollins.

is often experienced through incoherent or erratic breathing. In difficult or stressful situations one of the first things to 'go' is our breathing. When we are frustrated our breathing tends to be a series of mini breath holds or what is known as 'glottic stops'. The same is true of panic, anxiety or anger – all of which involve a different type of disordered breathing.

This wastes energy and causes unnecessary wear and tear on the body and yet it can be rectified in a matter of minutes. The B.R.E.A.T.H.E. skill is designed to enable us to generate a rhythmic breathing pattern which increases the power output of the heart and drives other biological systems to synchronise with it. Effectively we are using our breath to consciously control the output of the body's power station, triggering entrainment which in turn conserves energy and optimises physiological efficiency.

BREATHE is an acronym so it is easy to remember:

Breathe

Rhythmically

Evenly

And

Through the

Heart

Everyday

The key aspects of breath to focus on are:

1. Rhythmicity – fixed ratio of in: out breath
2. Smoothness – even flow rate in and out
3. Location of attention – particularly focused in the heart area to trigger positive emotion

This is an incredibly easy and yet powerful technique that anyone can learn. We have successfully taught it to children as young as 3 years old and people as old as 80 years with equal success.

There are also Smartphone apps that can help you master this technique.[33]

The increased energy that such exercises will release in your body is the horizontal benefit of developing physiological coherence. This increased energy can create a platform for increasing development in the physiology line. Increased physiological development, as we are defining it here, involves increased awareness of your physicality, a more powerful presence, more physiological balance and greater recuperative powers. Although, on its own, greater physiological coherence does not necessarily lead to any vertical development in the other quadrants or lines, the increased clarity that can flow from it can create the conditions for vertical development in the other key lines.

The other lines of development have their own type of coherence. For example, emotional coherence is slightly different to physiological coherence. It, too, requires us to learn new skills (a horizontal phenomenon). Clarity about how to apply some simple emotional self-regulation skills then facilitates stable, predictable variability within the emotional line of development. In other words we learn to expand our emotional awareness and access to a wider emotional repertoire (or emotional literacy), thus increasing our emotional range and variability. Learning to consciously choose our emotional state rather than being led or ruled by whatever emotional state we find ourselves in, makes us considerably more emotionally intelligent. This in turn allows us to flex and adapt to all types of people and situations which is clearly a powerful ability in solving wicked problems. We gain emotional sovereignty and elevate our social capability and capacity (vertical development) which also facilitates the development of cognitive coherence and cognitive development.

Cognitive coherence is different from emotional coherence,

---

[33] Complete Coherence Ltd (2015) CardioSense Trainer™ (CST Mobile) (Mobile Application Software) http://www.complete-coherence.com/what-we-do/apps/

which is different from physiological coherence. But they are all, as we have seen, 'prepotent' – meaning that coherence in one will make the emergence of the next higher dimension more likely; and in turn, its coherence will make the emergence of the yet next higher dimension more likely. What they all have in common is the nature of the change. Thus coherent change, regardless of whether it is occurring in the physiology, emotional, cognitive or other lines of development, is characterised by healthy variability that is stable and coherent and creates a platform for growth and improvement.

This is a simple but far-reaching realisation; and the clear implication is that for an approach to wicked problems to actually work, that approach must be Integral; and for Integral to actually work, its elements must be coherent.

It is therefore vital to increase the coherence, the harmonious functionality, within all the key lines of development. In addition, it is also crucial to cultivate coherence between the different lines of development – not to mention between the quadrants – otherwise our ability to solve wicked problems may be very limited. Remember, having all the Integral elements present and recognised is one thing; having them present functionally or dysfunctionally is quite another.

We see incoherence or disproportionate development in the developmental lines all the time in business. For example, some leaders may be very developed in their cognitive line but very underdeveloped in their emotional, ego or values line. This lack of coherence across lines of development brings its own problems and can certainly impair progress. In fact, if anything, such incoherence across lines can be more troublesome than a general lack of development, as leaders with an overdeveloped single line can mistakenly assume that because of their brilliance in one line they are highly developed in all other lines of development and therefore don't need additional horizontal or vertical 'development'. Often nothing could be further from the truth.

Whether we are operating coherently or chaotically in any dimension has a profound impact on our results, our behaviour, our performance and our ability to solve complex and wicked problems. And vertical development can more readily be achieved through the conscious movement toward coherence in each of the lines of development and through the application of skills that not only add capability but significantly expand capacity. These vertical skills are well understood and widely available within the developmental studies community, and are present in virtually every major developmental model in existence. Such practices do not just extend present skills or *aptitudes*, they invite the emergence of higher-level skills or *altitudes* altogether.

When we are unobstructed by low energy reserves, reactive, negative or suppressed emotion, fuzzy thinking or ineffective behaviour, we are more productive, enjoy better relationships and are more influential. And of course when we become personally coherent at second tier, and the other stakeholders become personally coherent at second tier – and each of our 'I' lines are fundamentally coherent – then we are able to generate collective coherence and the coherently Integral 'WE' emerges and then truly astonishing things are possible.

Ultimately, coherence is the right amount and pattern of stable yet dynamic change across all the lines of development, all quadrants, and all levels, and enables us to access more of our potential as human beings. This involves a significant commitment to change and develop our interior dimensions just as much as we are already invested in changing and altering our exterior dimensions – either alone spells wicked, wicked problems.

Integral Coherence

Essentially Integral Coherence means there is a fluid balance in all of the elements of any particular 'Integral Address'. The Integral Address is the sum total of Integral elements present in any individual or collective. It defines the particular active quadrants, levels, lines, states, and types. All phenomena in existence have a specific Integral Address; this includes the degree of coherence in all four quadrants. In the Upper-Right, there is coherence in the 'true', including a physiological coherence driven by auto coherence in the heart and a biological systems entrainment. In the Lower-Right, there is coherence in functional fit – the individual has to coherently mesh with the many systems to which it belongs. In the Lower-Left, there has to be coherence in justness or rightness, a genuine mutual understanding within the interpersonal space and the many 'We's' that the individual is a part of – an ethical coherence. And in the Upper-Left, there has to be a coherence or mesh in 'truthfulness', which includes emotional, psychological, and spiritual integration. That again might seem complex – and it is, wickedly. But we have to remember that all of those elements are actually arising in any event – they are real, they are occurring, they exist – and we can either engage them consciously and coherently, or be blindsided by them in ignorance – thus ensuring our wicked problems remain wicked problems. Wicked problems are human problems and the difficulty in solving these intractable challenges is not necessarily the problems themselves, but the dysfunctional incoherence of the people trying to solve them!

Knowing how we can behave in the various quadrants or what perspectives we can view the problem from is incredibly helpful in finding genuine solutions to the problems we face. But, of course, human beings still determine those variables. It is down to the human beings involved as to whether we can create a full picture of the problem and formulate viable solutions or not. And yet if those human beings are stuck in one quadrant or are operating from a particular evolutionary developmental level, and that level is not sufficiently sophisticated, or significantly out of step with their progress in another quadrant, then we will be unlikely to ever make any real progress. This is a primary reason wicked problems so often remain truly wicked – the real issues are not being effectively addressed, or often even seen.

And we need coherence in the Integral Frame – across the dimensions and between the dimensions. If there is no real coherent connection between these different dimensions – both internally and externally – then it is likely that little will get solved because even if we manage to bring together a range of smart, enlightened individuals and highly trained experts to solve the wicked problems, if they can't 'play nice' together nothing will change. Our capacity for mutual understanding is one of the great human marvels.[34] If there is no individual coherence within the emotional, energetic and cognitive levels, among other elements, there is likely to be little coherence between those smart individuals in the room, and genuinely sustainable solutions remain unlikely.

If individuals are individually coherent – and also become interpersonally coherent – then they are much more likely to establish a powerfully coherent bond enabling them to sustain their efforts and become a more powerful force, as well as apply the Integral Framework in the coherent and balanced way it was meant to be used. As Margaret Mead once famously said, 'Never doubt that a small group of thoughtful, committed citizens can change the world – indeed it is the only thing that ever has.'[35] We would change this to 'never doubt that a small group of Integrally coherent individuals can positively change the world – indeed it is the only thing that ever has.'

The Talmud states, 'We do not see things as they are; we see things as we are.' Integral Coherence is therefore a rally cry to all the individuals currently involved in problem solving – wicked and

---

[34] Stolk, A., Noordzij, M. L., Verhagen, L., Volman, I., Schoffelen, J. M., Oostenveld, R., Hagoort, P., and Toni, I., 'Cerebral, coherence between communicators marks the emergence of meaning', *Proc Natl Acad Sci U S A* 2014. Advance online publication. doi: 10.1073/pnas.1414886111. www.mpi.nl/departments/neurobiology-of-language/news/cerebral-coherence-between-communicators-marks-the-emergence-of-meaning

[35] Mead, M. (1964) *Continuities In Cultural Evolution*, Yale University Press.

otherwise – to recognise that right now they might very well just be seeing things as they themselves are as opposed to how the problem actually exists in all its glorious yet often unrecognised dimensions. Only when we can appreciate that fact and actively seek to develop coherently horizontally and vertically across a number of mission critical elements of development can we ever hope to solve these issues – in other words, if we become Integrally Coherent. If we do, however, and if we do in enough numbers, then genuine breakthroughs are most definitely possible.

Coherence is profound. When present at any given level it can turn the impossible into the possible for that level, and when present with the Integral Frame can in many cases turn wicked problems into manageable problems.

Without this delicate balance between the right amount and type of variability, the movement or 'life' that resides within all systems, at any level, is too random, too erratic and too volatile, which can be destructive and lead to chaotic breakdown, not creative breakthrough.

The only way we will effectively solve and re-solve the wicked problems is if we sustainably breathe life and real world dynamism into the Integral Frame by applying Integral Coherence. There is no point throwing everything we have at something so that we are emotionally, financially, spiritually, physically bankrupt because these issues can't be solved once in some tick-box fashion. They need to be constantly solved and re-solved as they constantly evolve. This sustainability is therefore paramount in bringing the Integral Frame to life and *keeping* it alive.

By using the Integral Frame as the map and coherence as the force that brings the map to life, we can create something we have never had before – a chance to resolve some of the world's toughest problems.

We *are* all in this together; to resolve these wicked problems will need all of us, individually and collectively. We will need to coherently integrate all aspects of who we are and work together in this crucial endeavour, otherwise we will continue to have partial, incomplete, ineffective answers and we will all continue to suffer. The hope is that we realise that the wicked problems we face are *shared problems,* and if we embrace Integral Coherence we can very likely become sufficiently smart, flexible and sophisticated to finally manage them effectively.

Integral Coherence is the emphasis of the coherence inherent in the Integral Frame, to ensure that the people charged with solving complex problems have an accurate road map to the solution AND are sufficiently enlightened as leaders and as human beings to be able to utilise it for maximum effect. With such transformation we can change our world, and thus – perhaps – finally make a real difference to our own lives and the lives of those around us.

Part 3

Climate Change

A couple of years ago I (AW) spent a few days with my wife and four boys in Cornwall, south west England. It was a Sunday in early November, the air was crisp, the winter sun was beaming and the surf was roaring excitedly onto the beach. We decided to put on our wetsuits and wade out into the frothy water. This might sound unremarkable but for two facts – the sea around the UK is so cold that seals normally cling together to share body warmth; and I am a complete wimp about cold water and would normally never venture into the sea even in the middle of an English summer. But this time we all waded out – the water was so warm we splashed around for two or three hours and only finally came in because we were hungry. Tucking into a deep bowl of hot chicken soup and a doorstep of granary bread smeared with butter I glanced at the Sunday papers. A story about climate change caught my eye. Maybe it was the unseasonably warm water maybe it was something in the soup, but this story affected me.

For some time, I, like many others, had taken an interest in the climate change debate albeit from a distance. But when I finished this article I remembered thinking, 'Boy, this topic is incredibly complicated, how can anyone know what's really going on unless they are an active scientist in the field'. The article concluded with the sort of non-committal 'the case continues' journalistic close that can be deeply unsatisfying. I decided that I needed to find out the truth for myself and sought out some of the world's leading experts on the topic so I could conduct my own assessment of the 'inconvenient truth'.

Climate change is without doubt a wicked problem. Past commentators have always maintained that a wicked problem is almost impossible to define. This is however not true of either wicked problems or climate change.

The problem we face is that the Earth's temperature is rising. Various people, groups and organisations may argue about the extent of the temperature rise, what's causing it and what the symptoms and potential solutions are but there is now irrefutable evidence that the Earth is heating up. Our climate is changing, not in a 'millennial cyclical drift as part of the normal ups and down of the life of the planet' kind of change but more of an 'inexorable increase like we have never seen going back to the beginning of time' kind of change. If you visit any country in the world and ask the elderly people in that community what the weather was like when they were children all of them would probably tell you how much the weather has changed in their lifetime. Such living knowledge is important for two reasons: much of the acceleration has occurred within a couple of generations; and we will not adequately address the issue unless there are sufficient numbers of people who are convinced of its existence and importance.

In the UK for example most people aged 30 and over will remember when the winters were colder, with considerably more snow. For many of us winter is now much wetter and milder and this trend is predicted to continue.[1] Most countries that have in the past experienced extreme weather are experiencing these weather events much more frequently, whether that is more flooding, more drought, more earthquakes or more hurricanes or tornadoes.[2] If we watch the national and international news, there barely seems to be a month that goes by without some natural disaster arriving on someone's doorstep somewhere around the world. As we were writing this chapter, parts of the US have had more snow in a few days than they would normally have in an entire year. For example, many residents of Buffalo opened their front door to a wall of snow after receiving a record-breaking 7 feet in just three days.[3] Typhoon Hagupit led to a million people being evacuated from vulnerable areas in the Philippines in 2014 just 12 short months after the previous super Typhoon Haiyan

---

1 www.changingclimate.org.uk/pages/changing_climate/74-milder-wetter-winters

2 Carrington, D. (2014) 'Extreme weather becoming more common, study says' *The Guardian*, www.theguardian.com/environment/2014/aug/11/extreme-weather-common-blocking-patterns

3 Barrell, R. (2014) 'US Snow Storm Left 7 Feet Of Snow Outside These Doors', *Huffington Post*, www.huffingtonpost.co.uk/2014/11/21/snow-door-pictures_n_6198054.html

that caused widespread damage and the loss of more than 7000 lives.[4]

Human beings are intelligent and we've developed numerous meteorological approaches to determine the validity of the global temperature increase. Using ice cores, tree rings, glacier length, pollen remains, ocean sediment as well as detailed weather and temperature data going back many hundreds of years, we have pieced together a very clear picture of the Earth's climate going back hundreds of thousands of years.

Historical records show that our climate systems do vary naturally over extremely long time frames. And certainly climate variations up until the Industrial Revolution in the 1700s could largely be explained by natural phenomena such as changes to solar energy, volcanic eruptions and natural alterations to greenhouse gas concentration. But the changes since the 1700s have been occurring far faster and are more significant than any previous demonstrable changes. As a result, extensive, robust scientific enquiry has stated categorically that it is very unlikely that these natural phenomena alone are to blame for the change – especially the climate change from the 1950s onwards.[5]

The Earth's temperature depends on a delicate balance between the energy entering and leaving the planet's system. When incoming energy from the sun is absorbed by the Earth, it warms up. Some of the sun's energy is reflected back into space, which reduces that warming effect, and when energy is released back into space from the Earth, the Earth cools down. The data we now have clearly demonstrates that this delicate balance is being disrupted, causing the Earth to heat up more than ever before, and that's the wicked problem we face.

---

[4] BBC News Asia (2014) 'Typhoon Hagupit: Storm weakens as it nears Philippine capital Manila', www.bbc.co.uk/news/world-asia-30370012

[5] United States Environmental Protection Agency 'Earth's temperature is a balancing act' www.epa.gov/climatechange/science/causes.html

If we accept, as anyone who has studied the evidence in detail and can take an objective view does, that the planet is heating up, what should our response be? The rest of this chapter will explore this problem from the perspective of the six wicked problem properties so that we can fully appreciate what we are up against. The purpose is not necessarily to educate you on climate change; after all we, as authors, are not climate change scientists or profess to be experts in this particular area. We do however have considerable experience in understanding how any issue, including wicked issues, are interpreted, seen, and experienced differently by all the various stakeholders and how every element of the Integral Framework helps us to understand what is really going on. And that is one of the things that makes this issue especially wicked – the enormous variety in actual interpretations of the 'same' set of phenomena. And we do have some understanding of 'wickedness' and therefore propose a way for tackling wicked problems that can best be illuminated through the thorough explanation of a real world wicked problem. We've chosen climate change because it is widely considered to be one of the most pressing wicked problems we face. In this chapter, we will outline the basic facts of climate change and its related problems – as agreed to by the vast majority of scientific experts. We will also sprinkle the types of solutions that a more Integral Approach would suggest for these issues. This will start to give you an idea of just how, in many cases, Integrally Coherent solutions are probably unlike any you have heard to date. Then, in the next chapter, we will pull together these suggested solutions into a coherent overview.

Like all wicked problems, climate change is/has:

- Multi-dimensional
- Multiple stakeholders
- Multiple causes
- Multiple symptoms

- Multiple solutions
- Constantly evolving

If you are clear about how these properties interact and work within wicked problems, then feel free to jump ahead to the 'wise' solution offered in the next chapter. Otherwise buckle up and get ready to have your brain overheat in your very own mini-internal climate change.

Multi-Dimensionality of Climate Change

Considering that all of life is occurring in multiple dimensions, then clearly climate change is also occurring in multiple dimensions. Those dimensions include the internal, subjective world of 'I', the interpersonal collective world of 'WE', and the external objective world of 'IT'.

The 'I' Dimension

If we start with 'I' – your internal, subjective world is different from ours. Ours is different from each other. No two people experience life in exactly the same way. We each have different values, different interests, different beliefs, attitudes, intellectual capability, maturity, educational, cultural and religious background, all of which influences the way we experience the world. As such, virtually everyone has a different view and opinion about climate change. Some believe, some don't; some care, some don't; some are taking action, some aren't. So one of the many reasons that climate change remains largely unsolved is that there is, as yet, insufficient internal commitment from enough people to force a change on a large enough scale that will make a difference. This is partly because many people live their lives believing there is little they can personally do about such wicked problems; or it's not their job; or it's the job of other people, experts in the field, already working on this. Such abdication even amongst big business is the norm.

For example, many multinational insurance companies do not debate the issue of climate change and how to reverse it at their 'strategy away days,' despite the fact that they increasingly have to pick up the tab for homes wrecked by increasingly turbulent and unpredictable weather patterns. In other words, something that is profoundly affecting their bottom line results isn't even being discussed at the very highest levels. Most insurance companies are much more likely to talk about how to increase their insurance premiums to cover the escalating risk or how to avoid offering policies to people in 'hurricane alley' or areas now at risk of flooding. Granted, this situation is beginning to change with multinational reinsurance companies such as Swiss-Re and Munich-Re. These pioneers are having more robust conversations with other insurers about the need to be proactive in this area if they want to spread their risk through reinsuring their risk. But unfortunately, this is still not the norm in the industry.

So if insurance companies at the sharp end of the consequences of climate change do not debate what actions they should take to reverse the problem that is directly impacting their profits, then what is the likelihood of other companies less directly involved taking action? Either way, if not enough people 'feel' a sense of urgency, or realise that the course we are on could lead to disaster for ourselves or our grandchildren (not to mention other species), then why would they take action? If we are to solve any wicked problem there has to be an internal desire for change in the hearts and minds of men and women around the globe. In other words, there has to be a genuine shift in the 'I' and collective 'WE' – the shared values, needs, or motivations – of humanity itself, or at least significant sections of it. So one of the critical factors rarely discussed in the climate change debate is the sense of disempowerment or frank indifference to the agenda. We must address this if we are to make significant progress. And that, of course, depends upon actually motivating people – and that depends on engaging their actual values, needs, drives, and passion – or engaging the Integral Framework across the board as it applies to real people in the real world.

The 'WE' Dimension

In the collective interpersonal world of 'WE,' some join environmental groups or become members of a 'Green' party. Some believe that if we don't all come together we won't make it and we won't solve the challenges we face in time. Creating some collective momentum around the climate change agenda may look very different for all of us. Of course, it is different for all of us, depending on the way our mind sees the problem and how far we have ascended through the eight major levels of adult development, both of which are part of the 'wickedness' of the problem. We may reflect on what level of cultural development our tribe, family, business or society is operating from that enables us to largely ignore the issue. We may decide to initiate conversations not about climate change but about extreme weather, recognising that the language itself may be impairing progress. Polls show for example that 'global warming' is much too alarming for many people; 'climate change' is more acceptable.[6] Or we may choose to join mass action around the issue of, say, air pollution – certainly these collective demonstrations have been occurring in India and China, to give only a few examples, where large swathes of the population resonate with the importance of the general issue.[7]

6 Kirshenbaum, S. (2014) '"Climate Change" or "Global Warming?" Two New Polls Suggest Language Matters', Scientific American [Online] http://blogs.scientificamerican.com/plugged-in/2014/12/15/climate-change-or-global-warming-two-new-polls-suggest-language-matters/

7 Hayes, J. D. (2014) 'Anti-pollution protest in China turns bloody', Natural News, http://www.naturalnews.com/044783_anti-pollution_protest_paraxylene_China.html#

Some may recognise that the multi-dimensionality of the collective perspective on climate change is not limited to climate itself. They see that cultural development needs to happen to help the agenda come into sharper focus for the population. We've seen that development, in general, moves from egocentric (it's all about me) to ethnocentric (it's all about my tribe) to worldcentric (it's about all of us) dimensions; and global warming, which most definitely is a worldcentric issue, demands worldcentric-thinking capacity to truly begin to grasp and understand it. After all, a hedonistic, thrill seeking, live for the moment culture or sub-culture is never going to debate the agenda, let alone do something about it. Therefore, we may wonder whether the appropriate action in our community, however we define community, is not actually to talk about climate change but to explore how we more effectively come together as a community to create change. Because even if we have the collective intention and desire to do something, if our debate ends up in a circular squabble, then we will likely fail to make a difference on the climate change agenda or anything else we feel passionate about for that matter. Alternatively, it may occur to us, if we want to galvanise others and work in the collective space, that to do so may require us to change our leadership. For example, we may need to focus not on climate change per se but our ability to create followership. What qualities do we have that could create the desire in others to join our efforts?

Those of us at postmodern level 6 will tend to share a 'planet-first eco-centric view'. We would take an ethical stance that humans are but one of numerous species, all of which have equal rights and are equal strands in the great Web of Life. We would believe that exploitation and domination of the planet is not only suicidal but deeply immoral. Therefore 'progress' at the expense of 'planet' is categorically rejected. Even if we just focus on humanity itself, we owe our future generations a liveable and sustainable planet.

A modern level 5 individual will focus on the rational-scientific data, and try to persuade others, not for moral but for scientific reasons. Applying the merit and achievement prized by this stage, they will focus the discussion squarely on economic factors. Can we make climate change adaptations in ways that do not destroy or even significantly hurt the economy and human progress? To level 5 individuals what could possibly be more important than giving our children an improved, better, more progressed, more profitable and affluent future?

Those at traditional level 4, with its ethnocentric and often fundamentalist-religious stance, might have some trouble grasping the exact nature of a worldcentric global issue like climate; many will simply think that climate change isn't occurring – they don't believe it. Others, who are members of some fundamentalist religion, will tend to agree to take action, but only because 'this land is mine, God gave this land to me' – and thus taking care of creation is solely up to them, and destroying the environment is a sin against God's creation and their role as the caretakers or divine stewards, of that creation. This stewardship stance, of course, infuriates postmodern eco-centric views, which see it as the epitome of an ego-centric view and human-centred pride and arrogance, exactly what has caused the climate problem in the first place. But this level 4 ethnocentric fundamentalist stance is no mere footnote. Many researchers have found that it makes up some 60-70 per cent of the world's overall population. For example Robert Kegan estimates that three out of five Americans are not up to 'modern' (level 5) thinking. This group, of course, responds in kind to the postmodern criticism, seeing postmodern liberal ethical looseness as the core of human sin, whose believers are all bound to an eternity of hellfire, so who cares what they think anyway?

And egocentric level 3, of course, thinks only of itself, and it will tend to ignore worldcentric global issues entirely, unless and until they bang directly on its door, threatening its own survival. 'This climate change thing could kill me?' – and then they will join action that seems appropriate.

Many researchers have found that the newly emerging Integral levels (7/8) seem to contain at least two sub-stages, although, as mentioned earlier we usually treat them as one major level. This level currently represents approximately five per cent of the population. Certainly a higher percentage of Integral individuals are found in many leadership positions in virtually all disciplines, and this 'higher development' has in many cases been directly correlated with a greater capacity in leadership. In relation to climate change, this Integral level will realise what we are trying to convey now – that real change in the real world isn't just a matter of following facts, it's a matter of values and interpretations and understandings of those facts. This level sees climate change not just as 'IT' material, but 'I' and 'WE' material, and each of those three dimensions has a significant number of genuinely different levels and views. Plus these views are at least as important in the resulting action that the individual or group takes as any set of facts are. Besides, 'facts' themselves – as we will see – will vary according to those interior levels and interpretations. And yet those interior views, those interior truths, those interior 'facts,' are virtually always overlooked.

But in order for any level of development to fully take any course of action, that action has to make sense in terms of the factors at play at its own particular level. Just from the brief explanation we gave above of five very different climate-change motivations coming from five major but very different levels, we can see that the reasons given for actions must be presented in language that will resonate with a given level, or else that level will very likely disagree. In fact, it will most likely ignore the suggested action altogether.

Thus, if the Pope wants to explain climate change in terms of a stewardship model; if rational businesses want to start correctly understanding that steps to help the climate problem will not necessarily hurt their profits (and might actually help them); if a postmodern eco-centric individual wants to see climate change as a deeply ethical and fundamentally moral change – fine! Each of those explanations are true enough for each of those levels of development. They will see the world that way or not – no matter what we say. And thus languaging action in a way that actually resonates with, is coherent with, and thus truly motivates their level is the only sane, effective, integral course to take. And, we will see, this is true for every element in the Integral Meta-Map.

So which perspective is correct?

So which of those many realities is ultimately correct, ultimately real? All of them are. That is, all of them have a piece of the truth, and all of them definitely need to be coherently addressed. But the 'most true' level is fundamentally the highest level generally available that has yet to emerge in evolution to date. This is because the most sophisticated level embraces more of the data, more of the perspectives offered by lower levels and therefore includes and transcends those truths.

In the Middle Ages when the centre of gravity was at level 4 'mythic-literal', what was true was what the Bible said was true. There was no possible higher authority, and those who violated it were quickly introduced to interesting organisations like the Spanish Inquisition, where the 'real truth' was laboriously explained and demonstrated to them.

With the emergence of the level 5 Enlightenment, truth switched from mythically revealed to experientially and scientifically discovered. Rational-empirical truth became the highest truth, and there was no possible higher authority than that. In fact those accused of denying scientific truths were often charged with believing in nothing but 'myths' – truths from the previous, now-seen-as childish level 4, on a par with Santa Claus and the Tooth Fairy.

With the subsequent emergence of the level 6 postmodern view – pluralistic and relativistic –cultural pluralism (and 'multiculturalism') became the highest truth. 'Postmodernism' means just what its name suggests: it is 'post' modern – it comes after modernity and 'moves beyond' modernity in significant ways (it is also called 'post-Industrial – it is 'beyond' the modern Industrial age).

And again the previous level was dismissed. Science was out. It literally had no more authority than poetry, both being simple social constructions. For the postmodernist, there isn't a single, pre-given, universal truth. Rather, all knowledge is 'socially constructed'. Knowledge is not a perception but a conception, an interpretation – and what is true for one culture is true for that culture, and what is true for another culture is true for that culture. There is no single 'metanarrative' or 'Big Picture' that is true for all cultures. Remember however, postmodernism, contained a fault line called a 'performative contradiction'. It maintains that its own view was definitely superior, while also maintaining there are no superior views anywhere. It claims it is universally true that there are no universal truths. Thus, its own universal Big Picture denied universal Big Pictures!

But this became easily the highest truth in the postmodern world at that time, especially within academia and it still powerfully lingers today, for better or worse. Those denying it were accused of being oppressive, marginalising, domineering, imperialistic, and guilty of trying to force 'their truths' on everybody else, the essence of oppression. All three of those truths ('mythical-literal', 'rational-empirical' and 'pluralistic' or 'multicultural'), were at one time, quite literally, *the very highest truths that were acknowledged by humanity.*

Just take a moment to think about that. These 'truths' still represent 'the truth' for individuals and groups who are developed to those same levels today. Clearly showing, once again, the importance of vertical developmental in what humans consider 'facts', 'truths', 'values' and 'realities' – all of which change, develop and evolve, ceaselessly. Yet millions of people around the world have 'dug into' a particular level and refuse to consider any 'truth' other than their own; and they are certainly not changing, developing and evolving ceaselessly as they should or could be.

And finally, in today's leading edge world, about five per cent of the population have evolved to level 7/8 or the Integral level. This is the highest truth to emerge to date. Of course, it is also destined to eventually be superseded by yet-higher evolutionary levels. Whereas all the other levels believe their level alone has significance; the Integral level is the first that believes all levels have some significance – if nothing else, as necessary stages in overall human development. Even those born in an Integral society are still born at square one. Everyone has to start their growth and development at level 1 and move up from there in all of their lines. If the individual continues 'Growing Up' to the highest present-day stages, he or she will reach the Integral level (in one or more of whatever lines are growing), which, because it 'transcends and includes' *all* of the previous successor levels, contains the 'most amount of truth' of any level yet to emerge. Just like a cell transcends and includes molecules, and molecules transcend and include atoms, and atoms transcend and include quarks – each of those is real, but each 'higher' entity is more inclusive, more comprehensive, more whole, contains more realities and thus 'more truths'. Or as Hegel, one of the first evolutionary philosophers, put it, 'Each level is adequate; each higher level is more adequate.' Likewise, each level is true, each higher level is 'more true' (molecules contain molecular truths plus atomic truths plus quark truths; yet cells contain cellular truths *plus* all those other truths – molecular truths and atomic truths and quark truths – hence, 'more truth').

Unfortunately the fact that 'Integral contains more truths' is irrelevant to every single level that has previously emerged, each of which is convinced that its level's truth and values alone are real. Put that in a wicked problem and see where it gets you!

The Integral level is the first to emphasise the significance of all other levels, while all other levels deny significance to every level other than their own. So, taking science as an example, even if science is done at an Integral level (which is increasingly happening right now) and it produces the 'most true' facts, in order for those facts to be understood and acted on at previous, junior levels, they must be interpreted and presented in terms that those junior levels can comprehend. So even if an Integral level scientist is adamant on the nature, extent, causes and cures of global warming, those facts have to be languaged and presented in at least five different ways to five different level groups of people, if those facts are to actually motivate a large percentage of humanity in the first place.

Thus, an Integral level view of climate change would intentionally and conscientiously 'interpret itself downward' into an ecocentric view for level 6. For example, an integral individual may soften the explanation or even omit the idea of developmental levels because an eco-centric person would believe such notions are 'domineering' (because they confuse growth hierarchies with dominator hierarchies – in the former, each higher level becomes more and more inclusive; in the later, each higher level becomes more and more dominating and oppressive). Similarly an integral individual would make the case on climate change in terms of rational progress and profit for level 5 and likely leave out 'interiors' which level 5 individuals don't often resonate with. The integral individual would fashion a traditional stewardship view for level 4 individuals and create a survivalist view for level 3 individuals. Overall to make progress it is vital to make the argument level specific and easy to understand varying the details considerably (although not fabricating any) by using the entire Integral Framework to fashion coherent interpretations for individuals at different locations in the Integral matrix.

This is far from pandering to individuals. It's putting the argument in the *only* language they will fully understand – and thus be motivated to act on. Why on earth would we not do that? This is not manipulating people, it is much closer to clear and viable communication.

But the way it is now, regardless of what level they originally come from, most environmental arguments simply end up resorting to a survivalist (level 3) view, arguing that human life itself depends upon making significant changes now while the other side argues that the science for that is overblown and exaggerated and the problem is really not that dire (if it exists at all). As a result the debate goes round and round. Most arguments end up at a level 3 survivalist bottom line simply because level 3 is the lowest common denominator, guaranteed to be present in virtually all humans, and thus this is an argument that, if won, can decisively carry the day. In contrast, for example, the postmodern level 6 moral argument is believed by virtually none of the lower levels and thus most postmodernists don't even try using it anymore. It used to be a quite common argument, but they just give it up since so few others actually connected or resonated with it in any way – although they still talk that way among themselves.

The 'IT' Dimension

As we've begun to indicate, an internal change in intention or desire within one individual or even a large number of people is not enough. Creating a shift in culture and building collective momentum is not enough. Both are certainly necessary steps in the right direction – yet there's still more in a truly Integral reality. Ultimately such inner transformations and changes in the collective must lead to a real change in the external objective world of 'IT' for any genuine progress to be made. The rational objective dimension is all about behaviour and what we are actually doing about climate change. Again the differences in people's actions in the world are enormous – even just using the five different motivations we gave above, we can see an enormous range of 'IT' behaviour. Some will do nothing. Some may think about climate change occasionally but only when there is a news report of yet another drought or wild fire in some country thousands of miles away. Even then they won't necessarily take any action unless the drought or wild fire affects them personally. As a result they don't engage with climate change or take it seriously; and even if they do, they don't really care that much because it is not affecting them or their loved ones yet. Others may watch documentaries and seek to read up on the topic so they can separate the fact from the fantasy. Some might get more involved, take more care with their recycling, use their bicycle more often and their car less, or exchange the four-wheel drive for the Prius. Some may start to lobby big business and demand that companies have a corporate social responsibility (CSR) policy or a proper Sustainability Plan in place – and they will do this as a matter of deep principle. Some may even test the veracity of such corporate statements to determine whether the company is just 'green-washing' to deflect attention from their unitary focus on profits. Some may make the effort to figure out whether a company's CSR plan represents a set of genuine programmes of sustainable action. Some may go even further and pressure companies to sign up to international sustainability groups such as the World Business Council for Sustainable Development (WBCSD).[8]

In 2009, 29 WBCSD members produced a report, *Vision 2050*, that plots a path to a world in which nine billion people could live well within the boundaries of the planet. They are now developing *Action 2020* to rally the efforts of business to deliver three critical promises:

- Economic Promise: The need to completely change the way we keep score in business and address financial capital issues.
- Environmental Promise: The need to rethink how we approach planetary resources to address the natural capital.
- Social Promise: We need to reset the inequalities in society across the globe and change social capital.[9]

This type of thinking is a significant step forward, but it is still basically a variation on just the Lower-Right PESTLE factors, or 'ITS' systems. To these, minimally, we need to add a 'Cultural

[8] www.wbcsd.org/home.aspx

[9] www.wbcsd.org/action2020.aspx

Promise', namely that business attempts to the best of its ability to ethically fit in and integrate with the local cultural values, meanings, and motivations of the area in which it is operating. This is a simple curb to 'business imperialism' (and we say this from an essentially pro-ethical business stance). There also needs to be a 'Personal Promise' or promise to help promote the self-actualisation and self realisation of each and every individual under their umbrella – all the concerns of Theory Y we discussed in Part Two. Without this personal promise there is a real risk that the plan will not be sustainable.

It is clear that some take their personal and collective or commercial climate change responsibilities seriously, some do not. Again the diversity of action and behaviour prompted by climate change is as diverse as the human race trying to solve it.

And since most of us do not even realise the multi-dimensional nature of reality (whether quadrants, levels, lines, states), we are only ever trying to solve the problem we face from one dimension – usually the one we are stuck in most of the time and thus assume everybody else is there as well. Even the most advanced thinking, such as that done by organisations like the WBCSD, rarely covers all the dimensions.

In short, it is clear that the collective action on climate change is itself multi-dimensional – and a multi-dimensional response is part of any effective action plan. Regardless of what version of that multi-dimensional view we decide to use, the simplest unavoidable factor is that humans have a variety of world views and belief systems, and these are crucial in their deciding what courses of action they will take. Taking these multi-dimensional viewpoints into account is clearly a component of any conceivably successful action plan.

In the end it doesn't really matter if you decide to recycle – we all need to recycle. It doesn't matter if even a few thousand people decide to fall off the grid and create their own energy from compost and sunlight – we all need to change behaviour, exert pressure on politicians and businesses to find new sources of energy so we can move away from the ones that are doing the damage. And this is true even if you happen to be one of the people who does not believe that the burning of fossil fuels is part of the problem. Oil, coal and natural gas are not sustainable energy sources because there is only a finite amount available on the planet. Sooner or later we will have to find alternatives.

Although there is still estimated to be some 1300 billion barrels of oil located in proven fields around the world that will only last us for about 40 years based on current consumption rates. Plus that's optimistic because much of that oil is located in places where extracting it is physically or commercially impossible. It may be that new, more accessible sources may be found, or that new technology will make the inaccessible oil accessible; but it is unlikely. It is estimated that roughly 6400 trillion cubic feet of natural gas reserves still exist around the world which would last just short of 60 years at current consumption levels; but again much of that is inaccessible. New ways of extracting natural gas such as fracking are currently being explored but these are controversial and can lead to additional environmental challenges above and beyond climate change. There's a lot more coal left – the equivalent of 3100 billion barrels of oil which could last us 120 years at current consumption levels. But it is environmentally devastating, not just to climate change but the landscape, it is labour intensive and expensive to extract.[10] Plus our consumption rates are increasing so it is likely these estimates are optimistic as we consume more and more energy.

The point is that even if you believe that climate change is nonsense, what we currently use is a finite resource, which means that it will run out – the only question is whether it will run out before or after we have turned the planet into a futuristic Sci-fi horror movie.

In addition to the multi-dimensionality of 'I, WE and IT' there are

---

[10] http://energyclimatetransportation.blogspot.co.uk/2011/03/fossil-fuels-how-much-is-left.html

even more dimensions, because all three dimensions are affected by global megatrends. As we discussed in Part One, these have traditionally been thought to be trends within the world of 'IT' – but they actually affect all three dimensions. Using the PESTLE acronym, which gives us a fairly decent summary of the mega-trend changes in the Right-Hand 'IT' and 'ITS' quadrants, we can illuminate additional relevant dimensions of climate change by drawing on all four real dimensions, not just the exterior ones.

Should you want to dive more deeply into these PESTLE mega-trends to fully appreciate their complexity and implications the political, economical, social, technological, legal and environmental aspects of climate change are explained in more detail in appendices 1 – 6. Although it is extremely illuminating, packed with 'a-ha moments' we acknowledge their exploration is not for the fainthearted so have removed this material to the appendix so you can read them if you feel inspired to do so or press on. The crucial point to remember if you chose to press on is that each dimension or lens through which you view the problem illuminates different, often competing, contradictory challenges from within that single dimension, not to mention the interdependencies and contradictions that occur across all the multiple dimensions. When seen from this perspective alone it's very easy to appreciate why wicked problems are so intractable. And the complexity continues....

Multiple Stakeholders of Climate Change

There are multiple ways to think about stakeholders in any organisation. With reference to business, for example, Mackey and Sisodia list what they see as six major groups, all of which are important and need to be consciously included: customers, staff, suppliers, investors, the community, and the environment

Figure 3.1: Shifting the gravity

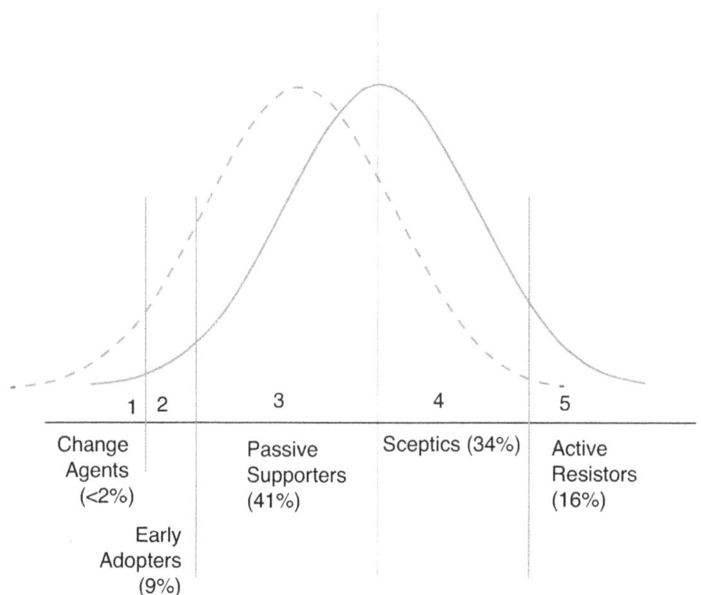

as 'inner stakeholders'; and 'outer stakeholders'.[11] The latter include competitors, activists, critics, unions, the media and government.

It is also possible to type stakeholders in terms of how they respond to change. There are essentially five viewpoints that multiple stakeholders may coalesce around the process of change itself (see Figure 3.1).

This distribution is based on what has been called the 'Innovation Adoption Curve',[12] although the percentage of stakeholders in each of the five populations may be slightly different in the

[11] Mackey, J. and Sisodia, R. (2013) *Conscious Capitalism: Liberating the Heroic Spirit of Business, Boston*: Harvard Business Review Press.

[12] Rogers, E. M. (1962) *Diffusion of Innovations*, New York: Free Press.

climate change debate. The five stakeholder populations could be described as:

1. Change agents
2. Early adopters
3. Passive supporters
4. Sceptics
5. Active resistors

If we are to resolve the wicked problem of climate change one of the great number of things we need to address is to shift the gravity of this stakeholder population. This means that, like most other parameters we are covering, virtually all of us need to change. For example, let's look at the sceptics. Some sceptics don't believe climate change is a problem because it is nothing more than a natural cyclical phenomenon and therefore we don't need to take action any time soon. Other sceptics may acknowledge that the planet is heating up, but refute the evidence that human beings are causing it and will argue that our influence has been exaggerated. These sceptical stakeholders believe we should be paying more attention to other more pressing wicked problems such as poverty or the spread of dangerous disease such as HIV/ Aids or Ebola. In addition to the large percentage (~34 per cent) of sceptics there is a significant minority of stakeholders (~16 per cent), the 'active resistors,' who are promoting the idea that there is no man-made increase in planetary temperature. So while there are significantly fewer sceptics than there once was, the remaining sceptics and active resistors have powerful backers and plenty of cash to cultivate doubt.[13]

Then there are those stakeholders that have largely embraced the compelling body of mainstream academic research. The majority (~41 per cent) of these could be described as 'passive

[13] Oreskes, N., and Conway, E. (2010) *Merchants of Doubt*, London: Bloomsbury.

supporters.' They accept the fact of climate change, but they are either taking no action themselves or at best are members of some 'green' organisation. There is even a term for these passive supporters – a 'slacktivist'.[14] A combination of slacker and activist, a slacktivist may support a social issue or important cause such as fixing climate change but do little other than post the occasional social media post and yet take personal satisfaction from the feeling they have contributed.

As the name would suggest, passive supporters are essentially passive, placated in the knowledge that they support the agenda. In some ways these stakeholders may be blocking progress more than the sceptics because they perpetuate the view that no proactive action needs to be taken, despite very strong evidence suggesting urgent action is what is required.

It is often said there is a 'chasm' between the passive supporter population, who often only take action if the problem is affecting their lives directly, and the 'early adopters,' who are looking for a breakthrough. The early adopters tend to be more active and have often been engaged with the agenda for some time. Within this population is a much smaller percentage of 'change agents', who are proactively working consistently on many fronts, all reflecting their particular Integral Address.

The Intergovernmental Panel on Climate Change (IPCC) could be considered to be the leading change agents and have had an enormous influence on world thinking, although the sceptics would suggest they have too much influence. Unfortunately, a few change agents have become radicalised activists and they may be inhibiting progress by being too polemic in their approach. These individuals tend to be ones who intensely fuse the facts with their particular values. This can result in them being excessively animated from one value set. The problem is that

[14] Robertson, C. (2014) 'Slacktivism: The Downfall of Millennials', *Huffington Post*, www.huffingtonpost.com/charlotte-robertson/slacktivism-the-downfall-_b_5984336.html

with at least eight different value sets, excessive advocacy of just one is likely to alienate seven others. It is a difficult dilemma: the more passionately you advance a particular cause, the more motivated those with similar values will be, but at the same time the greater the risk of alienating others. But to water down your values presentation so as to not 'offend' or 'alienate' anybody, is to effectively not really motivate anybody with any real drive. This difficult, sometimes near impossible, balancing act is one of the things that makes wicked problems so wicked.

Planetary Sensitivity by Stakeholder Group

In an attempt to unravel the scientific complexity that bedevils the climate change debate, some scientists have identified that the most critical factor at play is the positive feedback loops that can cause an acceleration of the damage that has already occurred. This is a phenomenon called planetary sensitivity. It has been suggested that if we really want to understand the true nature of the problem, we need to understand the critical nature of planetary sensitivity in estimating the true impact of accelerated global warming.

Think of it this way. If you have asthma, you are probably allergic to house dust mites, and this allergy makes your airways sensitive and overreactive. This immune sensitivity significantly exacerbates the problem. How sensitive your airways are will ultimately determine the severity of your asthma and how impaired your breathing is. If you are extremely sensitive, your asthma is described as 'brittle' and your risk of severe and debilitating breathing problems is much greater. Planetary sensitivity is very similar. In the airways of asthmatics, the inflammatory process is the body's attempt to rid itself of the house dust mite allergens. So if the allergic reaction to house dust in your airways is making your asthma twice as bad as it would otherwise be then your sensitivity level would be two times.

Similarly planetary sensitivity is a measure of how much the planet's attempts to correct the increased temperature is exacerbating the problem. The scientific debate as to how 'sensitive' the planet is to greenhouse gases is currently around 2.5 to 3.5 times. Thus the planet's attempt to correct the increased warming is multiplying the warming by 2.5 to 3.5 times, making the problem that much worse. Any scientist who suggests it may be greater than this is making a career-limiting statement but some have suggested it's as high as 7. Whether the planetary sensitivity is 2.5 or 7 is critical, of course, as it completely alters how soon we could hit a tipping point (or whether we already have) where the planet is unable to cope and we enter an irreversible terminal decline characterised by a 60 metre rise in sea level and all sorts of other climatic disasters.

The current international debate around greenhouse gases is about the upper safe limit being 440 parts per million (ppm) of CO_2 in the atmosphere. As of May 2015, the published view is that we are at 403.70 ppm.[15] The 440 ppm figure is based on a 'planetary sensitivity' of 3.5 (not 7) which will create a 2°C temperature increase. Hence the general belief is that we still have room in the 'sky-fill' site to dump more CO_2. However, if the planetary sensitivity is in fact 7 times, not 3.5, then the safe upper limit is 330 ppm, which we passed over 50 years ago, around 1960. In fact, some authors have suggested the planetary sensitivity is actually 7.8, which is even worse than the worse estimate.[16] In their view the sky-fill site is already overflowing and we actually need urgent reduction measures. If the higher figure is correct, then it is only a matter of time before turbulent weather becomes the global norm. In fact, some stakeholders believe it's

15 http://co2now.org/

16 Wasdell, D. presentation (2013) 'Sensitivity, Non-Linearity and Self-Amplification in the Global Climate System', The Annual Conference of the Club of Rome, Ottawa, 20 September 2013.

already too late and that we had better concentrate our energies on preparing to adapt to the change that is coming regardless of what we chose to do now.[17]

Clearly how to reconcile these significantly different stakeholder perspectives is part of the wickedness of this and other wicked problems. Not only from the perspective of who is involved and how to bring those divergent groups together, but how do we create a framework where each view can contribute to the solution. Each stakeholder's opinion and their view of the truth will clearly influence the solutions that they promote. So not only do we need to create a framework that allows all stakeholders to participate, but we also need a framework that allows the multitude of suggested ways forward to be integrated.

Anything less basically empowers the sceptics and active resistors to continue to block progress. In order for an integrated framework to succeed, we need to consider the possibility that each answer is true but incomplete. Progress will require us all to change. The challenge is that behaviour change is notoriously difficult to facilitate individually and even harder across large populations. This further empowers the sceptics and the resistors. It also reinforces the view of the passive supporters that it is someone's job to create the breakthrough. In short, we end up dependent on a very small percentage of individuals to resolve the problem.

In addition to the spectrum of opinion from change agents to active resistors, there are also different types of specific stakeholder populations involved in climate change. They include but are not limited to:

---

[17] Giddens, A. (2008) *The politics of climate change*, Policy Network Paper, www.fcampalans.cat/images/noticias/The_politics_of_climate_change_Anthony_Giddens(2).pdf

- Government
- NGOs
- Business
- Individuals
- Scientists/Experts

Government

Government is a major stakeholder group when it comes to climate change and there are multiple divisions within government that will influence and overlap around these issues. Within those divisions, locally, nationally and internationally, there will be individual politicians or government employees who may hold very different personal opinions about climate change.

Government policy will shift regularly as the political power shifts from one party to another with an unpredictable shift in emphasis on different quadrants, levels, lines, and so on. In Australia, for example, the Labour government led by Julia Gillard introduced a carbon pricing scheme in response to the fact that Australia has the world's highest carbon emissions per capita and is the world's second biggest coal exporter. The scheme required anyone emitting over 25,000 tonnes of CO_2 or equivalent greenhouse gases per year that was not involved in the transport or agriculture sectors, to obtain a permit. This initiative meant that the heaviest polluters paid for the damage they created, which only seems fair considering the profits they generate. Commonly referred to as the 'carbon tax', it came into effect in July 2012 and heralded what many individuals saw as a positive step forward from the Australian government in taking its climate change responsibilities seriously. In 2013, Tony Abbott's Right-wing Liberal Party came to power, buckled under the political pressure from big business – especially big mining companies – and the carbon tax was repealed by the Australian senate in July

2014. A move that was widely criticised around the world. In the UK, Britain's longest-serving Environment minister, Lord Deben, issued a statement stating that the repeal of the carbon tax would push Australia backwards in addressing the challenges of global warming and accusing Tony Abbott of recklessly endangering the world's future, adding, 'The fact is almost all the rest of the world is now fighting climate change. From Mexico to South Korea and China to South Africa, they are moving ahead, doing more and tougher things. Only Australia and to some extent Canada, but particularly Australia, is actually going backwards... Australia now has miserable targets. The idea that you're only going to decrease your emissions by five per cent by the year 2020 is way out of line of any other advanced country and that's a very sad thing.'[18]

Australia went backwards almost entirely because of partisan, protectionist politics and big business lobbying.

In November 2014, the United States and China agreed to limit carbon emissions following decades of talks on the subject. Under an agreement, the United States will reduce its emissions by a quarter by 2025 and China will reach a maximum in its emissions by 2030, cap them, and then decrease them. At the signing ceremony, President Barack Obama said, 'As the world's largest economies and greatest emitters of greenhouse gases, we have a special responsibility to lead the global effort against climate change.'[19]

Of course, the added complexity in finding a genuine solution to climate change is that the solution must involve all governments, not just one or two. Governments are of course elected by the

---

[18] Alberici E (2014) Australia is going backwards on climate change Lateline http://www.abc.net.au/lateline/content/2014/s4042037.htm

[19] Taylor L, Branigan T (2014) US and China strike deal on carbon cuts in push for global climate change pact The Guardian http://www.theguardian.com/environment/2014/nov/12/china-and-us-make-carbon-pledge

people, certainly in democracies; and as US President Jimmy Carter found out, the electorate often does not want to hear bad news that they will have to tighten their belts or change their habits in order to solve a problem that many would prefer to pretend does not exist.

During his term as the thirty-ninth President of the United States, Jimmy Carter made four televised speeches including one prophetically warning the American people that, 'We simply must balance our need for energy with our rapidly shrinking resources.'[20] In another he questioned America's rampant consumerism and materialism suggesting that, 'Human identity is no longer defined by what one does, but by what one owns.'[21] Carter urged the American people to appreciate that the US was not a land of limitless resources and that learning how to manage those limited resources sustainably was the key to long-term prosperity. But the electorate didn't like the messages so they got rid of the messenger. They preferred the Hollywood version delivered by the actor turned politician Ronald Regan. Regan refuted the message, denied the science and swept to power by telling the America people what they wanted to hear. Carter was scientifically right, politically naive. Regan was scientifically wrong, politically adroit – but he funded what the Left would see as the Hollywood myth with an explosion of federal debt that would never abate.

And the position is made even more complicated by the fact that industrialised nations, even if they were motivated to take severe action to reverse the catastrophic trend we have started, can hardly suggest to the developing world that they must change their ways. This 'don't do what we have done' argument is very

[20] Miller Centre of Public Affairs University of Virginia Transcript of Jimmy Carters Address to the Nation on Energy April 18 1977 http://millercenter.org/president/speeches/speech-3398

[21] Miller Centre of Public Affairs University of Virginia Transcript of Jimmy Carters 'Crisis of Confidence' speech 15th July 1979 http://millercenter.org/president/speeches/speech-3402

difficult for emerging nations to accept. Developed nations have already secured many of the advantages of industrialisation, and suggesting to emerging nations that they should not follow the same path looks like an attempt to maintain economic superiority. It is incredibly difficult to tell the governments of the developing world, 'Hey, we know that we have got rich exploiting the planets natural resources, but we've seen the error of our ways and would like you NOT to do it because it's playing havoc with our collective weather systems. Oh and by the way we're actually going to continue to exploit the same natural resources and use the same toxic manufacturing practices for at least another 10 years!'

NGOs

On top of the myriad of interconnected government departments and the number of governments that need to be involved in the creation and implementation of a workable solution, there are also thousands of Non-Governmental Organisations (NGOs) involved.

Some are directly involved in climate change and others are affected by climate change. For example, there is evidence that climate change is going to have a significant knock-on effect on food production and could exacerbate poverty and hunger – both already wicked problems in their own right.

In 2009, a report produced by SIGWatch, who track the activity of NGOs to help inform business of global trends, reported on where NGOs were concentrating their campaigning resources, and climate change knocked every other issue off the environmental activist agenda. After climate change, NGO priorities diverge strongly between North America, Europe, South America and Asia.

NGOs in North America are most worried about oil and gas drilling, protecting the Arctic, the impact of coal mining, and mercury pollution from coal-fired power generation. European

NGOs are more concerned about corporate social responsibility, road building, cattle ranching in rainforests, pesticide residues in food, and storing nuclear waste. In South America, NGOs are focused on the environmental impacts of aquaculture, mining, hydroelectric dams, plantation forestry and the impact of resource extraction on indigenous people; while Asia-Pacific NGOs have above average concern about palm oil, aquaculture, pesticides in textiles and coral reef conservation.

Environmental NGOs are far more numerous and wealthier than their counterparts in human rights, animal rights, or third world development.[22] As such they have a powerful stakeholder voice. Many NGOs centrally are composed of change agents or early adopters, and have many members who are passive supporters. NGOs are one of the areas that have the highest percentage of postmodern, pluralistic, multicultural level 6 individuals and values – and as such, many of them are at constant variance with level 5 business and level 4 traditional values.

Business

Business is also a major stakeholder in climate change that needs to be brought to the negotiating table if any long-term sustainable solution is to be found.

Of course, the debate about whether business is a stakeholder in the first place depends on what you believe regarding the causes, symptoms and solutions for climate change. Mainstream science is in no doubt that business is a major stakeholder in climate change, not least because the problem has accelerated significantly since the Industrial Revolution.

It follows therefore that business needs to be included in any workable solution. The problem, of course, is that ever since 1970

[22] Holt, A. (2009) 'Climate change tops the agenda for NGOs', *Charity Times*, www.charitytimes.com/ct/NGOs.php

when Milton Friedman wrote an article in the *New York Times* stating that the sole purpose of business was to make money for its shareholders, business has sought to do just that.[23] When the leader of the Chicago School of Economics suggests that any business executive who pursued a goal other than making money were, in his words, 'unwitting puppets of the intellectual forces that have been undermining the basis of a free society these past decades', business listened.

The push to maximising shareholder value was given an 'action plan' in 1976 when finance Professor Michael Jensen and Dean William Meckling of the Simon School of Business at the University of Rochester published a paper identifying the 'principle-agent problem' and proposing a solution that would change business forever.[24]

The authors believed that the shareholder (principal) was often unfairly disadvantaged by senior executives (agents) because they would pay themselves high salaries, run up expense accounts and generally create unnecessary 'agency costs' that would therefore dilute the return to the shareholder. It was a logical argument, although the authors didn't provide any evidence that the principle-agent problem actually existed in business at the time. Nonetheless, they suggested that the best way to solve the principle-agent problem was to make senior leaders shareholders themselves. That way they would have a compelling reason to align their interests with the shareholder so that maximising shareholder value also meant maximising their own personal return. In other words, if the agents became principles then there couldn't be an agent-principle problem

[23] Friedman, M. (1970) 'The Social Responsibility of Business is to Increase its Profits', *The New York Times*.

[24] Jensen, M.C. and Meckling, W. H. (1976) 'Theory of the Firm: Managerial Behaviour, Agency Costs and Ownership Structure', *Journal of Financial Economics*, vol. 3, no 4, pp. 305-360.

(even though there was no evidence that the principle-agent problem existed in the first place).

It was a game changer. And it offered a way for senior leaders and shareholders to animate Freidman's earlier vision and turn shareholder value into a commercial reality and the driving business force it is today.

Clearly delivering shareholder value is important in business and for global economies, but it has also resulted in some seriously toxic side effects. It can destroy long-term shareholder value by inadvertently shifting focus from real market returns to predictions of expected future income, thus resulting in shorter and shorter time horizons. These shortening time horizons have distorted executive behaviour and make it virtually impossible for senior leaders to look much further into the future than the next couple of quarters.

Climate change requires stakeholders to look much further into the future than the next few months! Senior leaders now live and die by the value they deliver, the costs they save, the revenue they generate. Accepting liability for causing climate change could therefore have significant financial repercussions for business – especially those that are heavy polluters.

This is undoubtedly why so few businesses are following the guidelines of the US Security and Exchange Commission regarding informing investors about the risk of climate change to the corporate bottom line. Of the 3895 US public companies listed on major stock exchanges at September 2013, only 27 per cent talk about climate change or global warming in their annual reports. Business is a notoriously big user of fossil fuels – the principal source of CO_2 emissions which means that sooner or later those businesses are going to have to address the issue or face stiff financial penalties or even consumer boycotts. Those penalties will impact shareholder value significantly and yet it is hardly even mentioned. Even the 1050 publicly-traded businesses that talk about climate change were weak on specifics, with 70 per cent indicating that global warming could affect existing operations, or that environmental regulation on CO_2 emissions might affect operations, but not their bottom line.[25]

Most businesses take the view that the climate debate is beyond their remit or influence, or they will do what the market requires so they cannot be accused of dragging their feet on sustainability. Few companies are proactively pushing for changes to the way global markets see sustainability, despite a number of organisations urgently advocating this approach.[26] Business leaders can easily justify that the problem is someone else's – governments, intergovernmental agencies, NGOs, it is anything but a corporate problem.

It is also hardly surprising that business, especially big energy business, funds some of the scientists and NGOs seeking to disprove or at least cast doubt on the causes of climate change. For example, over a few short years Exxon Mobile channelled more than $8 million to forty different organisations that challenged the scientific evidence of global warming.[27]

Of course, to add to the complexity, 'business' is not a single entity; there are millions of businesses worldwide. In regard to climate change, some are making a positive impact, some are neutral, and some are having a profoundly negative impact considering what we already know from higher-level science about the causes (more on that in a moment). Plus those businesses are located all over the world, operating under different political, legal and governmental jurisdictions.

Those areas are ones that, of course, Integral Coherence has much to offer....

---

[25] Rosen, L. (2013) *Ever Heard of the Heartland Institute?* The World Future Society, www.wfs.org/blogs/len-rosen/ever-heard-heartland-institute

[26] www.wbcsd.org/home.aspx

[27] Oreskes, N. and Conway, E. (2010) *Merchants of Doubt*, London: Bloomsbury.

Individuals

We, as individuals, are also stakeholders. We may wear different hats as we struggle to understand what is going on and what side of the argument we agree with, but we are still stakeholders. Plus what we consider 'stakes' in the first place will depend on our Integral Address – the quadrant, level, line, state and type that we operate from.

To add to the complexity still further, our opinion and willingness to act or change behaviour will be dependent on the hat we are wearing at any given time. As consumers, we may behave one way, activating a certain set of Integral elements; and as parents, we may behave another, activating a different set; and as employees or business owners, a different way again, reflecting yet another set. This is of course amplified because the stakeholder group of 'individuals' also occupy all the other stakeholder groups. Business is made up of individuals, governments are made up of individuals, NGOs are made up of individuals, scientists and experts are individuals and they all wear a number of additional hats that can lead to conflict of interest and crises of conscience.

As consumers, we want stuff. We want to buy the new technology and the latest smartphone – even though it needs to be recharged every single day. We have tablets, laptops, multiple TVs, and we want the appliances that make our lives easier and more enjoyable. All of these products we have come to expect and rely on are intensely energy dependent. We might consider walking to the corner shop to buy milk, but it is just easier to hop in the car and drive. And of course we want to be able to afford to buy all these things. We will happily scour the Internet for hours if we think it might save us some money on the new washing machine or the new fridge freezer. But what do we buy? Do we buy the washing machine that has an energy rating of A+++ that uses the least amount of energy and water possible, or the washing machine that has an energy rating of D which does not but is considerably cheaper?

We have families and we need to budget and balance the books in the same way a business or government needs to balance the books. There are pressures from our children about what they want; and as parents, we may worry about the future we are leaving them, but if money is tight and we have to decide which products and services to buy, our concern for climate change may not be as high as our immediate concern of balancing the household budget.

When we are deciding where to go on holiday, do the air miles we need to travel to the destination and therefore the carbon footprint we leave behind even enter the decision-making process? Or are we more concerned about the nightlife, how many swimming pools are at the hotel, and what the Trip Advisor reviews say?

Very often, the hat we are wearing (our Integral Address; i.e., exactly what Integral elements are active) at any given time will influence our opinion on climate change and what we are or are not prepared to do about it. This can add a very significant dimension to the wicked problem itself. Often there's a disconnect between what we feel inside is the right thing to do and our behaviour. We may feel that we need to engage and take climate change seriously but we may also convince ourselves that as one person, our efforts make no difference and therefore our lack of action is justified. Or we may simply run all sorts of reconciliations in our mind designed to placate our passivity.

This 'hat wearing' is present in all of us. Many of today's leading sciences are driven by Integral-level 7/8 cognition. But this developmental line often runs significantly ahead of virtually all other lines. This means that a leading scientist can be at level 7/8 in cognitive intelligence, and at lower levels – 3, 4, 5, 6 in emotional intelligence/development, moral development, ego development, and so on. As a result his or her scientific *talk* can be Integral level 7/8, while their *walk* is considerably lower. But almost all leading scientific theories and discoveries are done by the leading-edge of human development and evolution itself, namely Integral level 7/8 with its cognitive capacity to grasp 'systems of systems of systems'. This evolution *from* the leading-edge changes the leading-edge view of virtually every discipline it touches, and most of the leading experts in almost all fields are operating, at least occasionally, from this 'highest level' cognition now presently available, whether that is string theory in physics, bioengineering in medicine, self-organising systems in evolutionary biology, or Integral theories of multiple methodologies in philosophy.

The higher-level science and the data generated by our leading-edge environmental sciences is 97 per cent convinced that global warming is a fact; that most of it is caused by human activity (the 'anthropocene'); that greenhouse gases are the primary culprit; that the main problem can be addressed by reducing our emission of those greenhouse gases (such as CO_2 and methane); and that we are already perilously close to various 'tipping points' that could indeed render human life anything from difficult to impossible. Those are the closest things we have to 'facts' in this area; believe them for whatever reasons you want and whatever values you embrace – but believe them. They are the closest we have come to a physical *reality* to date (that is, a physical reality as seen, enacted, and interpreted by Integral cognitive level 7/8.) A hundred years from now, when level 9, 10, or 11 is the highest leading-edge level of evolution generally available, then the 'highest truth' in various disciplines will come from that level; until then the 'highest truth' is delivered by level 7/8. That is the 'edge' *that* Integral Coherence leads from.

Of course, as with any wicked problem, there are some individuals on both major sides of the argument, such as wealthy industrialists, business leaders, and influential politicians that can have a greater impact on reversing the rising global temperature than others, but that does not let any of us off the hook as individuals.

This is where the Integral Approach can be so helpful – in letting us see how individuals at different developmental dimensions in all the elements of the Integral Framework will inherently see and experience the problem in different, sometimes wildly different, ways. Those ways can either be taken into account or blindly ignored. If consciously taken into account they allow us to adjust our actions accordingly. If ignored we will be blindsided by them, by elements that are arising in the real world whether we realise it or not. One thing is certain: not realising they exist ensures they will remain wicked indeed. Either way they cannot be changed dramatically or quickly.

Scientist/Experts

Ironically, in the 1970s, just when the notion of shareholder value was gathering pace, scientists and experts were beginning to express serious concerns about climate change. Those studying the area had already proven the link between increasing CO_2 and rising global temperatures. This, of course came right after the 1960s, where every major scientific prediction was for an inevitable coming ice age! Obviously concerns that we were causing climate change by what we did, the products we bought, the lifestyle we enjoyed, the cars we drove, and the appliances we used was not good news for the businesses who supplied those products or facilitated that lifestyle. It was not good news for consumers or parents who were buying those products while simultaneously worrying about the future their children would inherit.

As stakeholders scientists and experts have played a crucial role in climate change and our understanding and misunderstanding of it. Following World War Two, everyone had become much more aware of the work of scientists following the creation of the atomic bomb. Science had helped to end the war albeit at a horrific cost, and scientists became the new rock stars. The scientists involved in those high profile enquiries became influential and rich.

Science was established as the shining light, a beacon of truth that we could turn to as a way of understanding the challenges we face, so we can make better decisions. Science was telling us that climate change was real and that we needed to take action to prevent permanent irreversible changes. This was, however, an unpopular proposition not least because it would massively impact the pursuit of shareholder value. Unfortunately, rather than embrace the science and collaborate on a solution, influential stakeholder groups with significant vested interests simply set out to attack the science and the scientists and experts that were trying to clarify the issues. What began was a deliberate organised campaign of denial and obfuscation to cast doubt over the scientific findings.

Keep in mind that in many cases, these were not deliberately 'evil' people, nor were they deliberately lying. For example, individuals at levels 3, 4, and some at 5, actually believed what they and their experts were saying. This is exactly how the world looked to their level's 'facts' and the values that were driving them. This is one of the items that makes wicked problems so wicked – the actual *sincerity* with which most of the dimensions in the multi-dimensional mix are honestly embraced and believed. The vast majority of people in these types of arguments would all pass lie detector tests.

By the time climate change became an issue, using science to defuse science was a well-known and highly effective technique. Known as the 'tobacco strategy' – a campaign of setting scientists and experts against each other – has worked extremely well in defending economic interests in everything from cigarette smoking to acid rain to ozone depletion to global warming and again, many of these people have sincerely believed what they were saying. It is like a fundamentalist sincerely refuting evolution and the existence of the fossil record. They aren't lying or deliberately trying to 'obfuscate,' although it can certainly look like it to higher levels. It's merely their sincere interpretation of the 'facts' and their values as experienced through their particular level of development.

Originally used to confuse the public about the dangers of smoking cigarettes and extend the life of the tobacco companies, while simultaneously shortening the life of their consumers, the tobacco strategy was a staggering commercial success. By 1950 science had proven without a shadow of a doubt that smoking was dangerous to health. So 'Big Tobacco' recruited high ranking, well known and well connected scientists to spearhead research into disproving or at least casting doubt over the facts. Their purpose was not to research smoking and the ramifications of smoking on a person's health, but to develop 'an extensive body of scientifically, well-grounded data useful in defending the industry against attack.'[28] The goal was to fight science with science – or at least the gaps and uncertainties in the existing science.[29]

Yet again, ask yourself, did the doctors who were personally advertising cigarettes really think they were directly promoting death? That they knew they were promoting death and deliberately did it anyway? As doctors? Or did they actually see the 'facts' differently, hard as that might be to believe by those of us who know better. Whatever we decide on this issue, the point is simply to remember the vast differences there are between the realities of the different Integral elements – different truths and values at different quadrants, levels, lines, and so on, and the need to always keep those differences in mind when addressing wicked and complex problems.

Consumers, confident they could turn to science for verified answers did not know who to believe. Some scientists said it was harmful to health others said it was not. The smokers, already addicted to the product, did not really want to stop so they liked to hear that the negative health effects of smoking were as yet unproven – even as they died in the thousands! Government, which was receiving billions in cigarette excise tax, did not

[28] William D. Hobbs to J. Paul Sticht, BN: 504480340, Legacy Tobacco Documents Library

[29] Oreskes, N. and Conway, E. (2010) *Merchants of Doubt*, London: Bloomsbury.

really want to believe it either, because it was a lucrative form of revenue. And of course Big Tobacco didn't want to believe it because then smokers would believe it and stop smoking.

The Tobacco Strategy has been used many times by influential individuals pulling the strings from behind the veil, and it's been successfully used to deflect attention and protect business and government interests for decades.

Scientist and experts clearly have a very important role to play in understanding climate change, but when the science is being funded quietly by entities that are not interested in the truth (at least, not any truth other than their own) but rather in fostering enough doubt to prolong the 'debate' and prevent legislation that will damage their financial interests, then it can be very confusing to know who to listen to and who to ignore.

Of course, blind trust in science is just as debilitating as no trust. The IPCC is the world's leading authority on climate issues and includes a group of some 1300 independent scientific experts from around the world. And yet when they delivered their first assessment of the state of climate science in 1990, the language they used was considered too strong and too alarmist and they were immediately subjected to a full frontal attack by various influential groups with powerful and lucrative vested interests. These interests' access to media allowed them to bend the narrative and cast doubt where none existed, and yet the general public largely bought it. Even as late as 2006, 44 per cent of Americans still did not believe in global warming, despite the fact that almost all climate scientists did. In 2007, 64 per cent of Americans still thought the science wasn't settled![30]

The reason the first IPCC assessment was alarmist was because the collective scientific community independently studying climate change concurred (from its leading-edge at the time) that

[30] Oreskes, N. and Conway, E. (2010) *Merchants of Doubt*, London: Bloomsbury

we really needed to be alarmed by the science! We needed to sit up, take notice, and do something to fix it while there was still time to fix it. Instead the tone was pounced on and they were accused of sounding the global fire alarm when all that had occurred was a chip-pan fire!

In over their heads

This is where it is also worthwhile to remember Robert Kegan's findings – that some 60 per cent of Americans are not yet capable of worldcentric rational thinking, but rather are at ethnocentric or lower levels of development. Ask them to address global worldcentric issues and they are simply 'in over their heads'. Therefore additional, exceptional measures, often including level 3 egocentric survivalist reasons, are required to convince such individuals.

This is one of the most astonishing findings of developmental studies, namely how dramatically 'truth' and 'facts' change from level to level and dimension to dimension in the overall Integral matrix. If you take a child of four or five years old, and put two glasses in front of them one tall and thin, the other short and fat, with the short, fat one full of water; and then, in front of the child, pour the water from the short glass into the tall, thin glass, the height of water in the thin glass will be much greater than it was in the short, fat glass. Pour the water back and forth several times, so the child can see that it is the same amount of water, but it gets 'higher' or 'lower' depending on the shape of the glass; then ask, 'Which glass has the most water?' Virtually all children that age will say the tall, thin glass has more water. Being at level 2 or 3 they cognitively lack what is called 'conservation of mass and volume.' But do this experiment when the child is six or seven years old (cognitive level 4), where the child does possess the capacity to follow 'the conservation of mass and volume', and all of them will correctly say, 'They have the same amount of water.' Now the funny part: show the child videos of when they said 'the short, fat one has more water', and they think you have doctored the videotape. They simply cannot imagine somebody being that stupid, and certainly not them. They are shocked. But that type of thing happens all along the developmental scale. We simply cannot remember what the world looked like at a previous level of development, we cannot imagine it. We see the world, and its 'truths' and 'facts', through the present level that we are more-or-less exclusively identified with, and all other levels are simply wrong. This is what is meant when the Talmud states, 'We do not see things as they are; we see things as we are.'

It is only at the Integral levels that consciousness becomes so highly developed that it can take a truly multi-perspective stance and thus have some sense of the significance of other levels. At this level, and for the first time, we realise that all levels are basically sincere but also are hamstrung by certain inherent limitations, limitations that are only overcome at the next-higher level... indefinitely. But including some aspects of all of those levels becomes a primary motivating factor in any truly Integral levels. This ability to transcend the binary right/wrong mind-set is revolutionary and unprecedented in all of human history.

The fact is, multiple stakeholders make wicked problems really messy. But, of course, it continues to get more complicated....

Multiple Causes of Climate Change

When we begin to understand the interdependencies, complexity and conflicts of interest within the stakeholder groups – not to mention the actual different levels and dimensions of what is considered 'weather' and 'climate change' in the first place – it is easy to see why there are so many different ideas about what is causing the global rise in temperature. Not to mention the fact that there are at least eight different levels of the actual meaning of 'global temperature'.

It is worth clarifying three basic types of approaches that people take to the debate about the multiple causes of climate change.

The types of approaches could be characterised as, but are not limited to:

- What problem?
- If there is a problem, it is a natural phenomenon
- The problem is caused by human activity

What Problem?

At one extreme there are some stakeholders that suggest there is no such thing as climate change (the 'sceptics' and especially the 'active resisters'). One of the noisiest and best funded is the Heartland Institute. In 2013, the Heartland Institute released a 1200-page report under the banner of the Non-governmental International Panel on Climate Change (NIPCC). This very official sounding body with a name and acronym very similar to the IPCC is made up of the Center for the Study of Carbon Dioxide and Global Change, The Science and Environmental Policy Project and The Heartland Institute.

The report has three lead authors with another 50 chapter lead authors and contributors and reviewers from 15 countries around the world. This 1200 page document, which would require deforestation to print, states that it provides the 'scientific balance that is missing from the overly alarmists reports of the United Nations' Intergovernmental Panel on Climate Change' (IPCC). It claims that the IPCC is selective in its review of climate science, ignores key studies, and that their studies and conclusions are biased and exaggerated.

You can even order your free 'Crisis or Delusion' poster from The Heartland Institute which lists all the climate change sceptics.

Whether you believe this position is bonkers, true, or you just do not know is not the point. The point is that it is the current and strongly held view of some stakeholders. It may be that these stakeholders genuinely believe this position and there are definitely some that do, or it may be that this position simply suits their political views, personal values or commercial purpose. Certainly if we scrape the surface to see who is funding the Heartland Institute, it would appear to be little more than thinly disguised self-interest. If we look at who is pulling the strings we find 'Libertarian groups, social and political conservatives, and industry lobbyists such as those behind Big Oil, Big Coal and Big Tobacco'.[31] It is probably not a coincidence that the people working hardest to disprove climate change are the ones that benefit the most from the status quo. Clearly if there is no problem then there is no need to change our behaviour or do anything different, or impose taxes or tariffs on those that are polluting the planet. So for these guys at least, and many like them, there is no climate change problem in the first place.

Natural Phenomenon

The sceptic's only concession on climate change is that even if the planet is heating up, it is not 'our fault'; that is, it is not caused by human activity and behaviour.

These stakeholders believe that variations in solar energy are causing it, or perhaps changes in the reflectivity of the earth's atmosphere. They claim that the greenhouse effect is a natural process and that changes in global temperature have been happening for thousands of years and therefore we just don't need to worry.

What makes this argument so potent is that parts of it are true (as is so often the case), and those who embrace this view will, consciously or unconsciously, cherry-pick data and science to back up their claims. The earth's climate has changed. In the last 650 000 years there have been seven cycles of glacial advance

[31] Rosen, L. (2013) *Ever Heard of the Heartland Institute?* The World Future Society, www.wfs.org/blogs/len-rosen/ever-heard-heartland-institute

and retreat, with an abrupt end of the last ice age about 7000 years ago. Most of these significant climate changes have been attributed to very small variations in the earth's orbit that have then changed the amount of solar energy the planet receives.[32] In fact, the whole issue of solar energy is also often cited as a natural cause of climate change.

The greenhouse process is a natural process that helps to ensure our planet is habitable. Heat from the sun, which is obviously very hot, is emitted toward the earth in high energy short wavelengths that penetrate the earth's atmosphere. About 30 per cent of the sun's incoming energy and heat is reflected directly back into space by the atmosphere, clouds, and surface of the earth. The remaining 70 per cent is then absorbed into the earth's system and heats up the planet so life can exist here. In the other direction, the earth emits energy into the atmosphere. Because the earth is cooler than the sun, the energy is emitted in the form of infra-red radiation, at wavelengths longer than the incoming solar energy. The greenhouse gases in the atmosphere absorb a lot of the long-wave energy preventing it from immediately escaping from the earth's system in space. This captured energy then warms the earth's surface and lower atmosphere. This atmospheric increase in greenhouse gas concentration has amplified the natural greenhouse effect by trapping more of the energy emitted by the earth, causing the earth to heat up.[33]

So it is true that the planet benefits from a natural greenhouse effect, but the increased concentration of gases is trapping too much of the heat, which is therefore heating the planet too much. The sceptics argue that this is probably because of variations to solar energy. But that explanation is, according to the vast majority of scientists, simply not possible.

---

[32] NASA, *Global Climate Change: Vital Signs of the Planet: Evidence*, http://climate.nasa.gov/evidence/

[33] United States Environmental Protection Agency, *Causes of Climate Change*, www.epa.gov/climatechange/science/causes.html

Atmospheric scientist Ben Santer has proven beyond reasonable doubt that natural climate variations leave different patterns and traces than warming caused by greenhouse emissions.[34] This is a good example of 'systems of systems of systems' thinking, or a leading-edge level 7/8 view. At the level of just 'systems,' the changes look identical (and in terms of simple system changes, they are identical) which is why some scientists, particularly those at 'systems' levels, will promote that view. But look deeper and subtle shifts, at the level of 'systems of systems of systems,' begin to announce themselves, and the 'truth', and the 'facts' once again change, shifting upward to 'more truth'.

There are two parts of the atmosphere surrounding the planet. The troposphere is like a warm blanket that hugs the earth's surface and keeps us cosy, and the stratosphere is the thinner colder blanket above. It is therefore the stratosphere that is closer to the sun. Consequently if variations to solar energy were causing the earth to heat up, then the stratosphere would be warm. Ben Santer proved that it is not – it is cooler than the troposphere – and that result is impossible to explain if the sun's variation alone was a valid cause for climate change.

But is Ben Santer one of the change-agent scientists or a sceptic? After all, we have already stated that it is sometimes difficult to know which camp scientists and experts are in. But it seems unlikely he is a sceptic. Ben Santer is one of the world's most distinguished scientists – the recipient of a 1998 MacArthur 'genius' award. He has done more to illuminate the data on climate change than just about anyone on the planet. Unsurprisingly, therefore, he has also been brutally, and in the views of many unfairly, attacked by those who have sought to discredit him and his science.[35] Since the vast majority of scientists (coming from

---

[34] Oreskes, N. and Conway, E. (2010) Merchants of Doubt, London: Bloomsbury.

[35] Oreskes, N. and Conway, E. (2010) *Merchants of Doubt*, London: Bloomsbury

the more leading-edge levels) agree with Santer, his views seem the most likely, at this time, to be the more accurate.

Human Causes

The fact that the troposphere is warming up but the stratosphere is not, along with other science, strongly indicates that human beings are causing climate change. In their Fourth Assessment Report, the IPCC concluded that there is a more than 90 per cent probability that human activities over the past 250 years have warmed the planet.[36] Ninety-seven per cent of climate scientists agree that climate-warming trends over the past century are very likely due to human activities.[37] Suffice it to say it is now very close to conclusive!

We are largely responsible for the increase in greenhouse gases. Greenhouse gases include water vapour, carbon dioxide (CO_2), methane, nitrous oxide, and chlorofluorocarbons (CFCs). One of the biggest drivers for the rising level of CO_2 in the atmosphere, amounting to 91 per cent of the total, is the burning of fossil fuels and our unquenchable need for energy; and this need for energy isn't going to disappear anytime soon. Most modern economies have become extremely dependent on fossil fuel. Given this dependency it is hardly surprising that energy companies have a disproportionate influence on the global economy and will offer extreme resistance to anything that can threaten their position or their revenue stream – such as arguments about the negative impact of fossil fuel.

Methane is created through the decomposition of waste in

---

[36] NASA, *Global Climate Change*: Vital Signs of the Planet: Causes, http://climate.nasa.gov/causes/

[37] Anderegg, W. R. L., et al (2010) 'Expert credibility in climate change', *Proceedings of the National Academy of Sciences*, vol. 107, no. 27, pp. 12107-12109 www.climateaccess.org/sites/default/files/Anderegga_Expert%20credibility%20in%20climate%20change.pdf

landfills and agriculture. Rice cultivation which generates considerable amounts of methane is particularly problematic, especially considering that China, the largest country by population on the planet, sees rice as the mainstay of its diet, as do many other Asian countries. In other words, the demand for rice is not going to suddenly drop. In addition, the rearing of animals, especially ruminants such as sheep, cattle and goats, creates vast quantities of methane. So the decimation of our forests to make way for cattle production causes a double whammy – a loss of CO_2-cancelling trees and the increase of methane-creating livestock. Plus, to make matters even worse, land-use changes with deforestation for food production leads to the melting of snow and ice which reduce the 'surface albedo', or the amount of sunlight reflected from the ground back into space, therefore heating the planet still further.

Methane is actually a stronger greenhouse gas than CO_2, but there is, at this time, significantly less methane produced than CO_2. Agriculture or food production is also responsible for the creation of nitric oxide through soil cultivation, especially when either organic or commercial fertilisers are used.

And finally we invented CFCs that create holes in the ozone layer. Although highly regulated now under the Montreal Protocol, there was a time that every fridge-freezer and air conditioner in the world had CFCs inside, keeping milk cold and humans cool and quietly eating the ozone layer.

On top of all that, the sheer number of human beings on the planet is adding additional pressure. As we approach 8 billion people, those numbers obviously put huge pressure on our natural resources; more people consume more products and more people eat more food, which puts more pressure on food production and agriculture. Yet agriculture produces a significant amount of greenhouse gas; not as much as the burning of fossil fuel but a significant amount nonetheless.

And while we may not all need the energy guzzling products and services we consume, we are not that keen to give them up. The social and economic costs of climate change will be significant. It is also important that the policies and solutions we arrive at are perceived as equitable by society and do not end up penalising those less fortunate or those who do not have a strong political voice. Such considerations simply add to the interdependencies and complexities that a solution needs to address.

As is the way with wicked problems, many of the factors that contribute to one problem are also separate wicked problems in their own right. Over-population is an example, and it too has multiple (and multi-dimensional) causes. It is created, in part, by a lack of education. There is, for example, clear evidence that women with more schooling tend to have smaller, healthier families. Throughout the world, more education is associated with smaller family size. In a number of less developed countries, women with no education have about twice the number of children as women with ten or more years of school.[38] International aid programmes are often heavily focused on education and ensuring that girls are educated, because cross-country studies show that even an extra year of schooling for girls reduces fertility rates by five to ten per cent.[39] Educated women are more self-confident and take active control of their fertility, therefore reducing the number of children they have, which of course also impacts other separate but connected wicked problems, including poverty and health. When women do not have control over their fertility and do not understand it, then they will invariably have far more children than they want or can afford. Without the financial resources, time or energy to care for those children, they are not as healthy as children from smaller family units. Plus children who do not feel loved or wanted are much more likely to suffer social problems

---

[38] United Nations, Department of Economic and Social Affairs, Population Division, (1997) *Linkages Between Population and Education*, New York: United Nations, December.

[39] UNICEF, *Girls' education: A lifeline to development*, www.unicef.org/sowc96/ngirls.htm

and be less educated themselves, which can then perpetuate and exacerbate the problems.

Of course over-population is also caused by religious beliefs that prohibit contraception and make it difficult for women within those religious cultures to gain access to education or preventative medication. The Catholic religion, for example, suggests that a woman can engage in family planning if she has a reliable knowledge of the cycle of female fertility and a willingness to abstain from sexual union at certain times. So what happens to the women who do not get even a primary school education, who can barely read, never mind have a reliable knowledge of female fertility? What about the women who live in cultures where they are essentially considered as property? How much say do those women have in their fertility cycle or abstinence? This issue is of course extremely controversial. We could argue that the world has changed considerably since these religions gathered pace, and that the religions themselves need to evolve with the people who practice them. Certainly within Christianity, the Anglican faith has embraced changes that allow followers to take active control over their fertility, but that argument would be nothing short of blasphemous to many religious leaders – especially orthodox Catholics.

Unfortunately when women are forced – either through poor education or religious beliefs or cultural ethics, to have more children than they want or can afford, then there are serious knock-on effects for the family, the wider community and the planetary temperature.

In 1995, US criminologist James Alan Fox predicted that the rate of murders committed by teenagers was going to spike. His best-case scenario was a rise of 15 per cent and his worst-case scenario predicted murders of this type would double. Citizens were already worried about crime in the 1990s and the Clinton government of the time took these predictions very seriously, and considered ways to avert this apocalyptic future. But then something odd happened – crime rates fell. Instead of increasing by 15 per cent or 100 per cent, teenage murder fell by 50 per cent in five years. So why did it fall so significantly so quickly? There are, of course many theories, and the reality is that it fell for a number of reasons; but one reason is particularly interesting and thought-provoking. Twenty years earlier, a young woman called Norma McCorvey brought a lawsuit seeking to legalise abortion in the US. She was a poor, uneducated alcoholic who had already put two children up for adoption. In 1970, she had found herself pregnant again, but abortion was illegal in all states of the US. People of influence adopted her cause; her identity was changed to Jane Roe (Roe v. Wade), and in 1973 abortion became legal in the US for the first time. The reason the crime rate suddenly dropped in the 1990s was because the children who would grow up in poverty, unwanted and unloved – and who would likely end up in a life of crime – simply were not being born in the first place.[40] Women were no longer forced to have children they could not afford or didn't want, so the criminals just did not exist.

For some, with strongly-held religious beliefs, this idea is abhorrent, and abortion is still a violently contested topic in the US and around the world today. It is also a political landmine. But the 'life at all costs' perspective is a good example of what is usually a sincerely and deeply held belief – most often from a traditional religious level 4 – and is invested with enormous passion because it is embedded in the very value structure of the individual, organisation and culture. Higher levels generally argue that such a belief ignores the view that it may be more abhorrent to bring a child into an already seriously over-populated world when that child is not wanted, not loved, not cared for properly, not educated and not nurtured. A child with such an unwelcome beginning, who experiences an unsupported, isolated upbringing, has very little chance of becoming anything other than a miserable and potentially violent human being. The 'life at all costs' principle will, for some, trump the suffering that will

[40] Levitt, S. D. and Dubner, S. J. (2005) *Freakonomics*, London: Penguin.

be inflicted on the poor child born into terrible circumstances. Of course, life or child abuse is a very difficult choice. It is often this accumulating, expanding enormity of the challenges we face, where understanding one wicked problem leads us to another and another and another – each as complex and interdependent as the last, that make them so overwhelming and intractable. Not to mention that each of them has components embedded in numerous different Integral Addresses, each contributing to the problem in its own way, and many of them enormously resistant to any quick changes. The only way to get at one of these issues is to get at all of them – Integral Coherence. Otherwise it is just a circular causal merry-go-round.

Of course when we are searching for causes, they are often extremely divisive and when we fail to understand the overall Integral sources of this, it often brings out the natural human tendency to blame someone else. Of course fault-finding and finger pointing takes us further and further away from any genuine collaborative solution, and makes compassion and co-operation all the less likely.

Multiple Symptoms of Climate Change

As with most wicked problems, understanding the nature of Integral interdependencies between the different climate factors is a massive task in and of itself, without having to deal with all of the 'one size fits all' approaches, not to mention campaigns of obfuscation orchestrated by various one-dimensional stakeholder groups.

The effects of CO_2 mingle with Arctic methane release, water vapour reflection, solar energy effects, and many other factors to create a complex spaghetti-like matrix of interconnectivity and feedback loops at just the physical level alone. These feedback loops themselves interact in a complex way. Taking all of these factors into consideration, the overall effect of the physical feedback loops is to accelerate the effects of global warming. There is little real doubt that we are heating up the planet somewhere near 300 times faster than at any other time in our history. John Schellnhuber from the Climate Research Institute in Potsdam put it this way, 'The possibility of a tipping point in the earth system as a whole, which prevents the recovery of stable equilibrium and leads to a process of runaway climate change, is now the critical research agenda requiring the concentration of global resources in a 'Manhattan project' style of engagement'. He concluded, 'All other work on impact assessment, mitigation and adaptation depends on the outcome of this over-arching issue'.[41] However, the consequences of this dramatic temperature change are far from straightforward.

Wicked problems do not just have one or two symptoms, they have multiple symptoms; and for climate change the symptoms, just focusing on the physical level alone, include but are not limited to:

- Extreme weather events
- Rising sea level, ocean warming and acidification
- Shrinking ice sheets, declining Arctic ice and decreased snow cover
- Increased disease

Extreme Weather Events

Not all extreme weather events are symptoms of climate change, but many are. There have and always will be storms and heatwaves and droughts, but the amount, frequency and severity

[41] Wasdell, D. presentation (2013) 'Sensitivity, Non-Linearity and Self-Amplification in the Global Climate System', The Annual Conference of the Club of Rome, Ottawa, 20 September 2013.

of these extreme events are increasing.[42]

The number of 'record high' temperature events have been increasing around the world. There is more rainfall and more storms. Hurricanes and other tropical storms get much of their energy from warm ocean water, and as the ocean gets warmer (another symptom of global warming), the storms get more frequent and more violent – with faster winds, heavier and more rain. When these storms strike, higher sea levels (another symptom) result in greater storm surges and coastal flooding and damage. Increased temperatures and evaporation also means that tornados are more frequent and stronger. Of course these storms cause significant damage, destruction and loss of life.

As the Arctic warms up, wind patterns are also becoming disrupted, altering the course of the jet stream – making it 'wavier' with steeper troughs and higher ridges.[43] It was this alteration of the jet stream that plunged the UK into a nationwide 'white-out' in January 2013 when a NASA satellite image showed the entire British Isles under snow.

Weather systems are also moving more slowly, which in turn increases the chances of long-lasting extreme events like droughts, floods, extreme snow, heat waves and wildfires.

And although we are not focusing on it here, it should always be kept in mind that not only are these dramatic changes affecting the physical dimension directly (and thus the physiological needs and dimensions of humans), they are also capable of exerting effects and potentially negative influences on virtually all higher levels and dimensions of humans existence via 'prepotency'.

---

[42] The Third US National Climate Assessment http://nca2014.globalchange.gov/highlights/report-findings/extreme-weather#submenu-highlights-overview

[43] Mulvaney, K. (2013) '10 Signs Climate Change is Already Happening' http://news.discovery.com/earth/global-warming/10-signs-climate-change-is-already-happening-130422.htm

This multi-dimensional impact of physical weather events is one of the items that make severe climate change so difficult for human beings to adapt to. Humans have higher developmental levels that most other animals do not possess exposing us to numerous extra levels and dimensions of painful suffering.

Rising Sea Level, Ocean Warming and Acidification

Another symptom of climate change is rising sea level and changes to the ocean, both in terms of temperature and acidity. Using core samples, tide gauge readings and satellite measurements, it has been deduced that the Global Mean Sea Level (GMSL) has risen by four to eight inches (10 to 20 centimetres) over the past century. However, the annual rate of rise over the past 20 years has been 0.13 inches (3.2 millimetres) a year, roughly twice the average speed of the preceding 80 years.[44] This is causing coastal erosion and loss of land mass. This trend is of course extremely worrying – especially if you live near the sea! Thousands of coastal cities, like Venice, which witnessed historic flooding in 2008, face serious problems. In Indonesia, 24 islands have already disappeared off the coast of Aceh, North Sumarta, Papua and Riau. In the capital city of Jakarta, the main international Soekarno-Hatta Airport could be below sea level as soon as 2030.[45]

As well as the loss of land mass, rising sea levels can have a devastating impact on coastal habitats, polluting fresh water aquifers and agricultural soil, as well as causing the loss of plants, fish and birds. This of course has a negative impact on food production.

---

[44] Sea level Rise, National Geographic http://ocean.nationalgeographic.com/ocean/critical-issues-sea-level-rise/

[45] BBC (2014) *Indonesia: Rising sea 'threatens 1,500 islands'*, www.bbc.co.uk/news/blogs-news-from-elsewhere-26337723

Rising ocean temperatures and acidity are also negatively impacting marine life. Coral is dying and fish stocks are dwindling, which has a knock-on effect for the people who rely on either for their livelihood. In developing nations, fishing provides an income and food source for many who are then adversely affected when fish stocks diminish.

Shrinking Ice Sheets and Decreased Snow Cover

Clearly if the planet is warming up then the cold parts of the planet become warmer and ice sheets melt, which in turn increases the sea level. The Arctic Ocean around the North Pole is covered in ice all year around, although there is obviously some thaw in summer. However, the amount of summer ice is now the smallest it has ever been since scientists started measuring the ice with satellites in the 1970s. Plus the ice is thinner.

In 1995, the Larsen-A ice shelf on the Antarctic Peninsula collapsed. Sixty kilometres to the north, the Prince Gustav ice shelf collapsed and several more have disappeared in the last decade. The Antarctic Peninsula, the region that reaches northward toward the tip of South America, is the most rapidly warming part of the southern hemisphere, with temperature increases of about 2.7 degrees Celsius over the last 50 years. In fact, in the Antarctic Peninsula, the degree of melting is a unique phenomenon in at least the last 1000 years.[46]

This is also having an adverse effect on wildlife and some species, such as polar bears, as they struggle to survive.

Plus these massive ice sheets and snow-covered land mass reflect a lot of sunlight back out to space, therefore preventing the planet from overheating. Shrinking ice sheets and less snow

[46] Mulvaney, K. (2013) '10 Signs Climate Change is Already Happening', http://news.discovery.com/earth/global-warming/10-signs-climate-change-is-already-happening-130422.htm

cover means that the earth is now absorbing that extra energy and therefore exacerbating the problem. This is an example of a positive feedback loop, where warming causes changes that lead to even more warming.

The loss of snow cover on land also impacts fresh water supply. Snow that forms in the winter, melts in the summer and fills up lakes, rivers and reservoirs that supply fresh water for towns and cities as well as agriculture. As the temperature increases, there is less snow cover and therefore less fresh water – all when the global need for fresh water is already significant.

One of the more recently announced concerns of Arctic ice melt has to do with methane gas, of which enormous amounts are now stored in the Arctic, kept there by the sea ice sheet. But the accelerated rate of global warming means that, as US Navy researchers reported, the Arctic sea ice sheet might disappear for periods during the summer as soon as 2016. In March 2010, *Science* reported the amount of methane trapped by Arctic ice is the equivalent of between 1000 gigatons and 10 000 gigatons of carbon dioxide. For comparison, the total amount of carbon dioxide emitted by humans since 1850 is 1475 gigatons.

This means that, according to a *Nature* July 2013 article, upwards of a '50 gigaton methane burp' is now 'possible at any time'. That means now. Such events would be catastrophic across the board. As well-respected climate researcher Paul Beckwith, at the University of Ottawa, put it, 'It is my view that our climate system is in the early stages of abrupt climate change that, if left unchecked, will lead to a temperature rise of five to six degrees Celsius within a decade or two' (from now, 2015).[47] This would make virtually all farmland, and most ecosystems, unworkable. The last 'Great Dying' occurred from a six degree Celsius increase, and killed 95 per cent of all life on earth. Humans would very likely be included and this is a matter of a decade or two,

[47] Quoted in Dahr Jamail, 'The Methane Monster Roars', www.truth-out/news, 13 January 2015.

not a century or two. It would be the death of humanity and the destruction of the human race via 'prepotency overkill'.

Increased Disease

The knock on effects of some of the other symptoms of climate change includes an increase in the spread of disease that can have a significant impact on human health. Warming climate, heavier and more frequent rain, more severe and long lasting droughts, and a rising sea level are spreading a variety of pathogens around the world.

Malaria is moving to the highlands. Lyme disease is spreading across the US northeast and eastern Canada. Outbreaks of cholera will increase as drinking water is contaminated. Director of the Global Health Institute at the University of Wisconsin, Madison, Jonathan Patz has expressed concern that many of the anti-poverty (another separate wicked problem) gains could be reversed because of the impacts of climate change. For example, heavy flooding as a result of rising sea levels and more frequent storms has been scientifically linked to increased outbreaks of diseases such as hepatitis A, giardiasis and norovirus infection occurring because of contaminated drinking water.

Diseases are also moving. For example, ciguatera is an illness that people get by eating fish that have a certain type of algae toxin; the disease causes nausea and vomiting and has negative neurological effects. Until recently it has never been found outside the Caribbean, but as global temperatures rise there have now been cases in the northern Gulf of Mexico. In 2013 there were 2474 documented cases of West Nile virus in the US, characterised by symptoms like headache, high fever and joint pains and which led to 114 deaths in 2012.[48]

[48] Lippman, D. (2014) 'How the Spreading Symptoms of Climate Change Can be Deadly', *Scientific American*, www.scientificamerican.com/article/how-the-spreading-symptoms-of-climate-change-can-be-deadly/

Changes to climate often change the way diseases behave and where they flourish. This, of course, has far reaching consequences for human health.

There are of course, many more symptoms such as reduced acreage of productive farmland; decreasing amounts of consumable water and reduced amount of human-habitable areas. The list of symptoms is almost endless, but what we have covered gives you a pretty good idea of the extensive networks that are involved.

From an Integral point of view, the cumulative impact of multi-dimensionality, multiple stakeholders, multiple causes, and multiple symptoms create a smorgasbord of potential solutions that all together add another, new level of complexity to the issues we face. Not just in working out what ones to choose, but how the various solutions will impact each other and other stakeholders, as well as the multiple causes and symptoms (the effect of 'systems within systems within systems'). What is imperative in all of this is to make sure that any map or model of this overall situation actually includes, in a coherent fashion, all of these variables, parameters, and dimensions. It is bad enough that this wicked multiplicity of factors is conspiring to wreak havoc on living beings, but impossible if agents trying to handle all this are generally ignorant of all these factors and dimensions to begin with.

Multiple Solutions for Climate Change

When it comes to the potential answers for climate change, again there are multiple solutions for every wicked problem. Invariably the solution presented will depend on the stakeholder group you ask and the causes that a particular stakeholder group believes is causing the problem or whether they believe or want to believe there is a problem in the first place.

The current multiple solutions for climate change include but are not limited to:

- New energy technologies and innovations
- Reduce the population
- Change human behaviour
- Increased corporate responsibility
- Legislation and evolved ethics
- *Integral Coherence* and the use of more inclusive models and meta-maps to guide our actions towards the evolution of consciousness itself. (How to actually implement this revolutionary solution is detailed in Part Four).

New Energy Technologies and Innovations

The climate change sceptics have long held that even if there is currently a climate change problem (and they are not admitting there is), then human beings are smart enough and innovative enough to solve it in due course.

And certainly huge strides have been made in the development of new technologies. Some such as CO_2 sequestration focus on dealing with a large source of the problem – CO_2. Sequestration captures waste CO_2 before it enters the atmosphere and transports it to storage sites, usually underground in geological formations. Other new technologies focus on the development of cleaner energy but each technology has its own set of concerns and challenges. There are several alternative fuel sources that we are exploring as a substitute for fossil fuel. These technologies are necessary not just because fossil fuel is damaging the planet, but because it is running out; and hopefully their continued development and widespread adoption can help us to reverse some of the damage that has already been done and provide a long-term sustainable solution to our energy requirements. These are straightforward system approaches, although they affect, directly or indirectly, all other quadrants, and all multi-dimensions to one degree or another. The main new energy options are:

- Wind
- Water
- Solar
- Nuclear

Wind energy

Wind power has a number of significant advantages. For a start, it is never going to run out, so it has enormous long-term potential. Plus harnessing the energy from wind does not pollute the environment. The infrastructure required to harness it and transport it to the grid does make a slight impact on climate change, but once the infrastructure is in place, the energy itself is pollution-free.

There are two types of wind farm – off-shore and on-shore. The off-shore wind turbines are located in the ocean. Although less of an eyesore, the corrosive properties of sea water mean the lifespan of off-shore turbines is shorter, resulting in higher replacement infrastructure costs.

On-shore wind turbines are located on land, usually in the countryside, on top of hills and in wide-open spaces. Obviously this particular solution has significant negative implications for the lucrative tourism industry in many places so it is not always a popular solution. Wind farms, especially the very large ones, are considered ugly – a *War of the Worlds'* intrusion on Mother Nature. They are also surprisingly noisy and can cause a danger to wildlife, although the wildlife impact can be minimised by appropriate site selection and by avoiding areas of high conservation or habitat value.

As at 2015, there are significant up-front costs associated with wind energy and most governments provide incentives to suppliers and landowners to encourage the creation of wind farms. These costs together with installation and infrastructure cost mean that the breakeven point for wind energy can be several decades after installation.

The biggest challenge with wind energy as a viable solution to fossil fuel is that the wind is inconsistent. There are times when there is no wind at all and therefore no energy is being produced, and other times when the wind is so strong that the turbines have to be switched off. So far there is limited technology for wind energy storage, which means that even if wind energy can be stored in massive batteries, it may only last a few days. If there is no wind for more than three days then the lights will go out!

Unless wind energy storage technology can be improved significantly, wind may never be a significant contributor to our energy needs, and other 'back up' systems will still be needed. There is potential to link up the various wind energy grids on the basis that it is probably always going to be windy somewhere, but that connection of infrastructure adds another layer of complexity and difficulty to the solution. It also involves multiple stakeholder groups across countries and governments, which raises its own additional set of challenges. Better energy management could also provide some respite for the inconsistency and unpredictability of wind as a source of energy.

Wind energy is still a new technology, and many people fear that wind farms are being created too quickly without the technology being thoroughly tested or alternatives properly assessed. It would be a travesty, for example, if our landscape was ruined by wind farms that did not actually produce or were incapable of storing the energy we needed. Who would take them down? Or would they just be left to rot in the countryside? The reality of any alternative fuel source is that there is currently a great deal of money in the area by way of government grants and incentives, and as soon as money is involved then the solution can become as skewed and warped as the problem it is seeking to solve. Wind energy has significant economic and environmental trade-offs, as well as technological uncertainty, which means it is by no means the 'clear winner'.[49]

Water energy

Hydroelectric energy is another renewable technology that harnesses the power of falling or moving water. Obviously we live on a planet that has a great deal of water – especially seawater – and wave or tidal energy technologies are seeking to tap into that potential. Wave power is much more predictable than wind power and it increases during the winter, when electricity demand is at its highest. Tidal stream energy is also predictable and consistent, which makes it a more stable proposition than wind.

However, salt water is very corrosive, which can increase the cost of development and replacement of wave energy technologies. Plus many of the existing technologies struggle when the waves are too turbulent or going in too many different directions. In 2013 a wave energy generator capable of harvesting energy no matter which way the sea is moving won the UK round of James Dyson's engineering award.[50] This type of energy generation is, however, still in its infancy, but it does have the potential to be at least part of the portfolio of solutions. In the UK, for example, studies have estimated that 12 per cent of the current UK electricity demand could theoretically be supplied by wave or tidal energy.[51]

Hydroelectricity is also generated by water – this time through

---

[49] Bassi, S. and Hicks, N. (2012) 'Onshore wind energy: what are the pros and cons?' *The Guardian*, www.theguardian.com/environment/2012/sep/25/climate-change-windpower

[50] Ward, M. (2013) 'Wave power generator bags Dyson award' BBC New Technology, www.bbc.co.uk/news/technology-24070071

[51] Gov.uk (2013) 'Wave and tidal energy: part of the UK's energy mix', www.gov.uk/wave-and-tidal-energy-part-of-the-uks-energy-mix

the creation of dams. The dams are either constructed on fast flowing rivers or a large man-made reservoir is made to create that fast flowing water to convert to energy. Hydroelectric energy has many advantages. It is a clean renewable energy source that does not pollute the environment with emissions. Once the infrastructure is in place the costs are constant and operating costs are minimal. Energy is created when the water is moving, and hydroelectric power plants have full control over when the water moves and therefore how much or how little energy is created. Plus the dams and reservoirs created for the production of electricity can be used for other activities such as water recreational activities or used to breed fish. This means that alternative economies are built around hydroelectric plants adding to the economic diversification in the area.

But there are significant downsides. For a start, they need a large area to build the dam and reservoir in order to produce the energy from the falling water. For example, when Canada dammed the Churchill River, 6988 square kilometres of land was flooded in the creation of Churchill Falls hydroelectric power station:[52] that is six times the land mass of Hong Kong!

Considering few of these unused uninhabited places still exist in the world, this usually means the destruction of the environment, forests, agricultural land and in some cases whole communities. When a river is dammed there are untold knock-on effects up and down the river. For example, the Mekong River sustains the world's biggest and most productive inland fishery in South East Asia, providing food and a livelihood for some 65 million people along its shores in Laos, Thailand, Cambodia and Vietnam. So whilst the damming of the Mekong may provide much needed clean energy, which may help to solve climate change, it will cause a new set of problems to those 65 million people and the environment. Ironically the solution that is at least in part hoped to

[52] Industry tap, *Largest Dams in the World*, www.industrytap.com/4856/largest_dams_in_the_world

solve our biggest environmental threat will itself create additional environmental and humanitarian threats. Such is the nature of a wicked problem – as soon as one problem is addressed, the solution will invariably create a whole series of new problems.

The decision by the Laos government to push ahead with the giant Xayaburi dam makes it the first of what could prove to be a cascade of 11 proposed dams on the lower Mekong. Of course, this challenge is made even more complex because the Mekong, like many rivers, flows through different countries controlled by different governments with different environmental agendas. When one government decides to dam their part of the river, it does not just affect their part of the river, which can in turn escalate political tensions across borders. As the President of Vietnam, Truong Tan Sang warned, 'Tensions over water resources are not only threatening economic growth in many countries, but also presenting a source of conflict.'[53]

Solar energy

Solar energy is another renewable and therefore constant energy solution. It is also abundant and doesn't produce any pollution. Like wind energy, there are some implications in the creation of the infrastructure, but once in place solar energy is very clean.

Solar energy is generally much less intrusive than wind turbines and do not cause a blight on the landscape. Plus it's silent.

Solar energy also has localised applications, which can allow individuals to install solar panels on their homes and businesses and sell the excess back to the grid. At least that is the promise; the reality depends on where you live and how much sunshine there is in your location.

---

[53] 'River elegy' (2012) *The Economist*, www.economist.com/news/asia/21565676-laos-admits-work-going-ahead-controversial-dam-river-elegy

This type of energy can be expensive, and the technology for storing solar energy is still not brilliant. Many of the current solar panels will create energy but that energy must be used as it is created. If it is not used immediately, then it is lost because it cannot be stored.

Although it is possible to store solar energy in batteries, these additional technologies are still largely experimental and relatively ineffective which means that, like wind energy, there needs to be a 'back up' for energy required when the sun is not shining.

Like wind energy, this solution will be revolutionised when the storage problem is properly solved so that solar energy can be stored. There is no reason this will not eventually happen, hopefully within a fairly short amount of time but it is not solved yet (2015).

Even if the storage problem for solar and wind power was solved tomorrow there is still the initial cost of switching to the new energies. Even if wind and solar power are both cheaper than, say, gasoline, the low-income factory worker in Philadelphia will still have to buy a new car, or have the present one refitted, both of which may be very costly. The farmer in England will have to buy a new tractor. Electric companies, or their own energy suppliers, will have to retool from coal and gas directly to electricity. Even the heating and cooling systems in houses and buildings around the world will have to be refitted. The cost of initially refitting, in essence, all of present-day society will not be cheap, and will effect individuals – in communities, towns, cities, states and nations – not only in the physical dimension, but also in emotional, mental, and spiritual domains too through the process of 'prepotency'. Such impacts need to be taken into consideration as part of the original plan to make these types of energy switches.

Nuclear energy

Understandably, most people are very uncomfortable with nuclear energy. Disasters such as Chernobyl in the Ukraine in 1986 and more recently Fukushima in Japan have escalated that discomfort considerably. In 2011 Japan experienced an earthquake which in turn created a tsunami which hit the Fukushima Nuclear power plant, which then started to release substantial amounts of radioactive material. That said, these two nuclear events have been the only nuclear incidents ever to measure level 7 on the International Nuclear Event Scale, and yet people are reticent about the potential of nuclear energy as a way to meet our needs and halt or reverse climate change. But there is a great deal of misinformation, fear and propaganda around nuclear energy.

The creation of the nuclear bomb was one of the most monumental projects of the twentieth century. Devastating and frightening, it also clearly demonstrated the power of nuclear energy. After World War Two, the 'Atomic Age' emerged, and we were told that atomic energy was 'a giant of unlimited power at man's command'. Of course there was a deep connection between the military, politics and the cultivation of nuclear energy for civilian use. Because of these connections, the science around the civilian use of nuclear energy and the military use of nuclear energy shared the same reactor physics based on uranium. But there are other ways to create nuclear power that do not use uranium at all.

One alternative is thorium. Thorium is more efficient, burns more completely, and is more abundant than uranium. But it is harder to work with, and harder to trigger and sustain a nuclear reaction which is required to extract energy. Perhaps the biggest reason thorium was not used was because thorium does not produce plutonium in a form that is readily used in weapons. When one of the largest, most influential stakeholder groups involved in nuclear energy were military stakeholders, the fact that thorium did not produce plutonium that could then be used in weapons was not a positive but a negative. Although influential scientists such as Alvin Weinberg, administrator at Oak Ridge National Laboratory during and after the Manhattan Project, recommended the use of a potentially safer way to create nuclear power, the decision came down to politics. Politicians needed to decide if they should explore the safer thorium or stick with uranium and they chose the latter.[54]

Who knows, perhaps if they had made a different decision, the nuclear power disasters of Chernobyl and Fukushima may never have happened, and nuclear as a technology may have been a viable option. Unfortunately, there is now so much bad press around nuclear that it is political suicide to even mention it as a potential solution to climate change.

As well as the potential for disaster, there is also the issue of nuclear waste. There are however scientists working on finding solutions to nuclear waste, which is a nasty by-product of nuclear energy using uranium. In France, they have made huge strides in a process called transmutation, where the half-life of radioactive heavy elements are reduced from tens of thousands of years to tens of hundreds of years by splitting them into lighter elements. This research is still in its infancy but shows great promise in dealing with the toxic side effects of nuclear energy.

There is also work being done in nuclear fusion, where the only by-product would be the creation of helium, which could be safely released into the atmosphere. Unfortunately, because of the bad press, fears and misinformation about nuclear power, there is very little money being spent on these options, especially when you compare them to other alternative fuel sources.

As UK TV scientist and presenter Brian Cox suggests, we seem to demand that the future is better than the past but we are not really prepared to pay for it. According to Cox, 'Americans spend ten times more money each year on pet grooming than nuclear fusion technology.' He goes on to say, 'Most of us are fortunate to live in democracies and democracies change when people have access to knowledge, when they understand facts and can make informed decisions, and therefore if you gave people

[54] BBC 2(2011) Horizon Episode 6 of 15 'Fukushima: Is Nuclear Power Safe?'

the science and facts about nuclear fusion and gave them the choice, they would probably happily brush your own cat and donate what they would have spent to those who are trying to find a way to generate unlimited clean energy.'[55]

Of course it is a nice idea, but if the discussion on climate change proves anything it proves that democracy or not, whatever stakeholder group owns and controls the conversation 'wins'. Ensuring that we all have access to truthful and complete information is difficult when so many groups and stakeholders are deliberately manipulating the information to support their own theories and self-interest or sincerely presenting the facts and values according to their own level of development. Theoretically, facts may be separate from values but they are not. In the real world, where people operate, facts and values always come prepackaged. As we have seen time and again, one interprets and therefore co-creates and co-enacts the 'facts' according to the values and overall Integral Address those individuals have. In America, left-wing voters, familiar with having their news presented through a left-wing lens, were shocked when Fox News began consistently presenting news and its 'facts' through a right-wing lens. This meant an entirely different set of facts altogether and these 'facts' still shock the liberals. Welcome to the world of developmental levels.

When working with all of the actual variables in a truly Integral Meta-Map, understanding the degree of interdependencies between the different climate factors is a massive task in and of itself – not to mention having to deal with campaigns of deliberate misinformation and fear mongering. Plus the reality is that, right or wrong, nuclear energy is a political hot potato and cultural opinion makes implementation almost impossible. Rather than really looking at this as a potential solution, most individuals blindly accept that it is dangerous and would not dream of voting

---

[55] BBC2 (2014) 'Human Universe: What is our Future?'

for a politician who advocated nuclear power as a viable option. As a result, democracy, or more accurately, what James Madison called 'the tyranny of the majority', itself becomes a wicked problem and can often stand in the way of the very solutions we are so desperate to find. Remember, according to Kegan, some 60 per cent of the American 'democratic' population is not capable of thinking in rational, worldcentric, 'modern' (level 5) terms which means the 'majority' itself becomes a wee bit wobbly as a source of solid decisions.

Clearly there is no magic bullet when it comes to the solution. Integral Coherence would therefore recommend a portfolio of different technologies to minimise the disadvantages of each.

Reduce the Population

Stakeholders who believe that climate change is caused and exacerbated by the sheer number of people on the planet will advocate, very simply, that we reduce the number of people on the planet.

As a solution, reducing the population is not an easy task. As mentioned earlier, the number of children in any family is considered a matter of personal choice or 'up to God' and it will often depend on a person's religious beliefs and interpretation. The Catholic Church, for example, is very much against contraception and abortion, and considering there are over one billion Catholics in the world, that particular stakeholder group is not going to agree with this particular solution. Even if they do agree that there should be fewer people on the planet, they have no viable means for achieving that goal. Considering their position, it is fair to assume that a good deal of the over-population is created by people who are happily or not so happily having eight, ten or more children. And if even half a billion people are having huge families, then we have a huge problem.

In the past, governments have got involved in seeking to reduce population, so we have experience of how this particular 'solution' can pan out. In 1979, China introduced the one child family policy in an effort to stem their rapidly rising population. At the time China had a quarter of the world's population but only seven per cent of the world's arable land. In addition, two-thirds of the population were under 30, which meant they were entering their child-bearing years. So China took decisive action and made it illegal to have more than one child.

Even before the one child policy, there was a cultural bias in China toward male children. This male bias still exists today in many other countries, including India and much of the Middle East. Very often female children are seen as a burden. They are perceived as subservient because of their role as homemakers and mothers, as opposed to the male children who earn money and ensure the family's social and economic stability. Considering this cultural bias, it is hardly surprising that when the one child policy came into effect, there was a surge in female infanticide in China. Faced with the ability to only have one child, parents would either abort female children or drown them when they were born. Or they would raise the girl but she would remain unregistered and effectively hidden from the authorities.

Over-population in China was a wicked problem, and while the one child policy helped to constrain that problem to some extent, it inadvertently created a whole slew of additional equally wicked problems. The Chinese government has even acknowledged the disastrous consequences of the gender imbalance the policy created in the country. It has created increased mental health issues and socially disruptive behaviour in young men, many of whom are unable to marry and have a family of their own because there are simply not enough women. The scarcity of women has also led to an increase in kidnapping and trafficking of women for marriage and the increase in commercial sex work.[56]

[56] Hesketh, T., et al (2005) 'The Effect of China's One-Child Family Policy after 25 Years' *The New England Journal of Medicine*, www.nejm.org/doi/pdf/10.1056/NEJMhpr051833

Again, this is just another example of how one solution to a wicked problem can have far reaching consequences that can end up being just as bad or worse than the original wicked problem the solution was intended to solve.

Change Human Behaviour

As individuals, there are many things we can all do to make a positive difference to climate change:[57]

- Recycle more
- Move closer to work and travel less
- Consume less – fix things when they are broken instead of buying new
- Eat less meat
- Unplug more and be more efficient with the energy we use
- Buy local food that has travelled fewer miles
- Reject heavily packaged products
- When building a new home or plant, make it energy efficient
- Plant more trees
- Turn off the air conditioner or heater when not directly in use
- Alter how we all think about climate change
- Create more inclusive and comprehensive meta-models of the many items that it would help to change in human behaviour or beliefs, and address those coherently

Of course this can all feel a little like grabbing an umbrella to protect ourselves from a typhoon – it is a bit futile! Besides, human behaviour is notoriously difficult to change. We might decide to recycle for a few months and make a real effort not to consume more than we need. But when our budget is stretched and we

[57] www.epa.gov/climatechange/wycd/

are struggling to make ends meet, most people will choose the cheapest option, not the option that is better for the planet. And those are rarely the same product.

If we have worked hard all year, then we are probably going to reward ourselves and our families with a trip to the Maldives instead of taking a break at home or not going on holiday at all. Air travel contributes to climate change. It was during the 1990s that the general public really started to hear about climate change in the media. Ironically, it was also the 1990s that saw an explosion in discount air travel. When faced with a cheap opportunity for some sunshine or a weekend in Paris or worrying about climate change, millions chose the cheap flight.

Climate change is one of those problems where we really are all in it together because we all live on the same beautiful blue marble planet. Of course it is easier to appreciate the challenges we face when we live on a Caribbean island and witness our beaches disappearing; but the fact remains that as many people as absolutely feasible need to participate in any needed changes. Granted, as a species, we don't have a great track record of averting possible disasters. Historically, at least, we tend to act only after the disaster has already occurred. It has been said that Noah was the only human in history that created the solution to a massive problem before the problem actually happened. Although, maybe we are getting better, as we write this in 2015 New York did prepare ahead of time for what was billed as the biggest snowstorm in the history of New York City – dubbed 'Snowmageddon', only it did not materialise.

But our simple point is that the more factors that we actually take into account, the greater the chance that real change will occur. Particularly, this includes not only the Right-Hand physical factors that need to be changed, but the Left-Hand values, beliefs, worldviews, and motivations that are driving actions in the Right-Hand to begin with. Enough with one-dimensional, flatland, 'one size fits all,' siloed and fragmented approaches – they are, rather literally, close to killing us all.

Increased Corporate Responsibility

Few would argue with the idea that business has been instrumental in creating an increase in global temperature. This appears true both in terms of emissions they create, and in lobbying politicians not to impose sanctions, tariffs and tax rises on the industries that are most responsible for the damage such as those that produce or use the most fossil fuels in their production processes.

Of course, not all business is contributing to climate change and in an effort to take their responsibilities seriously, numerous business leaders have in the past sought to beef up their corporate social responsibility (CSR). Unfortunately, like consumers, the commercial willingness to advocate a 'triple bottom line' approach, where success is based not just on profit but on people and planet too,[58] has in the past been very dependent on the wider economic environment. When business is thriving, corporations are happy to mention their efforts to address their environmental impact, and the internal PR department will gladly publicise any initiatives in an effort to win consumer brownie points. But as soon as the economy tightens and profits look less favourable, concern for climate change often falls away.

This is despite the fact that to date business is not required to pay a 'green tax' based on how much CO_2 they produce or planetary resources they consume. If they did, their net or 'true' profit levels would likely drop considerably. If they were taxed for their environmental impact, they might be motivated to reduce emissions or consumption to reduce their tax liability and make their business more environmentally sustainable. Similarly most businesses do not pay a tax for their social impact. For example, a number of towns have experienced increased unemployment when large retailers have moved in and created a retail

[58] Martin, R. L. (2011) *Fixing the Game: How Runaway Expectations Broke the Economy, and How to Get Back to Reality*, Boston: Harvard Business School Press.

monoculture, or worse still bought up local small retail properties, making people redundant, and then not proceeded with the opening of a planned superstore or creating the superstore only to close it a few years later.[59]

Part of the reason this does not happen is that their current cost base is relatively easy to calculate, but their true environmental and social impact is much more difficult to quantify. The good news is that some more enlightened firms such as Puma are starting to spontaneously look at 'triple bottom line' accounting. Bloomberg are starting to train their analysts in how to audit companies from a 'triple bottom line' perspective in recognition that this will, almost inevitably, become a reality at some point in the future.

Keep in mind that, if by 'planet' we don't mean the usual reductionistic idea of just the physiosphere or just the biosphere, but the 'whole' planet – including noosphere (mental dimension) and pneumosphere (spiritual dimension) – then the 'triple bottom line' (profit, person, planet) actually refers quite accurately to aspects of the three highest levels of human evolution and development to date. *Profit* is level 5 – business, achievement, profit; person is level 6 – pluralistic, 'HumanBond' or people-care; and *planet* as just noted, is level 7/8 – a total worldcentric Integral view. The drive toward a triple bottom line is simply the pressure that the emergence of levels 7/8 is having on the leadership in a large variety of areas, including business, science, and economics.

Increasingly business will need a 'social licence to operate' (SLO). The challenge, of course, is that a social licence to operate is a subjective concept, not a piece of paper. There is no application to be filled in and no issuing authority. The terms of the licence

[59] McCulloch, S. (2015) 'Tesco to close four Scottish stores as part of wider 43-store closure plan', *Daily Record*, [Online] www.dailyrecord.co.uk/business/business-news/tesco-close-four-scottish-stores-5058088

are also different for every business and vary considerably, even within the same industry. Ultimately the SLO is based on who your stakeholders are and what they think of you. In a world of social media and constant online connectivity that can change in a heartbeat, but most firms would have to flagrantly abuse their SLO before any real sanction from their stakeholders would kick in. As it is now, an SLO is basically a Lower-Left public opinion consensus on the social 'purity' of a particular business, and not a Lower-Right law or licence given by a recognised authority. But still, it is becoming extremely difficult for businesses to sweep their dirty laundry and dubious environmental practices under the commercial carpet.

For example, in 2012, Levi Strauss & Co. was able to largely avoid a PR and potentially commercial disaster by committing to go toxic-free. The company's commitment came eight days after Greenpeace launched a report called 'Toxic Threads: Under Wraps', and screened a documentary about a family struggling to hold factories in Mexico to account for the pollution Levi and other international brands were causing.[60]

Companies that are notorious polluters or cause environmental destruction in the course of their operations are being 'outed' by social media, tweeted and retweeted – which is spreading the story globally and definitely impacting sales. Companies that do not take their SLO seriously enough will start to be penalised as more and more consumers become more and more aware of the problems we face. As consumers become more educated, they will make better buying decisions and will increasingly demand that business take their concerns seriously. In fact a business's willingness to really embrace their responsibilities is likely to be a source of competitive advantage – certainly until legislation forces everyone to comply. What this amounts to is

---

[60] Klein, P. (2012) *Three Ways to Secure Your Social License to Operate in 2013*, Forbes, www.forbes.com/sites/csr/2012/12/28/three-ways-to-secure-your-social-license-to-operate-in-2013/

a significant evolution of consciousness and culture, and this is exactly what any decent education helps to accelerate. As that trend continues, more and more types of cultural consensus will arise (Lower-Left), eventually forcing more and more authoritative bodies to issue laws and regulations (Lower-Right).

Many of the most profound wicked environmental problems we face arise from our collective unwillingness to grasp the environmental nettle and look out into the future. For consumers that means buying the more expensive item that is better for the planet or not buying more stuff at all; and for business that means looking beyond quarterly or even yearly results to the way we use, protect and replenish our environmental resources.

Unfortunately, most businesses are so consumed with their own issues that unless they are forced to consider their environmental impact, footprint, and sustainability, they will continue to give the agenda scant regard.

In fairness, the quarterly battle for profits, market share, and cost management is so all-consuming for many executives that team conversations about environmental issues are often seen as fanciful or 'nice to haves' but largely peripheral. The need to return value to shareholders almost always trumps any environmentally sustainable approach. While such insular attitudes are beginning to change, many global organisations operate as if the environment gets in the way of their primary purpose, which most believe is profit and only profit. Some of the more enlightened organisations do have high functioning sustainability or 'corporate social responsibility' departments; but for many, such functions are really commercially defensive moves and in some cases just public relations tokenism. It is rare to find executive teams regularly debating the implications of environmental issues or climate change on their corporate future, never mind their own role as a force for sustainability in the world. This is despite virtually indisputable evidence and information on the subject.[61]

Again, and in fairness to most leadership teams, the debate on climate change is so incredibly complicated that it is virtually impossible for any senior executive to know what the appropriate response should be. The academic debate has become very confused, not only because there are many different, sincerely believed 'facts' in this matter, but also because specific vested interests have deliberately overwhelmed the discourse with a landfill of misinformation and deliberate toxic dumping of fallacious research into the debate.[62]

There are, however, shining exceptions. A handful of global corporations are demonstrating to the corporate world that it is entirely possible to increase profits and reduce carbon footprint at the same time. For example, Unilever's innovative supply chain boss Pierre-Luigi Sigismondi and CEO Paul Polman have been successfully doing just that for the past three years within their global supply chain. Launched in 2010, the Unilever Sustainable Living Plan is helping to drive profitable growth, save costs and create fuel innovation toward verifiable sustainable growth targets. The targets cluster around improving health and well being, reducing environmental impact and enhancing livelihoods.[63]

There is little doubt that business will need to get on board sooner rather than later and begin, like Unilever, to take their environmental responsibility more seriously. And if they cannot be relied upon to act responsibly and consistently regardless of the economy or the delivery of shareholder value, then legislation

---

[61] Wijkman, A. and Rockström, J. (2012) *Bankrupting Nature: denying our planetary boundaries*, New York: Routledge.

[62] Oreskes, N. and Conway, E. M. (2011) *Merchants of Doubt: how a handful of scientists obscured the truth on issues from tobacco smoke to global warming*, London: Bloomsbury Publishing

[63] www.unilever.co.uk/sustainable-living-2014/unilever-sustainable-living-plan/

– the force of cultural beliefs on social systems – becomes inevitable.

Legislation and Evolved Ethics

So far business has been free to address their environmental impact as they see fit. But that is changing as legislation formalises their requirements into law.

Although there are many different pieces of climate legislation in place that deal with the laws and regulations of greenhouse gas emissions, and many more being considered by countries around the world, most have so far stopped short of imposing penalties or higher taxes on businesses that pollute the planet.

As mentioned earlier, in 2012, Australia did introduce a carbon pricing scheme which required most businesses emitting over 25 000 tonnes of CO_2 or equivalent greenhouse gases per year to obtain a permit. The legislation was, however, repealed by the in-coming right-wing government in 2014.

The European Union operates the first and largest Emissions Trading Scheme (EU ETS), which provides an international system for trading greenhouse gas emission allowances covering more than 11 000 power stations and industrial plants in 31 countries, as well as airlines. The EU ETS works on the 'cap and trade' principle. A cap or limit is set on the total amount of certain greenhouse gases that can be emitted by the factories, power plants, and other installations in the system. The upper limit of the cap on the greenhouse gases that companies are allowed to produce is reduced over time so total emissions fall, and by 2020 this approach, if faithfully carried through, will see a 21 per cent fall from 2005 levels. Within the cap, companies receive or buy emission allowances which they can trade with one another as needed, giving them the flexibility to cut their emissions in the most cost-effective way.

Change often only really happens when we force people to change through legislation. Take the issue of plastic bags, for example. We have known that plastic bags take a very long time to decompose, if they ever decompose. We have known for decades that they are a major cause of pollution and cause significant damage to wildlife and marine life. We have been asked to be more responsible and we have been encouraged to buy a 'bag-for-life' at the local supermarket, but until the use of plastic bags was legislated and charged for by retailers we still used billions of them. In Wales, consumers have been asked to pay for their carrier bags since 2011, and this initiative has seen a massive 75 per cent drop in use.[64] The same legislation took effect in Scotland in 2014, and the change has been immediate and transformational. Clearly we should have imposed this legislation decades ago.

There is little doubt that tougher climate change legislation will emerge because it may be the only thing that really changes behaviour. To that end, the twenty-first United Nations' Climate Change Conference (UN COP21) will meet in Paris in 2015 with the objective of securing a legally binding and universal agreement on climate from all the nations of the world. Legislation definitely appears to be coming; it may not be 2105, but it is coming.

When it does, the legislation itself cannot be static; it will need to evolve and change as the situation evolves and changes, and that too adds another level of complexity into the mix. Legislation and evolved ethics also tie into our desperate need for improved political action and enlightened leadership.

There are multiple potential solutions for every wicked problem, and climate change is no different. Each solution sets the stakeholders charged with implementing it off in different directions.

---

[64] BBC News (2013) 'Plastic bag charge to be introduced in England', www.bbc.co.uk/news/uk-politics-24088523

Very often these solutions are not trial and error options because the implementation of each solution is itself extremely complex, far-reaching and costly. Each investment in one area can reduce the resources in another. Each solution is a 'one-shot' operation in that the solution cannot be retried or undone. Once a government has spent billions on wind farms or tidal energy, that 'solution' cannot be fully undone and the money reused. More often development within that solution needs to press on or be abandoned, which adds another stressful dimension to the wicked problems. But evolution occurs to some degree in every major element of every Integral Framework item – this issue is certainly no different. What is different is whether we remember to keep this in mind, or whether, again, we are unconsciously blindsided by it when it inevitably happens.

Climate Change is Constantly Evolving

Climate change, like all wicked problems, is constantly evolving. How it is viewed and how it evolves depends on how the highest level yet to evolve sees that reality. After all, we no longer look at the world as flat and yet every level up to and including level 4 most certainly did for hundreds of thousands of years! Today, we do not see atoms as being actual little planetary systems with a sun/nucleus and electron/planets actually orbiting around it, as level 5 did. Now we appreciate that atoms and electrons are made of quarks (level 6), or even strings (level 7/8), existing as probability waves. We no longer see gravity as action-at-a-distance, as level 5 did – now we see it as a curvature in the fabric of spacetime; and on and on and on. 'Real reality' changes level by level. And what we call 'reality' with any assurance is always what the most evolved level sees as reality – and that, of course, will itself change at some future point too, but at 2015 our level 7/8 version of reality is the best approximation of the 'actual reality' of climate and it is changing and constantly evolving.

Thus, the science around our understanding of the challenges we face and the interdependence within the problem are constantly evolving. For example, the safe level of CO_2 concentration in the atmosphere has changed over the decades.

But that is not the only sense in which climate is changing. Given that, as we noted earlier, there are at least eight different levels of exactly what 'climate' means in the first place, individuals are developing through those levels, each time changing their views about climate and weather change. In short, the stakeholders are constantly evolving, not just in terms of the type of stakeholder groups but also the people within those groups. Part of the wickedness of wicked problems is that solving them effectively crosses over multiple stakeholder groups in the public and private sector as well as countries. This makes it very difficult to address, especially when the people within the countries, governments and businesses also keep changing. We have already touched on the volatility of politics and how the perpetual changing of the political guard – and especially the changing of their Integral Addresses – can make finding solutions to these wicked problems almost impossible.

As we understand climate change better (using even better technology at even higher levels), the causes and symptoms are also constantly evolving, which means that the potential solutions we can consider and implement must also be constantly evolving. There will never be an end to the climate change problem, even if we gain consensus and universal agreement that tough action is necessary (which is extremely unlikely), the environment is a constantly evolving phenomenon and therefore it will need to be constantly assessed to ensure we manage climate change into the future and protect the planet for generations to come.

Summary

Climate change is just one of the many wicked problems we face and we have just scrapped the surface of the multi-dimensionality, multiple stakeholders, multiple causes, multiple symptoms, and multiple potential solutions. We have explored, very briefly, the constantly evolving nature of wicked problems; and yet we covered an enormous amount of ground. If you have stayed with us in this whistle-stop exposé of just some of the central issues then you probably feel like you have been smacked around the head with a baseball mitt!

It feels almost bruising as we jump from one issue to the next to the next. Reading about just one part of one wicked problem can feel utterly overwhelming. As the complexity and interdependency unfold before us it can feel as though the task of solving climate change or any wicked problem is just beyond us. And it is certainly easy to see why we have failed to solve them so far. They just seem too big, too complex and too intertwined – they seem impossible to tease apart, so we can effectively understand them, never mind solve them. Canadian educator and 'hierarchiologist', Laurence J. Peter once said, 'Some problems are so complex that you have to be highly intelligent and well informed just to be undecided about them.'

Wicked problems are those sorts of problems! But we must understand them and the six-property model that we have been using to dissect climate change – in the overall context of the Integral Meta-Model – is a significant step forward in seeking to do that.

This approach proposes a new and more inclusive model and meta-map that more accurately integrates the numerous different significant factors involved in the problem itself, thus more accurately outlining the actual modifications needed to affect climate change.

Now it is time to explain a little more about how to actually apply this Integral Coherence solution so we can solve and re-solve these pressing issues. It is this action and effort that may lead to an evolution of consciousness and culture across the board; this alone guarantees that 'shift' from resistors into proactors, thus resulting in more effective human action.

So having explored the multiple challenges inherent in a wicked problem such as climate change and brought the theory to life, it is now time to unpack how we actually convert the theory into practice.

Part 4

The Wicked Solution

Some years ago I (KW) was involved in an initiative to develop a new way of thinking to try to break through the adversarial nature of political debate.[1] As most people have witnessed, political parties tend to try to create clear differentiation in the mind of their electorate by pretending that what their opponents are saying is completely incorrect. Politicians on all sides of the political spectrum espouse an 'I'm right, you're wrong' view. It is extremely rare for any politician of any denomination to explicitly say that there is agreement or common ground with their opponents. Or, God forbid, the size of the difference in opinion between themselves and their detractors is insubstantial. We occasionally see a little more convergence of allegedly diametrically opposed views in times of crisis, on national security issues or other major challenges. But generally 'cross-party' agreement is rare. Even in societies where coalition politics is the norm (those that tend to have a voting system that embraces some degree of proportional representation) common ground and shared views are scarce. What tends to happen in coalition politics is 'horse trading' where you capitulate to my view on one issue and I surrender to yours on a separate issue. A sort of 'I'll let you win one if you let me win one' approach. In fact this 'you scratch my back and I'll scratch yours' trade-off is often seen as core to the political process. It is often perceived as fanciful or naive that politicians should reconcile their differences and come together for the best interest of the nation.

To repeat ourselves again, wicked problems are wicked because they involve people. So if we really want to breakthrough on the increasing number of intractable, wicked problems that beset the world, then we need to completely overhaul the way we address the people dimension. Basically we need to review *how* we bring people together; *who* we have in the room; the reason *why* each person is really attending; what exactly they are debating; the timing or the *'when'* of the meeting; as well as

[1] BBC News (1999) 'UK Politics: What is the Third Way?', [Online] http://news.bbc.co.uk/1/hi/458626.stm

where is the most relevant place to meet and is the environment conducive to progress. But these are all largely the nuanced external dimensions of brilliant meeting planning. They can be largely considered effective housekeeping. Real breakthrough requires a great deal more than this. A much more integrally coherent approach is necessary. A new way of approaching the preparation of the individuals, teams and organisations before people come together in the room with the intention of making genuine progress. This chapter will explore how the application of Integral Coherence may just be able to create that breakthrough – as well, of course, Integral guidelines for the meeting once it is under way.

Since solving wicked problems requires that we adopt an equally wicked solution, we must, from the start of the process, be cognisant of the multi-dimensional nature of the solution. The solution must involve multiple stakeholders, address the multiple causes, symptoms and potential solutions. The solution itself must constantly evolve as we solve and re-solve the issues as they evolve.

That is no easy task – unless you have a workable process that can facilitate the journey. This is true of complex, challenging problems as well as the really curly wicked problems we face. We need a map so we can successfully navigate difficult, treacherous terrain. We need to know where the shortcuts are and what detours to avoid so we can fast track the process and make progress where no progress has been possible before.

There are essentially five phases in the solution process:

- Map the problem by performing a thorough Integral overview including all of its Integral elements and dimensions.
- Map the network(s) to identify the key stakeholders, spectrum of opinion and organisations that need to be involved.

- Map the key stakeholders to understand their Integral multi-dimensionality and their respective strengths and vulnerabilities.
- Engage the key stakeholders individually and collectively to minimise the potential derailing nature of their vulnerabilities and amplify the positive dimensions of their strengths (i.e., understand their actual Integral Address and its overall impact).
- Involve an Integral Coherent facilitator(s) 'in the room', armed with a truly Integral Meta-Map, to facilitate the on-going process of solving and re-solving.

With this approach, roughly 80 per cent of solving problems – wicked or otherwise – occurs before the relevant stakeholders ever 'get in the room' together to discuss the solution. This might seem unusual because the typical assumption is that the problem can only be solved through discussion and negotiation. While that may be correct in one sense, it does not account for the fact that fundamentally wicked problems are in large part human development problems. We would not be facing the innumerable wicked problems we now face if the world's decision makers took a more inclusive approach that recognised the possibility of their own failings and limitations rather than approached the issues with an 'I'm right and you're wrong' certainty. If business leaders and politicians were more like the wiser, more mature versions of themselves than the immature, self-serving versions who have created the challenges in the first place, then we would certainly make much more progress.

Put in its bluntest form, solving wicked problems is a two-stage process. Stage one is to conduct an Integral overview and thoroughly map the problem. We need the Integral Frame to navigate the numerous potholes and derailers that exist in the interior and exterior of a complex situation.

Once mapped, stage two then ensures we get the right people in the room and that they 'Show Up' in their most healthy and coherently functioning to discuss those issues. We need those people to be mature, developed and sophisticated enough so that the right discussion around the right framework can take place. Coherence breathes life into the Integral Frame and the resulting Integral Coherence can facilitate genuine progress. Wicked problems have taken decades, sometimes centuries, to cultivate their unique wickedness, and yet they can be solved in a fraction of that time with Integral Coherence.

Map the Problem

Although inherent in the approach we have advocated throughout the whole book, it is worth pointing out that no genuine solution can be found without first thoroughly mapping the problem. If we intend to use the Integral Frame to guide us toward the most complete solution possible, we first must use it to gain the most complete and thorough overview of the wicked problem itself so we know exactly what we are up against.

This includes mapping the problem through all its Integral elements and dimensions to create a coherent map and possible ways forward – including both the problem and the change agents themselves (that is, *all* stakeholders).

Map the Network

Wicked or complex problems involve, among other crucial items, a core element of multiple stakeholders. When seeking to find solutions to extremely challenging problems there can be thousands of stakeholders representing hundreds of interests and stakeholder groups. It is clearly impossible to bring all those thousands of people into a room and expect success. It is impractical, inefficient and virtually guaranteed to fail. Thankfully it is also unnecessary – if you first map the external observable connections (Lower-Right) of the central players and the type of connections (Lower-Left) in all areas and dimensions that impact the wicked problem. We will review both of these processes.

In the case of climate change, for example, this process would start by identifying the most crucial members of the climate change network itself. Who is invested in this field? Who works in this area? Who cares about this problem? Who has a perspective that is important to bring to the negotiating table? Who has expert knowledge in this area? Who needs to be in the conversation? In addition to the 'usual suspects' of climate change, we should look to embrace the different types of stakeholder populations. In relationship to change, we highlighted five types of stakeholder populations (Figure 4.1), and representatives from every stakeholder group should ideally be included – from this type of stakeholder and all other relevant stakeholder populations.

Figure 4.1: Stakeholder groups

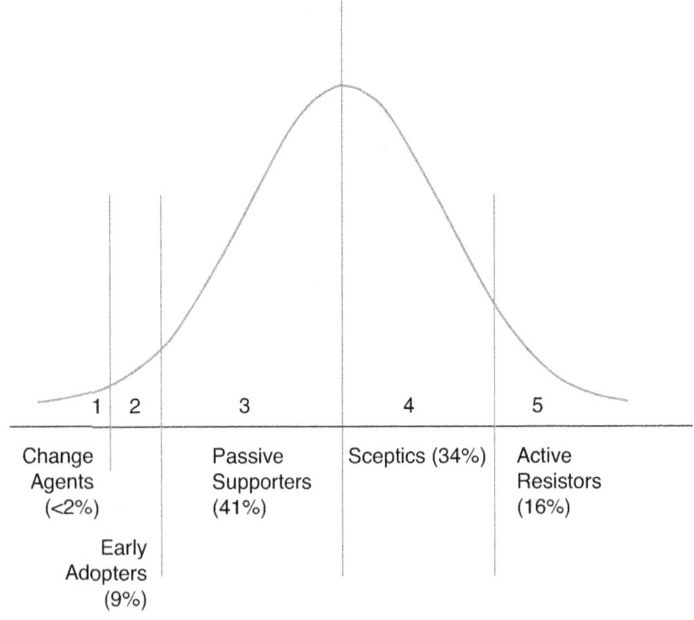

Once we have identified all the possible people who might be relevant to solving the problem, through the various stakeholder typing processes deemed appropriate, then the entire network –internal and external – is mapped. One of the central ideas of an Integral approach is that it is not just the exterior 'world' but the interiors of individuals and cultures that are all embedded in any view of 'climate' or 'weather' or any other wicked problem. Thus the overall approach suggested here starts with some typical exterior connections and interactivity, what is often referred to as 'network analysis'. This basically gives us a very crucial, Lower-Right understanding of exactly who is rubbing up against whom – where, when, how, and other indicators of social (exterior-system) interactivity. Once we have a detailed network analysis covering the basic 'facts' of exterior connectivity (which typical approaches usually consider to be 'all' the necessary data), we then add the real meat and marrow to the external skeleton by filling in the rest of the Integral Frame, especially its interiors. Such data reveals not just who certain stakeholders may *want* in the room, but also who *needs* to be in the room if the wicked problem is to be solved. It creates the most powerful inclusive map from an interior and exterior point of view.

It is imperative that we include people from every relevant stakeholder population, each of which tends to gravitate to a particular level and quadrant, which we will determine later. For example, we need to know who the key players are within the change agents and the early adopters, passive supporters, sceptics and active resistors. In the climate change debate, for example, there is no point getting the climate change scientists in the room if we do not also get the CEOs of the big energy companies and high profile active resistors. No real resolution is possible unless key stakeholders from all groups are present, *and* their multi-dimensional perspectives and the different levels or lens through which they view the subject, are appreciated and brought to the table.

Network mapping (the simple Lower-Right social interactions of the participants in the real world) allows us to appreciate the influence of the various stakeholders that are out there, where those stakeholders belong from change agents to active resisters and their exact patterns of interaction with each other. This first phase process is not just about creating a long laundry list of stakeholders from different types of stakeholder populations in the wicked problem, but also identifying what base of support those stakeholders have. Who is backing them? How much weight and influence do they have based on their patterns of connectivity? Who can they reach? Once we have successfully mapped the social network, detailed analysis allows us to identify the key stakeholders in that network. We already know that we cannot put all those stakeholders in a room, so we need to know which stakeholders to put in the room – and network analysis can begin to help us answer that question as part of an overall Integral Coherence analysis.

Network Analysis

In order to shift any system or solve any problem, we cannot just look at who is in the network or even who is connected to whom, but who has influence and reach so we can effectively get a handful of people in the room and yet those people will then in turn influence all the thousands or hundreds of thousands or even millions of other stakeholders in the entire network. This is what a truly Integral analysis will show us – starting with the patterns of interactivity in the Lower-Right.

In the climate change argument, for example, key stakeholders are likely to include CEOs of huge energy companies as well as key leaders from smaller yet influential NGOs, politicians, hardened sceptics and passionate scientists. The size of the organisation the stakeholder is involved in is not nearly as important as the reach and influence of that stakeholder or stakeholder group. What we are after are the individuals who exert disproportionate influence because of their market position, their knowledge, insight or influence into the wider market through, say, strong media contacts, widely shared reputation, and so forth.

The process of network analysis is based on complicated social networking theory. But it is possible to use a much simpler approach that can rapidly generate some very insightful data. So once we have the list of stakeholders in the social network, even if that list is not complete, we can then ask those individuals a few simple questions which can flush out some really key network insights.

When we have mapped the social networks in multinational organisations for example, we can identify approximately 40 000 useful data points in a matter of minutes just by asking the top 60 leaders seven simple questions. The questions can clearly be adjusted depending on the specific goal of the network analysis, but helping organisations to develop a new model of leadership, we have found the following seven questions provide further relevant insight into the Lower-Right correlates of three critical networks:

1. Functional Network
   Q1: Name the people you typically get work-related information from?
   Q2: Name the people you regularly collaborate with?
2. Emotional Network
   Q3: Name the people you feel energised by when you interact with them?
   Q4: Name the people you feel comfortable sharing sensitive information with?
   Q5: Name the people to whom you turn for support when things are tough?
3. Leadership Network
   Q6: Name the people you feel personally stretch your thinking?
   Q7: Name the people to whom you turn for leadership or guidance?

We have used this tool in business to suggest insights into the covert dynamics in the business as opposed to what the organisational chart suggests are the nature of relationships. These insights uncover the connections between people and their patterns of interaction in a wider setting to map and analyse the various stakeholders within a wicked problem. Or could address any Integral element to determine much of its Lower-Right correlates (remember, all Integral elements leave footprints in all the others, since they are all mutually interwoven).

For example, when mapping the climate change stakeholder network, we may discover that the CEO of a coal company may be functionally connected to the CEO of a clean energy company because they will probably know each other and share information; but they are probably not emotionally connected. The CEO of the coal company probably will not be connected at all to the CEO of Greenpeace. He or she may know about Greenpeace but they will not have a relationship with them. Greenpeace is probably seen as the enemy and vice versa. The leadership network flushes out who is influencing whose thinking on what front. Even the leaders of energy companies will be influenced in their thinking by someone – inside and outside the industry. The coal CEO may be influenced by a grandee of the industry. For example, Lord Brown used to run BP; now retired but working in private equity he is still likely to exert significant influence on some of his old protégées. The leadership network helps to identify the grandees of industry, the thought leaders in any area and the people who are influencing the thinking of others. But the population that is being influenced by a particular leader cannot, of course, be identified without doing an interior analysis, such as values: the CEO of the coal company is likely level 5, 'progress' and 'profit,' whereas the CEO of Greenpeace is likely level 6, 'eco-centric' and 'people oriented.' Without continuing our Integral analysis, we would never be able to know why one of those is considered a great leader to one group, yet nearly demonic to another. We want to keep these types of examples in our minds as we go through each of the social network analyses, so we can remember what the social network tells us… and what it does not.

Interpreting network analysis and deep network analytics (DNA)

In order to 'read' the network visualisations below it is important to know that a unilateral connection (represented by a single arc line) indicates that person A referenced person B but person B did not reference person A. A bilateral connection (represented by a wavy double headed line) indicates that person A and person B referenced each other, which makes that connection or relationship much stronger – it is a bit like a double bond in chemistry. The size of an individual node reveals the importance of that individual in the whole network.

This type of network analysis provides a clearer picture which allows us to see who is connected to whom and the strength of each connection (a single or bi-directional connection). In Figure 4.2 grey lines indicate who trusts whom and blue lines indicate who collaborates with whom on a regular basis. What is not shown on this initial visualisation is the level of development of any of the individuals involved, which quadrant the trust relates to, whether the individuals are coherent or chaotic, or a number of other Integral concepts. Nevertheless this simple 'system theory' type of network diagram can reveal powerful insights and track the functional fit or interactivity of various items. It shows us exactly how and to what degree each item is physically or functionally interacting with the others. As such, it offers crucial information about the Lower-Right dimension of each item mapped (as well as correlates of the other quadrants, just as, for example, an interior rational thought leaves a 'footprint' or 'correlate' in the Upper-Right brain, but cannot be reduced, or even fully seen, with mere brain activity). And such network analysis visualisations can be adjusted so that each node can represent an individual, a team or a whole organisation. As the network analysis builds, it can identify people who may not have been on the original key stakeholder list so they can be added to the assessment process.

Figure 4.2: Simple network visualisation of interactivity (collaboration and trust)

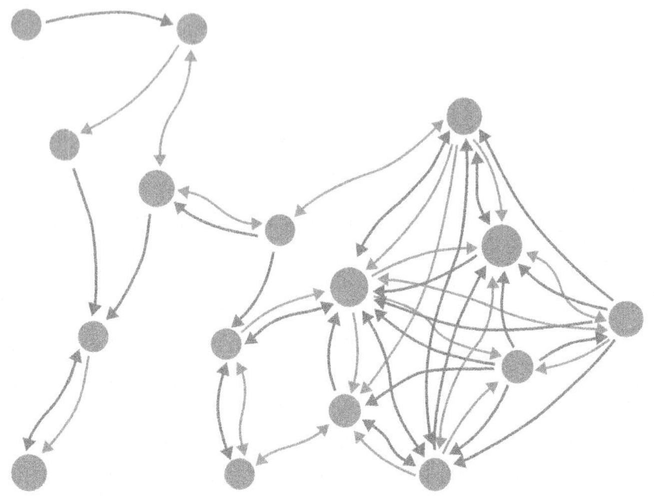

Once the data has been acquired and we can start to see the degree of connections in the Lower-Right, then it is easier to explore some of the deeper patterns of those connections in much more detail. Using 'Deep Network Analytics (DNA)', we can reveal the Lower-Right 'operating code' of the network (what Integral Meta-Theory calls 'nexus-agency') and illuminate still further who needs to be involved in finding a solution to the challenging problems we face – and many of the specific obstacles that must be overcome.

There are a number of widely used academic concepts that measure different types of deep social network analytic connections. Most of these concepts have different names such as 'tightness', 'density' or 'perstige', many of which are confusing to anyone who is not an expert or deeply immersed in the network analysis literature. Therefore to try and simplify the largely Lower-Right systems connections we have renamed these metrics to generate some clarity as to what they do and their relevance to organisations and problem solving.

Let us take a moment to explore these DNA metrics to show you how they can generate very useful insights into what is happening within our social networks. Normally when people think about their networks they tend to think simply in terms of numbers of connections. In other words – how many people are in an individual's 'little black book'? But the number of people you may be connected to may not be that important and it certainly is a poor measure of your influence or reach. A stakeholder may have thousands of contacts on LinkedIn or thousands of 'friends' on Facebook, but that does not necessarily mean the stakeholder is important or influential. 'Number of connections' thus gives us a fairly limited look at the deeper dimensions of the Lower-Right, or the depth and degree of overall interactivity. We can look deeper into the type of connections in the Lower-Right.

Figure 4.3: A further step in Deep Network Analytics (DNA)

Metric	How it is measured	What it means
Significance	No. people who referenced you	How connected you are
Symmetry	No. people you share a bi-directional ref with	Reciprocity of your relationships
Centrality	No. steps to reach whole network	How quickly you transmit to all
Clustering	No. triads you are in with bi-directional link	Strength of your alliances
Bridging	No. clusters you connect	Dependency of system on you
Influence	No. high quality connections you have	How easily you influence the system

Significance

'Significance' (and by this we mean Lower-Right significance) is simply a measure of numbers. This is the most straightforward of all metrics and is based solely on how many other stakeholders referenced you when answering those seven questions (or however many questions you have included in the set up to the analysis). Such data can give you a general initial handle on the Lower-Right or social connectivity. For example, the data shown in Figure 4.4 is taken from the top 60 people in a multinational organisation showing the number of references each person has across the different networks. As can be seen the CEO of this organisation had the most connections, 145 in total. The marketing and operations director then had the next highest number of references, followed by the finance director. In this particular company, this exactly matched the degree of impact each of these leaders is having on the business. The person who had the fifth largest number of references, and more than six other Executive Board members, is one of the rising stars of the company and had been identified as a future potential board member. This data helped to confirm the marketing executive's significance in the organisation.

Symmetry

'Symmetry' identifies how many bi-directional connections exist between one stakeholder and other people in the social network (Figure 4.5). So how many people did a stakeholder reference that then also referenced them when asked those seven questions? This DNA metric can be quite nuanced because an individual may have a bilateral connection with a person on say information but not on trust. The greater the reciprocity within a relationship the greater mutual strength of the bond (or degree of intense and constant hatred), and often suggests that the stakeholder and the other person see themselves as peers (or mortal and eternal enemies!) Figure 4.5 shows an example of high symmetry in the left-hand panel within the 'Information' network. In this example every connection is bilateral. In contrast, the right-hand panel shows the connections within the 'Stretch' network and all the

Figure 4.4: Significance visualisation

	Info	Collabn	Energy	Trust	Support	Guidance	Stretch	Total
1 CEO	12	6	46	12	11	29	29	145
2 Marketing	16	10	25	12	14	30	19	126
3 Operations	25	12	28	9	13	23	16	126
4 Finance	12	7	16	13	8	26	19	101
5 Marketing	17	15	31	13	10	10	2	98
6 People	11	10	8	17	14	12	14	86
7 Other	8	5	7	8	16	17	20	81
8 Commercial	13	8	12	5	8	17	11	74
9 People	10	9	6	16	17	6	8	72
10 Strategy	8	7	12	4	3	23	3	60
11 Operations	17	6	12	7	5	6	4	57
12 People	5	10	11	4	9	5	6	50
13 Finance	13	5	4	9	8	6	5	50
14 People	7	7	2	9	11	5	6	47
15 Finance	12	3	1	6	4	14	4	44
16 Operations	11	10	5	6	4	3	4	43
17 Finance	7	8	1	7	6	8	5	42
18 Commercial	16	11	2	6	3	3	0	41
19 Operations	12	11	10	3	3	2	0	41
20 Strategy	10	10	5	4	5	4	2	40

Figure 4.5: Symmetry visualisation

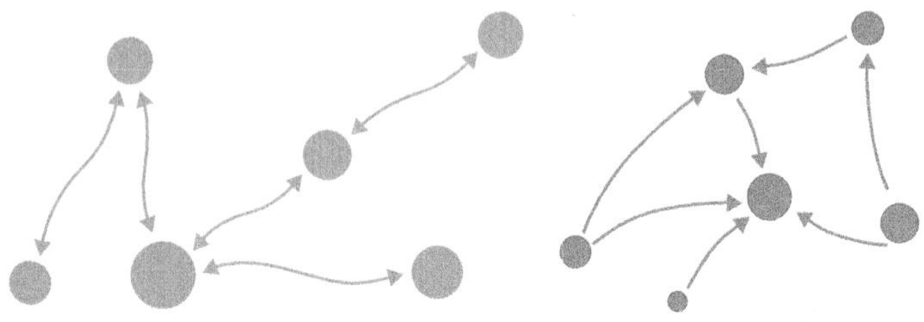

connections are unilateral, i.e. there is a low level of symmetry. Of course high levels of symmetry attest to the strength of relationships but do not reveal the belief that such strength is based on. For example, you would expect to see high levels of symmetry in a strongly fundamentalist congregation, where everybody feels everybody else is their 'brother' or 'sister' and acts accordingly. Ultimately we will need to know interiors of the people who are strongly connected to be able to determine the impact of such connections. High symmetry bonds could connect people who are deeply anti-climate-change but knowing the levels of symmetry at the outset can be extremely useful in the solution finding process.

Centrality

'Centrality' identifies how central the stakeholder is in the interactive network; that is, how many steps would the stakeholder need to make to get to the periphery of the whole exterior network (Figure 4.6). This is almost the reverse of the game 'six steps to Kevin Bacon' where someone names a person and everyone else has to connect that person to Kevin Bacon in as few steps as possible. Centrality seeks to identify how close a stakeholder is to the epicentre of the interactive network – the closer to the middle the more weight the stakeholder usually carries and the quicker they can then affect the whole network. Person 'A' in Figure 4.6 will clearly have a higher 'Centrality Score' than person 'B'.

Figure 4.6: Centrality visualisation

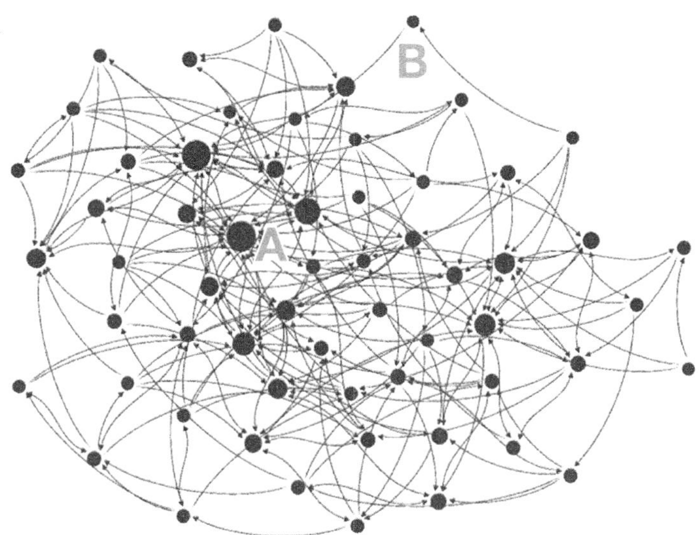

Again it must be remembered that if we only look at Lower-Right 'centrality' we do not know whether person 'B' is the most sophisticated thinker and at an Integral level of development in a predominantly egocentric or rational organization. It could be that person 'B' is more peripheral because they are operating at a higher level of development and much more leading-edge than person 'A'. Although if a highly evolved person B wants to influence a deeply ethnocentric network it would help for them to be more central.

Clustering

'Clustering' indicates the number of bilaterally connected triads a stakeholder is involved in (Figure 4.7). In other words, how many subgroups or clusters of three or more people does a stakeholder share a bilateral connection with? This indicates powerful alliances that can be extremely useful in solving problems or shifting a system or culture. In the example shown, the cluster between the same six people is visualised as part of the energy

Figure 4.7: Clustering visualisation

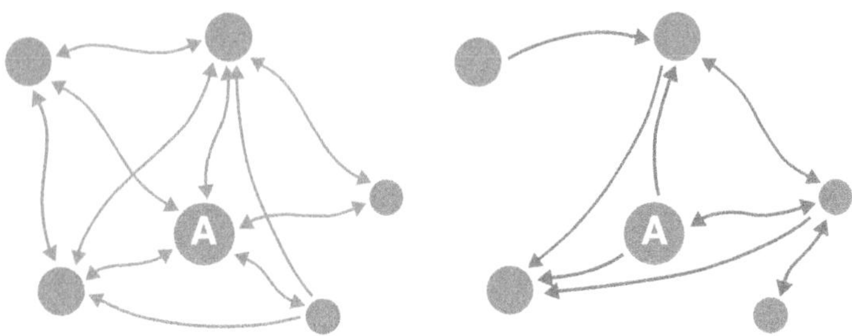

network. In the left-hand panel, person 'A' is connected to four clusters that have bilateral connections. In the right-hand panel (where we look at the collaboration connection, while maintaining the node size for energy) person 'A' only belongs to one cluster with a couple of bilateral connections. So the clustering score would be much higher in the left-hand panel compared to the right-hand panel.

Once again what we do not know from such external mapping is whether the people clustered together are positive change agents or strong resisters of the climate change agenda. When we combine such network analysis with other data that reveals an individual's development in other lines, then we can create even more useful insights that can help us drive change and transformation. So when we see 'clusters' we need to dig deeper to determine whether they are, in fact, a good thing or a bad thing, a help or hindrance to the agenda by performing a complete Integral Analysis.

Bridging

'Bridging' is also an extremely potent element of DNA because it determines whether a stakeholder is the bridge between key clusters (Figure 4.8). In climate change, for example there may be clusters of oil companies and clusters of coal companies and clusters of green energy companies, but there is also likely to be one or two stakeholders who are connected to senior

Figure 4.8: Bridging visualisation

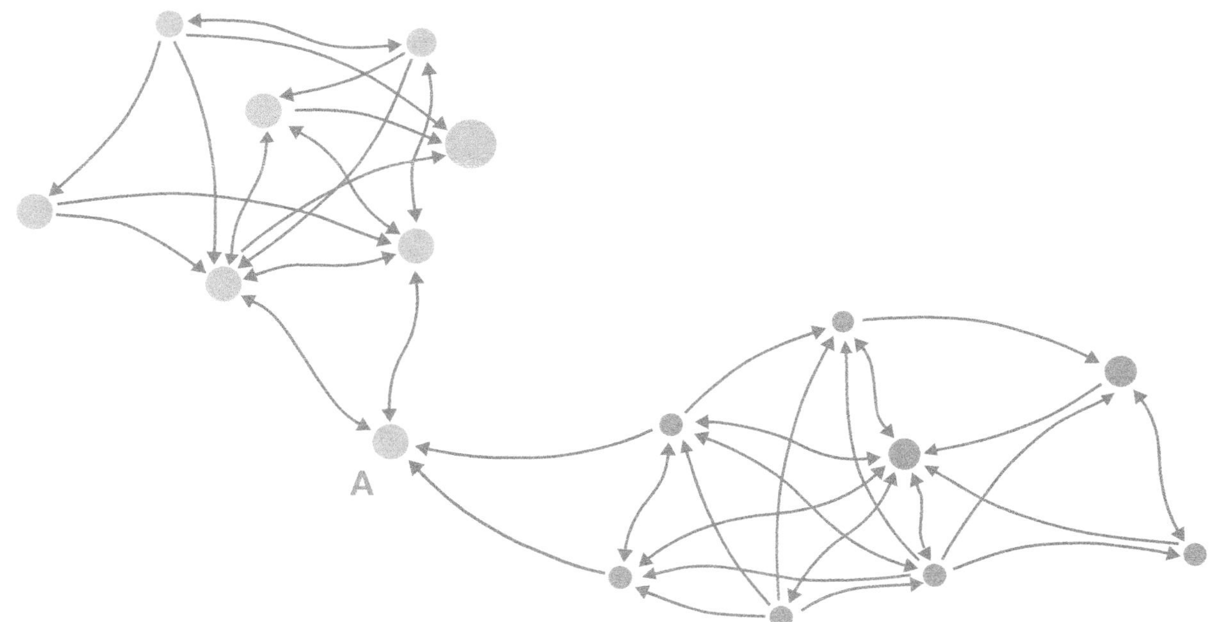

executives in each cluster. Those individuals are therefore disproportionately influential because they bridge often diverse communities within the network. It is also a strong indicator that such individuals are at Integral levels of development, in order to be able to hold various contradictory perspectives fully in awareness. If a stakeholder bridges a couple of key stakeholder groups – we only need to involve that stakeholder and that person will be able to influence both stakeholder groups without adding multiple other stakeholders to the negotiations. In the example above person 'A' is the only person from one department who bridges the two different departments. Therefore they can have a significant influence on shifting the centre of gravity in both departments on the particular network being explored (in this case collaboration).

It goes without saying that 'bridging' can be positive or negative, depending on its overall Integral Address. A great number of effective and active climate change resistors have notorious, even infamous, bridge connections. This still makes them proportionately more significant in the overall dialogue, but whether that significance will be a real help or a major hindrance depends, again, on a fuller Integral Analysis. So we must never forget to interpret this sort of network analysis in the context of people's overall Integral Address. However network analysis provides a powerful starting point and reveals the degree of interactive connectivity. Whether that is pulling in the direction of egocentric, ethnocentric, or worldcentric is not yet known and we will need additional information to know how we could drive a shift in the gravity of a network and solve a truly wicked problem.

Influence

Finally, 'Influence' seeks to identify a stakeholder's overall impact in a specific network. This DNA metric is really driven by the importance of who references that stakeholder. Thus the number of people a stakeholder is connected to may be relatively low but because the people who reference that person are highly referenced by many others this will significantly increase their influence within a network. Think of a Communications Director who alone is not that heavily connected but they have the ear and the trust of the CEO. As a result they can disproportionately impact the outcome because they have very high level of influence. A stakeholder will exert far more influence if the people that reference them are 'big fish', even if there are only one or two, than if countless 'minnows' reference the stakeholder. If Stephen Hawking references a stakeholder as the 'go-to-guy' for information in a particular scientific field, that is infinitely more influential than endorsement from a thousand high school science teachers!

Clearly the impact or influence here is that exerted on a given, specific network – which, like all phenomenon, will have an Integral Address. Think of the influence that Osama bin Laden had on Muslim fundamentalists – quite profound, but this does not make him somebody we would want on our side in too many issues. The reason we are tracking 'network analysis' in the first place is to get an indication of the functional fit, the interactivity, the connectivity – the *correlation* in the Lower-Right dimension – of any element anywhere in the Integral Frame. This is profoundly important 'orienting information' for any element in any individual, organisation, or system we are tracking. What we can never forget to do, of course, is attach that connectivity with the rest of the real universe – with the quadrants, levels, lines, states and types that will situate all of these 'connectivity items' in the rest of the overall cosmos.

Solving wicked or even highly complex problems does not require getting everyone in the room. It requires network mapping and Deep Network Analytics (DNA) so we can understand the network, rank the clout of those in that network and choose people from all populations who have the most clout within that population and across the network as a whole. But, as we have noted, such mapping only reveals the exterior dimensions of a network (Lower-Right quadrant). They do not reveal the interior left-hand dimensions or the levels of growth and maturity in the network in key lines of development of that network. Such understanding requires us to map the stakeholders themselves, in a continuing expansion of our Integral Analysis.

Map the Key Stakeholders

Once we have mapped the social network of the wicked problem, we need to conduct a much more profound and complete analysis, wherever possible, to determine the full Integral Address of each stakeholder. This gives us maps not only of the exteriors of the problem, but also of its interiors. Needless to say, the wicked problem intimately involves both of those dimensions, and both need to be taken into account for anything resembling a truly satisfactory re-solution.

In any Integral analysis, there are a very wide range of internal and external characteristics that can be brought to the final overview, map, model or view. In addition to the items just discussed, we recommend a minimum of:

- Key Stakeholder Dimensionality – does the stakeholder operate from the dimension of 'I', 'WE' or 'IT' – or integrate them all?
- Key Stakeholder Engagement via coherent vertical development – is the stakeholder coherent and what is the extent of their vertical development (their altitude) and coherence across the key lines of adult development relevant to that issue within each of those dimensions?
- Existing Stakeholder Relationships – what if any, is the nature of any existing relationships between the identified stakeholders? This includes the results of our initial Deep Network Analytics.

Key Stakeholder Dimensionality

In order to make the final stakeholder mapping we need to understand the multi-dimensional nature of the individuals we have identified as key stakeholders in the solution process. This process is two-fold – first, we need to determine if they are aware of the multi-dimensional nature of reality, and second, which dimension each key stakeholder is operating from most of the time – 'I', 'WE' or 'IT'?

For example, if a key stakeholder is almost completely focused on the 'IT' dimension, they will be consumed by what needs to get done – by the science, the data, the 'information.' As a result they may talk the good talk about all the things on the 'To Do' list that need to be completed, but unless they are aware of their interior motivation or 'I' dimension and appreciate the importance of the relational 'WE' dimension, they may not see things though. These individuals may sign a treaty or agree to a solution while in the room, but they may not drive through the implementation of any agreement once they have left the room because they may lack sufficient internal motivation to do so. Or the community they represent may decide it is legitimate to unpack what has been agreed on their behalf, a possibility that throws the whole agreement up in the air because they did not take this 'WE' dimension into account to begin with and were therefore blindsided by it.

It was this dynamic that most fundamentally derailed the Kyoto Protocol – an international treaty, which sought to commit those involved to reducing their greenhouse gas emissions on the basis that climate change was a real phenomena and that human beings were the main cause of the change. The objective of Kyoto was to reduce emissions to 'a level that would prevent dangerous anthropogenic interference with the climate system'. Although everyone in the room signed up to the Kyoto Protocol in 1997, there was little individual or collective interior commitment, so it was nowhere near as effective as it could or should have been. This is a classic example of the failure that occurs when the solution is created in the 'IT' dimension only. There was no real interior or collective commitment for the process beyond 'looking the part' and applying some window dressing to the efforts to combat climate change so the various parties could carry on doing what they were doing for a bit longer, safe in the knowledge that 'well, we agreed to Kyoto – we are taking action'.

This one-dimensional approach is a guaranteed derailer to the solution process and therefore must be identified before the stakeholders get in the room. On the other hand, recognised 'leaders' of the dialogue as it gets underway will almost always be those who have most mastered the 'WE' dimension and process, and can almost effortlessly integrate the 'WE' with the various 'I' and 'IT' dimensions that are present (and they will likely have the strongest and most influential connectivity indicators on the Deep Network Analytics). Individuals committed to their own 'I' dimension will almost always be implicitly recognised by the group and intentionally steered around. True success depends on the integration of 'I' and 'WE' and 'IT' not any one dimension.

Key Stakeholder Engagement

Next it is important to assess the verticality within the three dimensions of 'I', 'WE' and 'IT'. Chances are if a stakeholder is operating almost exclusively from the 'IT' dimension (which is extremely common in business and government) then the stakeholder will be well developed in that dimension but poorly developed vertically in the dimension of 'I' and 'WE'.

Vertical development or increasing the *altitude* across these three dimensions is the single most important factor in success in virtually any field, including solving wicked or highly complex problems. However, this *altitude development* is dramatically different from *aptitude training* or horizontal learning. The acquisition of additional skills, knowledge or experience is important but it is simply not enough, and it certainly does not step change capability. As we said in Part Two, 'horizontal development' simply 'adds more apps' whereas 'vertical development' upgrades the human operating system.

If we are serious about implementing workable solutions to the viciously complex problems we face, including wicked problems, we absolutely must upgrade the human operating system. This upgrade increases capability across the three dimensions so we can see further, understand more, become significantly more sophisticated and flexible in the way we approach and solve the issues we need to address. It stands to reason, therefore, that just how vertically developed the key stakeholders are will be a crucial factor in how encompassing and effective any agreement will be – and likewise, a serious lack of vertical development can and will derail that process. Hence the need for coherence – to ensure the stakeholders maintain potent access to the very best they are capable of at whatever level of vertical development they are operating from (and even better if that level is somewhere close to the leading edge). If an actual selection process is part of a particular gathering, a brief determinant of vertical altitude can be included in the selection parameters. Going further, if there are preparatory pre-meetings made available, individuals can register for quick courses in 'challenge and response,' Robert Kegan's term (among many other possible terms) for the process that engages vertical development. In the best-case scenarios, a significant amount of time may be spent working specifically on the vertical development of the likely participants prior to finally getting everyone in the room. This pre-meeting work can transform the chances of progress once the stakeholders meet. Any authentic vertical development work does not challenge or attack a person's particular beliefs, worldviews, or values, but simply creates a greater number of perspectives through which all of those can be viewed – and that, of course, changes everything – but gently, softly, 'off stage' and not in any violent head-on collision or attack.

Of course, in many cases, we have to work with the Integral Address of individuals as they are presented; and if this simply means working with people as they show up, and nothing more, then this would not include the opportunity to work with people in expanding their Integral capacities and altitudes. This is understood; but as the importance of overall consciousness development and evolution becomes clearer and clearer, those factors will increasingly be valued in leaders, representatives, and authorities in any field. And likewise, it is important to remember that we – various organisations, agencies, and governments – also want to present any progress made and protocols developed in a language that covers the full spectrum and array of values and worldviews, representing the numerous levels and stages of development in the broader stakeholder populations. What we are discussing here is the opportunity when a specific group of individuals from a wide range of disciplines are brought together to discuss and implement various protocols for solving the wicked problems we face. To the extent that there is some choice in the selection of the individuals that will attend, the point across the board is simple: select those with the highest, widest, greatest overall Integral Address. For every increase in every element of the Integral Frame, the odds of protocols reflecting the highest-level science being agreed to by the largest number of attendees increases proportionately.

What is an overall agreement or set of protocols anyway, except an agreement by the largest possible 'WE' collective (in the Lower-Left) to interact (in the Lower-Right) according to the behavioural dictates of that protocol. The best way to increase the likelihood of a more all-encompassing collective agreement is to increase the inclusive capacity of every individual participating in that collective. That means increasing the Integral Address of the collective, and the coherence of the individuals within that collective. Specifically, this might mean for example, working with various major lines of development to increase their overall altitude. As that expands from egocentric to ethnocentric to worldcentric to Kosmocentric, the chances of a yet larger and more inclusive 'WE' consciousness grows, thus increasing the likelihood of a widely inclusive and adopted set of protocols. If individuals remain in their own egocentric wishes or continue to represent nothing but their isolated and siloed ethnocentric group or organisation, the likelihood of an agreement that serves us all plummets.

We are simply arguing that, to the extent that there is a selection process for any meeting brought together to create items such as behavioural climate protocols, then including a potential member's overall Integral Address would be a crucial item. This Integral Address can be fairly easily determined by a panel of experts analysing any prospective member's public actions and statements; there now exist solid tests in every element – including quadrants, levels, lines, states, and types – to determine those elements in any individual with a high degree of reliability. This information would be made available to the facilitators of the process (see below) and also be used in any pre-meeting workshops that might be offered. Again, these workshops would not challenge or attack any member's beliefs, worldviews, or values, but simply give them various exercises and practices that could increase the capacity of their own awareness.

The specific goal is not to change any member's Integral Address – a person has a right to be at whatever level or dimension of the overall developmental matrix that they wish to be. A person's Integral Address is information, however, that is highly useful for any sort of viable facilitation process; and, if the particular member chooses to participate in any pre-meeting workshops that offer advancement in any areas in which they might be weak, doing so would increase significantly the likelihood of a more significant and deeper 'WE' space in which the meeting would take place. This would then increase the likelihood of a much more satisfactory resultant protocol agreement. We have spent considerable time demonstrating the real problems – even disasters—that can and do occur with lack of depth and awareness in each of the Integral elements (quadrants, levels, lines, states and types). These aspects of wicked problems lie on the side of the change agents themselves, and if we are ever to fully solve and re-solve any wicked problem, we will address not just the exterior problems but the interior problems driving the catastrophe. Either we will become consciously aware of these elements and take them into account, or we will be blindsided by them. They exist whether we are acknowledge them or not. So we either act with that awareness or wilfully ignore it which means that we wilfully choose not to solve the wicked problem. It now becomes our choice, not just our disaster and to us at least, that seems much, much worse.

All of the arguments that we have presented essentially demonstrate the importance of increasing the adequacy of each of the Integral elements – and we will put those items to conscious use, or we will continue to be smashed by them. We will have them, or they will have us. That is the entire argument. So far, they are winning, along with the wicked problems they support and often drive.

Existing Stakeholder Relationships

After the Deep Network Analytics and the overall Integral Address have been determined, it is also important to flush out any pre-existing relationships between the stakeholders – both positive and negative.

Obviously existing positive relationships are going to be less of a problem than negative relationships. In the case of climate change 'positive' would mean in favour of proactive climate change protocols, of one variety or another. Often positive existing relationship can help build intimacy and trust in the new stakeholder group of the present gathering, but the facilitator will need to be mindful of those relationships and seek to prevent cliques forming.

Negative pre-existing relationships, however, are likely to be strong hindrances to the solution process. Depending on the level of maturity or overall 'altitude' of the stakeholders involved it may be manageable. A mature human being should be able to sit down with the Devil and not feel compelled to try and annihilate the Devil; but it is a tough ask – especially if negative feelings run deep. If two or more of the chosen stakeholders have previous negative history they may refuse to be in the room with each other. In such cases compromises will need to be made because the toxicity they will create will derail the process before it has even started. Much of this lies in the hands of facilitator(s), as we will see below.

Engage the Key Stakeholders

Once the network has been mapped and the key stakeholders have been individually mapped to identify what dimension they operate from most of the time and how much verticality and coherence they currently have across the key lines of development, then those insights will determine an overall stakeholder engagement programme.

The specific form of this programme – and its degree of comprehensiveness and intensity – will vary enormously, depending upon exactly what degree of involvement the participants are willing to engage with, and the inclusiveness of the engagement itself. The general point is that some engagement with items such as individual developmental factors ('altitude') is much better than no engagement at all; and the more engagement, the better. Again, these engagement programmes do not in any way attack, challenge, or deny any person's particular beliefs, worldviews, or values; rather, such programmes simply aim to increase the degree of engagement by increasing the number of perspectives, the amount of altitude and the awareness of various items such as lines, and so on, that the person has access to. Most individuals, regardless of their level of development, find such conversations to be 'opening', 'clearing', 'freeing', 'liberating', 'clarifying.'

This step itself may seem unusual. In many cases we will be dealing with very senior, very seasoned individuals who may find the idea of additional personal growth potentially unwelcome. But if history proves anything, it proves that the current way of solving wicked problems does not work. We need change, not just in how we solve these problems but within the people charged with solving them. Our point has been, time and again, that if we are to actually work with the *complete* wicked problem instead of just partial slices of it, which is the general case, then we need to work with both the exteriors of the problem itself and the *interiors* of all of the stakeholders involved with the problem. This interior focus is the one approach that generally has *not* been taken to date, with the results obvious for all to see.

Vertical development is without question the next frontier of competitive advantage in business and represents a quantum leap in human capability that can then be turned to solving all manner of urgent and pressing issues. Robert Kegan, one of many well-known developmentalists working with this issue specifically, calls the organisations that do so 'deliberately developmental organisations', and echoes our notion that this is the leading-edge issue in organisational capacity today. This is indeed a real issue. For example, it is quite clear that, as we have previously noted, when it comes to the modern, worldcentric stage of development, some 60–70 per cent of the world's population is, to quote Kegan again, 'in over their heads' – not capable of a consciousness consistently generated by the modern stage of development.

What one version of this approach does is target very specific, highly relevant areas for development so that each stakeholder can effectively neutralise their own limiting behaviours while expanding their perspective and capability in each dimension. When all the stakeholders engage in this process of development prior to the initial meeting, then genuinely astonishing things are possible.

Of course, in today's world, there will be stakeholders who either are not given the opportunity to engage in developmental exercises or simply refuse to do so. In those situations an alternative may be found; and if not, it may be possible to reposition that person so that they are still involved behind the scenes but their rigidity or particular failings are not allowed to pollute the solution process. In any event, if their Integral Address is known, making this available to a skilled facilitator will help that facilitator to communicate more clearly with this person, and ensure that their authentic thoughts, feelings, and desires make it into the overall discussion with as much clarity and genuineness as possible. Having the Integral Address of each attendee will give the facilitator a master map to guide his or her actions with greatly increased skill.

This is something that can be done right now. The overall Integral Address of each attendee at a particular gathering can be determined and made available to the facilitators. The facilitators can then immediately and straightforwardly use the overall Integral Frame for each of the attendees as a solid meta-map to help guide and direct their facilitating process. There are already numerous consulting groups using the Integral Frame in exactly this fashion, and the results, as their own data shows, are spectacular.[2]

---

2 Among many others, there are A. Watkins, D. Hamilton, Integral Coaching Canada, 5 Deep, Meta-Integral, B. Brown, Integral Without Borders, etc.

Involve an Integrally Coherent Facilitator

Although perhaps 80 per cent of the solution to wicked problems, or indeed any really complex issue, takes place outside the room before the stakeholders ever meet,[3] once they do, the right facilitator is absolutely essential. Of course, even if various stakeholders have agreed to do pre-meeting preparatory work, a top-notch integrally informed and coherent facilitator is still required. All the network and stakeholder mapping can then be used by the facilitator on an on-going basis to navigate and negotiate the remaining 20 per cent needed for a breakthrough. It is their job to use the vast amount of data gleaned for maximum advantage. In our opinion, this means taking an Integral Approach to ensure that the solution process is not derailed by factors that remain unknown, unseen or unappreciated. The behavioural insights, for example, gleaned via Deep Network Analytics, can be used in the allocation of roles and duties in the meetings and between meetings. If one stakeholder has undeveloped information gathering skills and another has that skill as a strength or strategic strength then it would make sense to allocate information gathering to the person who already demonstrates a proficiency in that skill. In this example, the point is to match tasks with individuals who already display an advanced skill capacity central to such tasks. This requires no pre-meeting exercises or training, just the skilful correlation of a person's Integral Address with required duties – and this is a co-ordinating talent that Integral Facilitators are taught right from the beginning.

At the very start of the meet-and-greet session, the Integrally Coherent facilitator will know when to lean on the stakeholders with a level 6 pluralistic or 'human-bond' value system, who are especially effective at bringing people together and helping

---

[3] Watkins, A. 20 years of work in the field

everyone get to know each other; and when to use caution with them due to their likely deconstructive value system. When the stakeholders are in the room getting ready to strategise and create a plan, then the facilitator should be going to the stakeholders who operate at the second-tier or Integral values level, who are more driven by ideas and 'wholistic' innovation. That is not to say that the facilitator only asks those stakeholders but he or she actively focuses on those individuals to ensure that all the potentially best ideas are brought to light as early as possible – again, simply matching tasks to the Integral Address of those asked to do the task. If the facilitator started with the stakeholders focused on maintaining the status quo or driven by power, the former individuals would simply derail or dominate the conversation, the latter would continually push their opinion, agenda or point of view. When the facilitator knows all these insights about the stakeholders (i.e., knows their Integral Address), they act like a skilled orchestra conductor by using the data gleaned from the mapping phases to get the very best out of every individual stakeholder while managing the process toward solution and resolution. All of the items that often blindside typical consultants become points of opportunity for the Integrally Coherent facilitator.

These insights are also incredibly important in developing coherence and unity in the group. The primary role of the Integral facilitator is to increase the strength of the bonds within the room and help to bring about the shared space of second-person perspective, which is so critical to effective resolution. Any good Integral facilitator watches not only the second-person shared space, but the *altitude* of that space – ethnocentric 'WE' spaces derail global/worldcentric protocols more often than any other negative item.

Facilitating the Shared Space

When the stakeholders are eventually together 'in the room,' the goal is for everyone to work in the 'WE' space from a worldcentric altitude, and be able to access and operate from such a developed second person perspective. This is not a skill that many of us have naturally. As we explained in Part One, there are three perspectives – first, second and third. The most commonly used perspectives in the modern world are first and third. Stakeholders are therefore either passionately communicating from their first person 'me, my, I' perspective, where they are pushing their own agenda because they are right and everyone who does not agree with them is wrong. Alternatively they are helicoptering up to the dispassionate third person perspective by insisting that, 'the evidence states' or 'the data doesn't lie'. This third person perspective is very common in business and government because it abdicates any personal responsibility for the outcome. If the decisions do not work out, the stakeholder can blame the data and hopefully avoid being personally blamed.

If stakeholders are not permanently stuck in first or third then they may flip flop between both perspectives. In reality, however, what is often happening is that the stakeholder is moving from passionate advocacy to objective rational data which involves them cherry-picking the data that suits the passionate argument they made earlier.

But getting into second is not a simple answer. It depends on the maturity or altitude of that second person perspective. For example, in today's world, we have individuals who are stuck at the earlier stages of second-person-perspective taking. This is characterised by level 4, ethnocentric, fundamentalist, mythic-conformist views where everybody is my 'brother' or 'sister', particularly if they believe in the right God. If not, they are unbelievers, unclean, unsaved, infidels, and bound for hell or some such everlasting purgatory. Worldwide, a large majority of anti-climate believers are stuck solidly at this developmental level 4. They can step into a second person perspective of shared meaning but it is still pretty immature. The aim is to help such people find a 'WE' space that expands from just 'us' to 'all of us' – and a skilled facilitator has just that in mind with such individuals. If participants are stuck in a narrow ethnocentric-embedded identity, it is unlikely they will adopt any ideas or actions coming from some 'other' group – including the one generated at any particular gathering or meeting designed to move all of us forward. This is a central reason that an Integrally Coherent facilitator is so crucial to the success of such gatherings.

For any real progress to be made and real collaboration to occur when the stakeholders get in the room, then the facilitator must help those involved to access the gap between first and third person perspective and get into the shared space of second person perspective. Even more importantly, to make sure, once there, that its altitude is not ethnocentric but worldcentric. Most facilitators are trained to help get people into a 'WE' space, but without a fully Integral approach – including the developmental altitude – this can actually stall a meeting in an arrested development at ethnocentric-conformist, one of the worst possible, least productive, outcomes and also, sadly, one of the most common with typical, conventional facilitation processes. Without a facilitator that can help bring this about, who is able to call the stakeholders on their approach when needed and nudge them into more constructive communication space, then the discussions will almost certainly fail. Each stakeholder will hold fast to their opinion, or cling to the data, or remain embedded in the dogma of their ethnocentric identities. They will not really listen to each other, but wait for their opportunity to speak, or simply interrupt and talk over each other. We call this 'meeting popcorn' where ideas and discussion 'pop' out randomly in a meeting with no one actually listening to each other. What they almost certainly will not do is proactively build a shared commitment to find a workable solution that works for everyone (not just 'us' but 'all of us').

The second person perspective is the *shared* perspective and it is the secret to constructive and effective relationships – but only if the stakeholder group's overall centre of gravity (its altitude) is at level 5, beginning worldcentric or higher. The facilitator's primary role is therefore to foster this perspective, at such an altitude, with the key stakeholder group. Essentially this is achieved by encouraging the group to go into increased detail or pulling back to higher principles until they find some common ground that all the stakeholders can agree on. Easy to say, difficult to manage.

Think of this like a zip. When the facilitator is looking for common understanding, he or she is attempting to find where the stakeholders are connected or 'zipped'. Is the bottom of the zip undone or the top? Are there two or six teeth connecting in the zip?

We can see this dynamic in personal relationships where two people meet and the resulting sex is amazing. They are connected at the most basic physical level. That may be enough for a time, but if they are not emotionally connected or do not share the same degree of emotional sensitivity or expression, then eventually that 'relationship' will fizzle out because the zip was only connected at one point – sex. It was not strong enough to endure. At the first sign of trouble, the zip pulled apart and they went their separate ways. Alternatively two Oxford professors could meet and form a relationship, only this time the connection is not physical it is a cognitive connection. They totally 'get' each other at an intellectual level and for them the intense discussions they have are better than sex. They may also connect on behaviour as they both work in laboratories and do similar research. Plus they are driven by the same values and believe in the power of science to do good. These additional 'teeth' in the connection zip makes their relationship considerably stronger and they are better able to weather the ups and downs of the relationship. Their challenge may be to ensure any physical disconnection does not derail their relationship. So reaching a common understanding of what they want from the physical side of their relationship may be crucial to the longevity of the relationship.

In ensuring that the 'zip' is connected, it is vital to identify the points of connection and exactly where the disconnection occurs. This is where the value of an Integral Approach stands out brightly. Typical PESTLE type approaches just look for exterior connections (connections in the Lower-Right). But most central and enduring connections are interior (items in the Left-Hand). This is why the facilitator having the Integral Address of each stakeholder can be so profound – it helps the facilitator see ALL the points of both likely connection and likely disconnection, and hence they can navigate the interaction so as to strengthen the connections and mitigate or avoid the disconnections that can so often blindside the process. The disconnection may occur more in the details at a more fundamental level, or it may be necessary to pull back one or two levels and get close to the vision or purpose of any conversation to determine where the connection (or disconnection) is. The ability to work with connection and disconnection requires brilliant and artful facilitation from a highly developed expert who is gifted at creating a second person, worldcentric, Integral 'WE' space.

Even the most ardent climate change deniers probably do not want to go down in history as people who were actively involved in destroying the planet. If they realised that in 500 years they may be remembered in the same way as political tyrants are remembered today, they might indeed change their approach. If the collective come to the viewpoint that these ardent deniers are the enemy, such individuals might even conceivably end up in prison. While money can be a great insulator against the public mood, history is littered with examples of people who accumulated massive wealth only to see it forcibly taken from them if the society in which they exist determines that their actions have been excessively self-serving and destructive of the collective interest.

Besides, even the most vocal nay-sayers will be connected in the idea that they want the planet to survive for their children and grandchildren. They almost certainly already believe that they may just disagree about whether the planet is really in jeopardy and if so what to do about it. Surely everyone wants the planet to survive. A skilled facilitator will be able to go up and down levels, pan into and out of detail, in order to find 'teeth' that the various stakeholders can agree on and 'zip' together on. This is the point where an Integral Meta-Map becomes so useful.

Instead of overlooking or being unaware of most of the Integral elements, a skilled facilitator coherently applies the Integral Frame as a map of potential connection points – and potential disconnection points – instead of simply letting them play out in a hidden fashion under their own impulses and desires.

The facilitator's role is therefore to identify the variety of existing connectivity points that there are in the room between the major stakeholders, including the levels or altitudes of that connectivity. Are stakeholders connected at the basic data level or at a higher purpose level? And what are the connections and disconnections up and down the zip between the various stakeholders? Are there any clusters of people cohering around a certain point of view or value system? Are there two or three people who are connected at two or three points which make those connections stronger? If there are clusters, is there anyone who bridges those clusters? These interactions and dynamics are crucial in the on-going negotiations and the facilitator's role is to develop these bonds and foster connection and intimacy in the group. It also allows the facilitator to use the network mapping skills to understand the mini-network that has been created by the key stakeholders and how that is shaping up; and these new insights are used by the facilitator to dynamically steer the process and continually seek to connect more and more people at more and more levels.

That is where the real art of the facilitator kicks in. Facilitating second person perspective at a worldcentric altitude is a very subtle and skilled process particularly when it involves helping people move beyond their ethnocentrically embedded identities, similar to when the Church acknowledged, at Vatican II, that 'similar salvation [to Christianity's] can be had by other religions' – a clear move from ethnocentric to worldcentric, and for the first time in the Church's entire history. Some individuals can do this more naturally than others. But there are only a handful of developmentally mature, integrally informed coherent facilitators who are conscious of these perspectives. There are even fewer that are able to proactively move between the perspectives in order to clarify any misunderstanding with the intent of creating a shared view that honours all parties. The facilitator needs to understand all the critical lines of development in the room and all the levels on all those lines; be very coherent despite the incredible difficulties and challenges; and also know how to facilitate coherence in the room. They will skilfully cultivate a degree of entrainment in the room around the various lines and levels to really facilitate a solution and continue to solve and resolve the issues.

It is also worth noting that the Integrally Coherent facilitator does not need to be a technical expert in the topic being discussed, but they do need to have done their own developmental work across the key lines of development in all the quadrants (and possibly states and types).

The network and stakeholder mapping ensures that the facilitator has a good understanding of the Integral Address of each of the stakeholders in the room – where their major strengths and weaknesses lie. This includes whether they are either sufficiently vertically developed across the three dimensions of 'I', 'WE' and 'IT' or have done the work to ensure the necessary verticality. The whole point of Integral Coherence is to use these mapping processes to help business, NGOs, governments, education facilities and virtually any other organisation solve their most complex challenges and move forward quickly and efficiently. When led by a skilled Integrally Coherent facilitator, the likelihood dramatically increases that coherent vertically developed stakeholders are able to bring a new level of sophistication, innovation, speed of thought, and inclusiveness of vision to the negotiating table – as well as the social and emotional intelligence to 'play nice' and work effectively with the each other. And this potent combination – never before brought together in a single coherent frame – can literally solve virtually anything.

Other Possible Integral Elements

We have consistently mentioned 'states' and 'types' in this book. The simple point concerning states and types is that the more inclusive the map, the greater the likelihood of success in any venture. Any generally Integral Approach is a pragmatic selection among a variety of Integral elements, and while the more elements that are included, the greater the likelihood of success, this is not always pragmatically possible. We have therefore focused our argument on three of the most fundamental, most important elements, all of which should be, to the degree possible, included in any overall Integral Approach (namely, quadrants, levels and lines). But states and types definitely have their application strengths and we will simply summarise a few of them here to give the general sense and a more complete picture.

'States', as we saw during their introduction, are responsible for the process of 'Waking Up,' which is one of the two most central developmental processes available to humans (the other being 'Growing Up'). 'Waking Up' is a literal, developmental and metaphorical phenomena. Most stakeholders involved in wicked problems can discern the difference between being in dreamless sleep (but not the different depths of dreamless sleep) and being awake. They may notice that they often pass through the intermediary state of dreaming and they may even wonder about different degrees of 'awakeness'. People will often refer to being 'sleepy' or 'wide awake' for example. But 'Waking Up', in this context, does not just refer to the transition between deep sleep and being wide awake. It also refers to the different states of awakeness. So it is common for people to talk somewhat metaphorically about people not really being 'awake' (even though they are awake and talking to you). Being 'awake' in this sense is often meant metaphorically as in 'waking up to the reality of what is really going on' or 'wake up and smell the coffee'. What is being referred to is a quality of consciousness. People are awake but they are not really awake – 'the lights are on but no one is home'. What many may not realise is that this 'Waking Up' is not metaphorical it is actually developmental and being awake proceeds through a series of states of consciousness. These states are ironically often accessed using a more reflective, meditation or contemplation type of process, often with the eyes closed so they may look like someone is asleep!

The 'Waking Up' journey takes us through a series of well-established, well-defined stages from the ordinary, conventional, separate-self sense (or 'ego') all the way up to a state that is variously called 'Enlightenment', 'Awakening', '*Moksha*' (Liberation) , 'Metamorphosis', '*Satori*' (Awakening) or Gnosis (nondual enlightened awareness). The Sufis call this ultimate state 'the Supreme Identity', because it is said to be an identity of the individual with the Ground of All Being (Godhead, Spirit, Being, Emptiness). This state of Enlightenment is said to be the *sumum bonum* – the greatest good – of all human endeavours, and is claimed to put an end to all human suffering, while divulging an Ultimate Reality or Supreme Truth common to and in all sentient beings. It is said to connect people with their 'Source', their Ground and Goal, their Condition and final Truth, Unborn and Undying. This 'Supreme Identity' is universally said to include an identity not only with ultimate Spirit, but with the entire manifest universe as well – often called 'cosmic consciousness' or 'unity consciousness', a state of at-one-ment with everything that is.

The various types of 'Waking Up' experiences tend to be associated with what are known as the 'esoteric' or 'hidden' branches of the world's great Wisdom Traditions, whereas their typical, outward forms are called 'exoteric' or 'outer' and are much more widely known. The *exoteric* side of spiritual systems usually involve various sorts of mythic stories and narratives, miracles, magic and myths, tales of a Supreme Being and how one should act in order to be in a correct relationship with this Supreme Being. But the *esoteric* teachings are quite different. They are not belief systems or mythic narratives, but actual psychotechnologies of consciousness transformation – practices such as meditation that are not involved with learning new beliefs or myths, but rather focused on transcending all mental forms and concepts and directly discovering a radical identity or connection with the Supreme Reality – which is also said to be one's own True Self or Real Self. This Self is in direct contrast to what people think of as their 'self' – the 'skin-encapsulated ego,' which is merely a temporal, finite, relative and even illusory mortal coil, which is born, lives a bit, suffers much, then dies – unlike one's True Self, which is timeless and therefore eternal. This does not mean 'everlasting' but 'timeless.' To paraphrase Wittgenstein, 'If we take 'eternity' to mean, not everlasting temporal duration but a moment without time, then eternity belongs to those who live in the timeless Now'.

The methodology and practices required to 'Wake Up' to a full experience of the state of Enlightenment are actually quite rare, even in the East, and even rarer in the West. But of the two major developmental paths available to humans, the East specialises in one of them – 'Waking Up' – and the West specialises in the other one – 'Growing Up'. In fact, never in history have *both* of these developmental paths been practised together – which means, never in history have human beings trained their full potentials of development. Rather, they have specifically trained only a partial aspect of development – a fragmented, limited aspect, one path or the other path – in short, humans have trained themselves to be broken people, developed only in one or the other of the developmental paths open to them. With the recent rise of Integral Meta-Theory, both of these paths have been brought together and thus trainings in being 'whole humans' have evolved for the first time in history.

Individuals who are aware of both climate change issues and 'Waking Up' processes (including Zen, mindfulness, Vedanta, Christian mysticism, Neoplatonic practices, Jewish Kabbalah and Hasidim, Islamic Sufism, Taoism, Tibetan Buddhism, among others) strongly insist that only a 'Waking Up' process will give human beings the type of ('Kosmocentric') awareness required to deliver a breakthrough in our deep-rooted ecological divisions. The separation of the human Self from the rest of the living universe, often generates in us a sense that we are different from the universe and have some sort of right (or even duty) to rule over it, to control it, to dominate it. Without removing this deep-seated sense of separation – this subject/object duality – people who advocate the importance of 'Waking Up' maintain that all other approaches to climate change are doomed to failure, because they do not go nearly deep enough to get at the most fundamental cause – that split between human and Kosmos. Only something like an Enlightenment (and its 'unity consciousness') will be enough to place humans in their correct connection to the rest of the universe, and thus allow them to 'love the universe as you love your self' – because, ultimately, they are one and the same in the Supreme Identity. According to these advocates, this realisation of Ultimate Reality – and this realisation alone – will serve as the foundation to any real climate change that has the slightest chance of actually taking hold and sustaining permanently.

It is a very compelling argument but unfortunately the number of individuals recommending this course of action is, of course, incredibly small, simply because there are so few people who have actually traversed the overall path of 'Waking Up' – in any of its forms – and permanently discovered an Enlightenment or Awakening. On the other hand, there are a substantial number of individuals who have had temporary 'peak experiences' (Maslow) of these ultimate nondual or unity consciousness states – they are today often referred to as 'flow states', and there is a considerable amount of interest and research in these states. There is also a major branch of medicine that deals with the impact of these higher states on normal health and well-being.

There are serious environmental scholars who explicitly include states of consciousness – leading to Awakening – in their overall programmes of climate change and 'saving the planet.' These individuals are so absolutely adamant on the importance of consciousness development that they sometimes slip or even regress into 'absolutistic' thinking of ethnocentric levels. But aside from that, anybody who has had a direct experience of Enlightenment knows that such realisations are introducing them to some of the highest – if not the highest – states of being and awareness that humans are capable of.

So we include 'states' in order to cover this deeply significant element of human reality. As is always the case, exactly which of the overall Integral elements are included in any specific approach varies, and is up to the change agents or facilitators themselves driving the given approach as to whether to include them or not. Although we have not dwelt on Enlightenment states, the Integral Meta-Model has abundant room for these should individuals decide they are an important part of initiating a climate change that will really work. Of course, our opinion is that the more Integral elements are included in any approach, the greater the likelihood of the success of that approach.

The same can be said of various typologies. As we noted when we first introduced types, there are thousands of different typologies, virtually all of them giving important and useful data about any particular item being approached. Common typologies include everything from Myers-Briggs to Five Factors to Enneagram to – a mythic level 4 version – astrology. We suggested that selected typologies that particularly apply to a specific problem can be a very useful course of action. If we simply look at the typical names of, say, the nine major types of the Enneagram, we can see how different the approaches would need to be when working with different types. The types themselves are: the mediator, the perfectionist, the giver, the performer, the romantic, the observer, the questioner, the epicure, the protector. Now the notion of a type is that, generally, a person's type does not change with development – so somebody who is an observer at level 3 will basically be an observer at level 4, level 5, level 6, and so on. But you can imagine – just from the different names – how different the drives, the motivations, the defence mechanisms, and so on would be for people at those different types. These types tend to be less significant than, say, the basic altitude or level of development – a level 5 observer and level 5 romantic will have more in common than a level 4 observer and a level 5 observer

– the levels simply outweigh the types. But if you need more detail, more granularity, then those types can give you crucial information on many more differences that are present in these individuals – and tailoring a programme that will clearly appeal to one will be much more effective if all the type differences are taken into account. So do keep these possibilities in mind as you are creating any overall Integrally Coherent Map.

So the general point is that, to return specifically to the Integral facilitation process, the more completely the various members' Integral Address is determined, the much greater the number of elements – both for connection and for disconnection – the Integral facilitator will have available to weave their 'WE'-space magic. Quadrants, levels, lines, states and types – all are crucially important factors in an individual's overall Integral Address, and the more of them that are included, the much greater the likelihood of major success. Our simple reminder: abundant evidence has indicated that these elements are real, they exist, they are there; and thus we will either take them into account consciously or we will be blindsided by them – but one way or another, they will most definitely impact us – and already are, right now.

Concluding Remarks

We face significant problems in the world today. Those problems are escalating. The world we live in is changing rapidly and the complexity of the challenges we face is accelerating constantly. We simply don't have time to try and fail and try and fail indefinitely. Besides, constant and repetitive failure is soul destroying, costly and time-consuming. In many cases this repeated failure is costing countless lives. If you think about climate change, poverty, long-standing conflicts such as those between Israel and Palestine – people are dying in the thousands and hundreds of thousands because of our inability to really solve these challenges.

What we have outlined in this book is a radically different approach. An approach that identifies the key elements of human identity – each of which has an extraordinary amount of supporting evidence, but they have never *all* been brought together in a single, coherent, integrated scheme. They form the crucial elements of any wicked problem, as well as the significant items present in any change agents working on those problems. This Integral Approach further suggests that both of those phenomena must be dealt with simultaneously if any real and authentic change is to actually occur.

In terms of the real world, there is a whole range of different engagements possible using this basic Integrally Coherent Approach. If there is no pre-selection process possible – and no pre-meeting workshops offered (or if they are declined), analysis of the members' public statements and actions allows a fairly accurate determination of their overall Integral Address; Deep Network Analytics allows an understanding of their social interactivity (or Lower-Right behavioural) patterns. These alone, in the hands of a skilled Integrally Coherent facilitator, can enormously increase the smooth flow of the overall meeting process, allow a spotting of possible connection points as well as disconnection points; and suggested ways forward in creating second-person 'WE' spaces at worldcentric altitudes or higher. All of this can be done *right now* and without stakeholders participating in pre-meeting workshops or filling out any test measures. But some degree of Integrally Coherent mapping gives the facilitator a rigorous meta-map of all of the overall ingredients of the individuals participating in the meeting. This provides a true guide book to just what to expect, and not expect, from each participating stakeholder. This is an enormous advantage right from the start.

Going further, if there are pre-selection measures of this meeting put in place, then the 'DNA' and the Integral Address of potential members would be powerful indicators of whether the proposed member would contribute to a positive move forward or a negative resistance across the board; hence selections could be made with those parameters fully in mind. Further yet, the selection-process forms would allow individuals to indicate if they were prepared to engage in pre-meeting workshops when a Coherent Integral facilitator could help increase a participant's intellectual, emotional, and leadership capacities – and not just aptitudes, but altitudes. Those who engaged in the pre-work could be certain that they are likely to make the greatest contribution to the outcome.

Finally, the most advanced possibility for a best outcome would involve meetings being set up where basically all of the attending stakeholders have agreed to various types of pre-meeting workshops, where they could deliberately hone their vertical capacities and altitudes across the board in the interest of step changing the results of the process. Such a gathering would be expected to arrive at the highest-level science and the most inclusive 'WE' space agreements, across the most effective behavioural protocols possible for humans. Such a process would put into play the staggering amount of information that has been learned about human growth and development over the past 40 years, not to mention the 'Waking Up' process of the last two thousand years! The results that such an optimum process would generate can barely be imagined but would likely be truly spectacular.

Even if we achieve all of that, the selection of the right facilitators to guide the entire process is required. Being able to identify the right people for the job is crucial. Obviously they need to be Integrally Coherent with a deep understanding of the Integral Frame and a track record of working with the type of stakeholders involved, as well as an ability to maintain their own coherence while developing coherence in others. When such a skilled facilitator then uses the insights gained from the mapping process to dynamically steer the group away from potholes and into collective coherence, then we finally have a real chance to truly solve these issues, re-solve them in real time and literally transform our futures.

Epilogue

By making the Integral Meta-Theory available across virtually all human disciplines the number of different possible directions is truly limitless. To mention a few that we, the authors, are involved in, in our effort to maintain focus on the wicked problems we face and our need and ability to solve them, a series of books are already planned to follow this one. These books will be offered by both authors, with Ken continuing his world-famous string of books pioneering Integral Meta Theory itself (translated into nearly 30 foreign languages), and Alan and his colleagues pioneering their in-the-field real-world application of Integral Coherence across numerous lines, which they will present in a series of books (of which this one may be considered the Introduction). The upcoming books in the wicked and wise series will cover topics such as:

- Government
- Health
- Economy
- Education
- Food
- Capitalism

- Gender
- Trust

Ken Wilber, in graciously agreeing to co-author the first and foundational book of this series, will also be involved in several of the other offerings. If you would like to be kept in the loop regarding these various books and other titles in the series then sign up at http://www.wickedandwise.com/

Meanwhile, Ken himself continues turning out pioneering books applying Integral Meta Theory across virtually every major discipline humans engage in. He has two books shortly due out from Shambhala/Random House (Integral Meditation and The Religion of Tomorrow), as well as the much-anticipated follow-up to Sex, Ecology, Spirituality-namely, Karma and Creativity. There are some 7 books that are almost done, and those will be out shortly. He is active at several websites, including IntegralLife.com, IntegralInstitute.org, a very active group of Ken Wilber on Facebook, kenwilber.com, and CoreIntegral.com.

Alan, through his company Complete Coherence, continues to work with CEOs and senior executives in organisations around the world. He and his team have been helping to develop more enlightened leaders in business, sports, education and politics by coherently implementing different aspects of Integral Meta-Theory. This includes the development of a suite of Smartphone apps that can help us map our interior landscape and directly understand the significant influence our interior dimension has on our performance, results and wellbeing.

Ken and Alan plan on continuing their partnership works, one of the main ones being the "Ukraine Project," which can be found at IntegralSociety.org. This project came about after senior leaders in the Ukrainian government asked for "help in rebuilding Ukraine ground up, based on Integral principles"; and we are attempting to achieve just that, as friendly advisors to an Integral Society, not official office holders. You are warmly welcome to visit or even join any of these endeavours.

This is an extraordinary period in human history, where we are facing "the best of all worlds, the worst of all worlds." On the "best" side, humanity is indeed undergoing its 7th or 8th major transformation of consciousness and culture in its entire history. This transformation is however a first, the first truly integrated or Integral level of being and awareness, the likes of which has absolutely never appeared in history anywhere before this time.

On the "worst" side, the wicked problems that are rapidly engulfing us are the direct result of not using our emergent Integral potentials to directly solve these wicked problems despite the fact that these emergent Integral potentials can solve them! We don't believe that's a hype or an overstatement on our part, but a direct application of the full range of Integral dimensions to the full range of wicked elements in wicked problems. When truly wicked problems meet a truly wicked meta-model fully global in reach it dissolves the fundamental issues creating the problem in the first place - like matter and anti-matter brought together. It is no accident that global wicked problems came into existence at basically the same time as global consciousness-Integral consciousness came into being as well. They are illness and cure, problem and solution, disaster and resolution, all arising together and meant to confront each other head on-with the winner being the first one to act. Let us do everything in our power to be that first responder.

Appendices

Appendix 1: Political Dimensions of Climate Change

According to Labour peer and sociologist Anthony Giddens, the UK has 'no effective politics of climate change, especially at a national level where much of the action must happen. That is to say, there is no developed analysis of the political changes we have to make if the aspirations we have to limit climate change are to become real'.[1]

And the UK is not alone in this regard. Although 'Green' political parties have increased dramatically in membership and influence over the last decade, they are still considered a fringe party in most developed countries around the world. Most governments are dominated by left-wing and right-wing politics – each taking their turn in power.

In their present forms Labour or Democrat left-wing politics emphasise the collective and are more 'Green'-friendly than their right-wing 'business-centric' contemporaries. They rarely

---

[1] Giddens, A. (2008) *The politics of climate change*, Policy Network Paper, www.fcampalans.cat/images/noticias/The_politics_of_climate_change_Anthony_Giddens(2).pdf

go as far as the Environmental parties because they do not want to alienate business leaders and lose their votes, but are generally more willing to recognise there is an issue that needs to be addressed. Traditionally, a left-wing approach came into existence during the Enlightenment and emphasised individual rights against collectivist mythic Catholic beliefs. As everybody has noted there was eventually an almost complete turnaround in the role of government as far as the Left was concerned. What began as a level 5 modern 'individual rights' and 'human progress' orientation progressed into the postmodern level 6 stance (ironically level 6 actually disagrees with almost all of the original level 5 values – 'individual,' 'merit,' and 'progress' which are all now looked down on by postmodernist level 6). Today the Left is largely therefore an unstable mixture of both levels 5 and 6.

In its recent forms, Conservative or Republican right-wing politics emphasise the rights of business, deregulation and allowing the market to decide based on the laws of supply and demand. Traditionally, the Right represented the level 4 ethnocentric values, and its 'hard core' still tends to be fundamentalist, religious, family values, and often still ethnocentric (race, creed, religion, country). But as overall development continued to move forward, the 'progressive' branch of the Right moved forward as well, into modern level 5 individual rights (even libertarian) and economic progress, and that is where its mainstream tends to be today; although, as with the Left, the Right now has its own two fundamentally different levels (4 and 5) as the Left has its two levels (5 and 6). In both cases, getting these two branches within the same 'party' together is a constant source of turmoil and sharp disagreement, never mind trying to get all branches within both 'parties' to agree!

Both sides, of course, have their merits. The Right encourages individual and collective enterprise as a way of generating value and wealth which in turn can fuel an economy and allows everyone to prosper. The challenge of course is that business post Industrial Revolution is considered a major contributor to the climate change problems we now face – and this, in the eyes of many typical individuals, has pitted human well-being against environmental well-being. Imposing any type of sanctions or restrictions in this area would therefore be *politically* dangerous. This is where we can see cultural (interior 'WE') pressures bearing down on objective 'IT' facts. This makes acting on those 'IT' facts, even if scientifically the correct thing to do, potentially crippling to any politician proposing to do so. It is these political pressures – actually generated in the cultural norms of the Lower-Left – and not scientific pressures from the Lower-Right, that have effectively prevented widespread action on climate change.

Taking action is made even more difficult by the fact that business has not just made a great deal of money for various stakeholders, but it has also created a starving crowd of consumers. This is one of the Left's major criticisms of business (and 'capitalism' in general). As a species we are now extremely reliant on energy – most of which is created or supplied in ways that seriously exacerbate climate change. We expect to flick a switch and have access to unlimited power. We expect to be able to jump in our car and drive as often and for as long as we want. We have gadgets and gizmos, appliances and many energy-demanding comforts that we do not really want to give up. We may try and do our bit when the economy is doing well and we can afford our comforts, but during periods of economic uncertainty, when we are told that the changes we need to make will cost more, and we may not be able to plug in our iPhone every night, our collective ambivalence can skyrocket.

As a result climate change is a potentially fatal political football. No main party politician in the world would be elected by a clear majority if they sought to remind us of our need for sacrificial personal behavioural change or that we need to embrace the need to reduce our energy dependency, as President Carter found out to his cost.

The fact is it is impossible to separate politics from climate change because the narrative on planetary temperature changes depending on who holds the political power in a democracy – and particularly on the level they are coming from and the quadrant they are looking through. Not to mention the perpetual flip flop that plays out between right- and left-wing politics. A right-wing government (particularly when it draws on its level 4 values) questions the prevailing scientific consensus on the effects of climate change and often seeks to scale down the urgency of the problem and the severity of the threat assessment or shift political attention elsewhere, because if they don't they will lose political support from the business community who are keen to maintain 'business as usual'. Usually the right-wing government goes too far and is booted out of power by a disenfranchised electorate who then vote in the Left. The left-wing political party (this time drawing particularly on its postmodern level 6 values) again questions the prevailing scientific consensus on the effects of climate change but this time by seeking to scale up the urgency of the problem and the severity of the threat assessment in an attempt to bring about the changes that are needed. But *they* cannot go too far otherwise they will lose the business vote (and both the Right and the Left fight for the business vote due to the fact that both of them have one wing that embraces level 5 values. But nobody, for example, in the modern or postmodern Left ever goes after the fundamentalist religious vote, because both Left branches – modern level 5 and postmodern level 6 – thoroughly lack level 4 values and do not even pretend they want them). Almost always, whether for climate change, poor fiscal control or something else, the left-wing government goes too far and is booted out by a disenfranchised electorate that swings back to the Right – and the flip-flop cycle begins again.

Of course there are exceptions, but we can see the broad-brush politics involved are pro-business, anti-climate change action on the Right and the anti-business pro-climate change action on the Left – and neither is 100 per cent right and neither is 100 per cent wrong.

This democratic penchant for partisanship and short-termism is of course just one strand of an incredibly wicked problem which makes finding a genuine long-term consensus-built solution extremely difficult. In fact, the very nature of 'sustainability' is somewhat oxymoronic for most governments and corporations. How can we even think long term if societies, businesses and governments are dominated by short-term issues because their very survival depends on maintaining a short-term focus? In a democracy how can we create binding climate change decisions that will then override changes in government or business and not simply be reversed as soon as the 'other' political party or new CEO comes to power?

As Giddens points out, a return to long-range planning cannot mean stepping back to heavy-handed state intervention, which brings its own unique set of challenges. The role of the state, national, international and local should be to provide an appropriate regulatory framework that will steer the social and economic forces needed to mobilise action against climate change in what he calls the 'ensuring state'. In other words, the role of the state should be focused on stimulating others to action and then letting them get on with it. The ensuring state is then 'expected or obligated to make sure such processes achieve certain defined outcomes – in the case of climate change, the bottom line is meeting set targets for emissions reductions'.[2]

Of course, this depends entirely upon the state deciding in the first place exactly what any 'set targets' in any area are supposed to be. Theoretically this is best determined by taking the most comprehensive or Integral view one possibly can. This will happen in a few individuals whenever they rise to their very highest potentials. As evolution continues, the percentage of the population at Integral levels will continue to grow. Historically humanity has already progressed from states where its overall

---

[2] Giddens, A. (2008) The politics of climate change, Policy Network Paper, www.fcampalans.cat/images/noticias/The_politics_of_climate_change_Anthony_Giddens(2).pdf

centre of gravity was predominantly at level 3 (tribal), then predominantly level 4 (classical traditional), then 5 (modern), and now moving into 6 (postmodern). With each new evolutionary leap all the earlier levels remain as subcultures. The Integral levels now emerging (and already presently available in what Maslow called the 'growing tip'[3]) are the leading edge of human consciousness and culture evolution and development.

Those who are attempting to change that process – and virtually everybody is – will have the most success if they understand clearly the actual nature of the dimensions they are trying to change. They will language and present their interventions or change actions in a fashion consciously designed to resonate with, and significantly impact, the actual characteristics of whatever dimension they are intervening in. They will have more impact the more they understand the quadrants, levels, lines, states and types they are trying to change, and fine-tune their actions accordingly. (This is true whether working with molecules, individuals, organisations, or entire populations.) The more accurate they are, the more successful they will be. This includes utilising the most evolved, most senior, most leading-edge 'truths' in all the dimensions of the Integral Framework. It also includes understanding how the earlier, junior dimensions of development will interpret those leadingedge truths and languaging accordingly. In other words, the more coherent you are with each Integral element (including each quadrant and level) and the more coherently you lead from the evolutionary edge, the more successful you will be. This is the essence of an Integral Coherence approach.

---

3 Grof, S. (2007) *A Brief History of Transpersonal Psychology*, www.stanislavgrof.com/wp-content/uploads/pdf/A_Brief_History_of_Transpersonal_Psychology_Grof.pdf

Appendix 2: Economic Dimensions of Climate Change

The economic implications of climate change are enormous, far-reaching, and almost impossible to quantify. Nevertheless if we want to begin to understand the overall costs, we need to consider the multitude of issues spawned by climate change. One way of quantifying the cost is to break the problem down in terms of the impact of a temperature rise on people (including on all the dimensions in their 'I' and 'WE' domains), and specific 'IT' factors including food, water, oceans, ecosystems and weather. Any economic estimate should include the cost of the damage done by global warming as well as the cost of rectifying the problem.

Various authorities have, over the years, attempted to tot up the economic consequences of climate change. For example, according to the 2006 House of Lords Select Committee on Economic Affairs, the global one-off costs for controlling emissions and therefore the atmospheric concentrations of CO_2 will be anything from \$2 trillion to \$17 trillion. In addition the ongoing annual cost was estimated to be between \$80 billion to \$1100 billion, assuming these costs are borne in the first 20 to 50 years. In terms of cost per ton of carbon removed or avoided, the figures range from \$18 to \$80.[4]

More recently evidence has emerged suggesting that this UK government estimate massively underestimates the size of the problem, the cost may be significantly larger even to fix one aspect of climate change. For example, compelling evidence has revealed that the thinning permafrost around the Artic will cause

4 House of Lords, Select Committee on Economic Affairs (2005) 2nd Report of Session 2005-06 The Economics of Climate Change, vol. 1: Report, London: The Stationery Office Limited, www.publications.parliament.uk/pa/ld200506/ldselect/ldeconaf/12/12i.pdf

a release of methane from organic matter that is so substantial it will cost the world $60 trillion to fix the problem, or the equivalent of the total global economy.[5] This 'methane time bomb' could undermine the entire global financial system. If this methane were to be released as a single pulse the financial consequences could be catastrophic. More likely the release would be slower, creating fifty years of sustained economic damage and dire climactic consequences.

Previously it had been thought that the fact that the region around the Arctic no longer freezes in the winter would create an economic boom by allowing greater oil and gas exploration and enabling shipping routes between Asia and Europe to open up all year round. Shipping companies could cut their costs by 40 per cent as the distance travelled would be reduced by more than a third and reducing journey times by 10–15 days. In 2011 only four ships used the much shorter northern route sailing through the Bering Straits. In 2012, 46 ships took this route and in 2013, 218 ships planned to take advantage of the Arctic ice recession.[6]

But the financial benefits felt by the shipping companies are miniscule compared to the detrimental global economic consequences. The negative impact of the vanishing Arctic ice, which is now at 40 per cent of 1970s levels, will be felt right across the planet. Unfortunately many of the worse consequences will affect the developing countries in Africa, Asia and South America in the form of extreme weather, flooding and failed crop production. The fact that wealthy nations will be relatively insulated against the most severe consequences may create an even more dangerous sense of immunity as the problem may be mistakenly seen as an emerging economy problem.

---

[5] Vidal, J. (2013) 'Rapid Arctic thawing could be economic timebomb, scientists say', *The Guardian*, www.theguardian.com/environment/2013/jul/24/arctic-thawing-permafrost-climate-change

[6] Vidal, J. (2013) 'Rapid Arctic thawing could be economic timebomb, scientists say', *The Guardian*, www.theguardian.com/environment/2013/jul/24/arctic-thawing-permafrost-climate-change

The authors of the 'methane time bomb' paper, published in *Nature*, suggested that global economic bodies have massively underestimated the economic tsunami approaching us all; to date, the authors suggested global financial planners have only really acknowledged the possibility of the increased risk of oil spills as a result of increased shipping movements! Such woefully inadequate risk assessment is common when dealing with climate change. The authors state 'neither the World Economic Forum (WEF) nor the International Monetary Fund (IMF) currently recognise the economic danger of Arctic change.'

Of course, as with all wicked problems, not all stakeholders agree with the dire warnings of catastrophe.[7] But none of these scientists who reject the warnings are experts in the East Siberia Arctic Shelf (ESAS). The truth is that there is an emerging consensus among ESAS specialists based on continuing fieldwork that the danger of unprecedented quantities of methane release is very real. For example, research published in 2013 analysing a 500 000-year history of Siberian permafrost found that the tipping point for continuous Siberian permafrost thaw could be as little as 1.5°C increase in the earth's atmospheric temperature. The authors suggested that the loss of ice could 'potentially lead to substantial release of carbon trapped in the permafrost into the atmosphere.'

Let's look at the economic threat caused not by loss of Arctic ice but something much closer to home – the damage to property and infrastructure due to flooding. In the winter of 2013/2014 the south of England experienced its worst flooding in decades, costing an estimated £2.5 billion. Some estimates put the impact on the whole UK economy as high as £14 billion.[8] The south of

---

[7] Ahmed, N. (2013) 'Seven facts you need to know about the Arctic methane timebomb', *The Guardian*, www.theguardian.com/environment/earth-insight/2013/aug/05/7-facts-need-to-know-arctic-methane-time-bomb

[8] Davies, R. (2014) 'The Cost of the UK Floods', *Floodlist*, http://floodlist.com/insurance/uk/cost-of-2013-2014-floods

England is also the location of some of the finest arable land in the UK – much of which was under water for several months, wiping out crops and pushing up food prices. In fact, 'extreme weather' was cited as the single biggest challenge to food security in the UK during an Environment, Food and Rural Affairs (EFRA) Select Committee.[9] And that is true worldwide – not just the UK.

Obviously the implementation and administering of any potential solution has serious economic implications. How, for example, do we agree on an international framework for an economic response to, say, carbon trading?

Virtually all of the PESTLE systems have their artefacts, physical structures and infrastructures in the Lower-Right. They also have their motivations, purpose, goals, values to embody and protect and how much cost a population is willing to outlay in order to support them. All of those driving factors do not exist in the right-hand quadrants. Rather they exist in the Upper-Left 'I' and the Lower-Right 'WE,' quadrants. So the influence of PESTLE factors can only be fully understood by including all the quadrants in the analysis.

For example, level 6 eco-centric views have one of the lowest interests in 'profits' imaginable; they put 'planet' and 'people' massively ahead of 'profit', and usually see profit as driven by virtually nothing but ego-centric greed. Gordon Gecko's 'Greed is Good!' is the epitome of almost everything they think that level 5 is doing to ruin the planet, to ruin loving relationships between people, to ruin a 'care economy', to ruin a truly rewarding, ethical and forgiveness culture, one that will grow human beings to be their best and finest. They want a world with no ranking, no hierarchies, no domination, no oppression – a true 'partnership society' and 'care economy'. Treating the planet and all its inhabitants ethically, including renewable energy sources and

[9] Addy, R. (2014) 'Weather now biggest threat to food security', *Food Manufacturer*, www.foodmanufacture.co.uk/Supply-Chain/Weather-now-biggest-threat-to-food-security

understanding the 'limits to growth', and not oppressing any sentient beings at all, are primary drivers for this level. And the economic factors that they support will reflect these values directly. An economy driven by level 6 motivations is dramatically different from that of any other economy of any other level.

On the other hand, level 5 modern scientific rational perspective, particularly its personal forms as 'achievement', 'progress', 'accomplishment', 'excellence', sees profit as a primary, sometimes *the* primary drive for human beings. The rationale is that we all need to build sufficient financial resources so we can buy almost anything we may want. Of course, you can only buy items in the right-hand dimensions – cars, houses, liquor, medical care, food, planes, drugs, etc. – but you cannot purchase items in the left-hand dimensions – love, compassion, native intelligence, consciousness, care, etc. But individuals operating at this level often see their business' quarterly profit figure as the main driver of all economic and therefore societal activity. On Wall Street, CEOs can be legally dismissed for not meeting quarterly profit targets. But if they profoundly fail to provide a business atmosphere that supports and promotes personal growth and self-realisation in their staff, or fail to create a corporate culture that makes employees feel needed, included and engaged, or fail to adjust the range in salaries from lowest to highest in an equitable manner – no problem. No penalties at all. Modern economics as a discipline came into existence largely driven by this level (which is, after all, the 'modern level'), and the basic tenets of an economic model driven by this level still reflect a Lower-Right, 'scientific materialistic', rational-empirical systems view. In other words all individuals are viewed as having the same interior drives and are treated as single units in the great system driven by the invisible hand of self-interest. The assumption is that all people are basically motivated by money and this rather crude assumption is made into inviolable truth by level 5 economics. Of course, this economic truth is strongly challenged by economics from other levels – including a type of sharia or fundamentalist-religious economics from level 4 and a 'partnership, caring economy' of level 6.

Level 4, ethnocentric, mythic-conformist perspectives are moved by the truths as presented in their particular cultural 'mythic-literal' view. Wall Street caught on to this fact a few years ago with advertisements that said things like, 'What car would Jesus drive?' Fundamentalist religious groups are rarely directly sought as a market unless the company specifically targets them. Most businesses simply attempt not to rile a particular religious group, given the power of their boycotting capacities. Fundamentalist groups will be economically motivated to purchase items that fit with their version of divine truth; given that most of the great religions were created during the level 4 Mythic Era of humanity (at its height from around 3000 BCE to 1500 CE), many of them have an enormous number of restricted items, activities, behaviours, pursuits, ownership, vocations, and so on, making them as much a strong negative as positive force in any market. For example they often advocate no sex, no conspicuous wealth display, no erotica, no extravagant material possessions, no skimpy clothes, no alcohol, no cigarettes, no drugs, numerous dietary restrictions, limited access to various types of entertainment, no gambling, restricted days and hours of work, etc. With regard to climate change, as noted earlier, level 4 ethnocentric individuals will act in favour of climate change actions if they see them as part of a stewardship model endorsed by the leadership of their denomination. Otherwise, given the tilted slant of 'My Kingdom is not of this world', they do not place environmental issues high on their list of drives – economic or otherwise. This is why getting their leadership to adopt stewardship models is perhaps the best that can be hoped for in these cases, and is a small but significant part of any comprehensive or Integral approach (recall that some 60–70 per cent of the world's population is at ethnocentric or lower levels). In the meantime, the economic factors of this level reflect sternly the inherent limitations and specific values embedded in this developmental level. When left to its own devices, it tends to produce, even at its best, economic systems such as the feudalistic guild associations of the Middle Ages.

But all of this goes to show that economic theories that attempt to derive mathematically-based models focused on the exchange of physical artefacts and services anchored in the Lower-Right tend to completely miss what is actually driving economic behaviour in the actual world. They are powerless to predict what real people with real motivations will do in the real world – and basically fall back on versions of people acting with 'rational self-interest' – which is actually one of the least likely motivations for anybody ('rational', yes; 'self-interest', often; but 'rational self-interest', rarely).

Present-day economic models not only leave out Integral-level truths, they often do not incorporate the partial truths of other levels, even level 4, which was the beginning of introducing ethical demands into culture. Some developmental models call this stage 'TruthForce' because of its emerging desire to find universally good and true principles, such as the Ten Commandments, or the 108 vows of a Buddhist monk. But modernity (level 5) was marked by two major factors – one good, one not-so-good. The first was what Weber famously called 'the differentiation of the value spheres', by which he meant, the differentiation of art, morals, and science (that is, the differentiation of the quadrants – of 'I'/art and 'WE'/morals and 'IT'/science). When previously fused in the mythic-conformist church (of level 4), these quadrants/spheres were not free to pursue their own truths with their own methods. The churchmen did not have to look through Galileo's telescope; the Bible already told them what they would see. But the widespread differentiation of the Good, the True, and the Beautiful meant each of them could pursue their own truths and values and methods, and each of them began to make spectacular advances – the entire birth of the 'modern world.'

This differentiation has been called 'the dignity of modernity'. But within a century or so, the staggering advances of material science began to overshadow the other domains, and the value spheres not just differentiated but *dissociated* – flew apart, with science dominating the scene almost entirely. This has been called 'the disaster of modernity' (and the 'disenchantment of the world'). In particular, given this flat-land 'scientific materialism' background, the loss of morals as containing any sort of 'provable truth' meant that economics grew up in an atmosphere where 'the free market' tended to really mean 'free to do whatever it wanted' – ethics be damned – which many right-wing economic theorists still think is the only correct direction for economics to proceed. But even the staunchest believers in a 'free-market' realise, somewhere in the back of their minds, that markets are never free, and should not be. The market is not free, in the modern world anyway. For example it cannot sell human beings and yet several million human beings are 'trafficked' each year, sold in a 'free market' according to supply and demand, a perfect free-market system of catastrophic ethical horrors. Realising that the 'free market' has ethical constraints is an emerging realisation which began with 'TruthForce', and will become greater and greater as consciousness and culture become more and more inclusive. Thus the more people who are included as truly free humans, the more restrictions there are on their unethical treatment.

Nor are level 6 factors often included in present-day economic models, although there are plenty of level 6 theorists pressing for their inclusion. Factors particularly important to the postmodern multicultural values level are usually left out of most economic models, which level 6 theorists maintain distorts the models badly. Items not included in, for example, the Gross Domestic Product, include the economic value of mothering and fathering, of care-giving, of taking care of the elderly, the sick, the infirm – particularly items considered 'woman's work'. Yet the total economic value of these services has been estimated in the trillions. Another example, dear to the eco-centric views' heart, is carbon tax. Economic models do not include, in the price of any goods or services, the environmental cost that went into producing that product. What about a happiness index, as Bhutan has? The list goes on and on....

The central and crucial point that we are trying to make here is that what such exclusion reveals is that economics, like every other discipline that humans engage in, does not simply reflect a single, pre-given, same-for-all reality. What an individual calls 'reality' is co-created or co-enacted by the overall Integral matrix from which they are operating. This means that, even focusing just on levels as we have been in this particular discussion, that there are different systems of economics, politics, medicine, governance, science, cultural values, and so on, each generated by a major, different, evolutionary/developmental level of being and consciousness (we have outlined eight of those levels and have been emphasising five of them).

This varying view of reality applies as well to climate change, and more specifically to the *economic cost of climate change*, because what the economic cost actually is depends upon what you include in economics in the first place. There is not just the level 5 modern economic models that most people take as 'the one and only economics'. That economic model is as partial, fragmented, and broken as virtually any model imaginable, and calculating the 'economic cost' of climate destruction using that model alone will come nowhere close to calculating the actual damage to actual people in all the real dimensions in which they will be affected. As a cost estimate, most current economic models give only a small, partial list of the cost to some elements in the Lower-Right quadrant alone. That's it.

There are now several approaches to developing fully Integral Economic Models that are being developed, and they are already showing enormous promise – certainly covering more of the bases that actually drive economic behaviour and return than the currently used models. It is these types of models that will be needed to much more accurately take into account the economic aspects of climate change, because climate change does not affect only the Lower-Right quadrant – it affects, in one way or another, all of the quadrants (and levels and lines and states and types). For example there are significant currently ignored costs occurring from damage in the 'I' and 'WE' quadrant, such as not including a 'care economy', which ignores the billions spent in caring for individuals severely hurt by extreme weather events or not including a 'happiness index', which misses the positive values of having good, as opposed to destructive, climate. Economic models that leave these and other crucial factors out simply give us another fragmented, partial, broken view of reality, which will mislead more than illuminate.

Appendix 3: Sociological Dimensions of Climate Change

People are definitely paying more attention to climate change. It has moved onto central stage over the last decade or so. US Vice-President Al Gore's environmental documentary *An Inconvenient Truth* certainly helped to put the topic on the agenda for ordinary people and helped to raise awareness outside the scientific and academic communities. Although not always caused by global warming, significant natural disasters such as the Boxing Day Tsunami in Indonesia in 2004 and Hurricane Katrina in 2005, have served to remind us just how powerful and economically indiscriminate Mother Nature really is and how fragile we are in comparison.

Just how much of a problem climate change is and how much we as a species are prepared to do – and perhaps prepared to give up or adapt – will come down to our level of education on the subject and our access to reliable and accurate information. When we say 'accurate information' we mean data discovered and interpreted through the highest level of development presently available. We are not talking level 5 data – which gives 'systems' – nor level 6 data – which gives 'systems of systems' – we are talking level 7/8 data – which gives 'systems of systems of systems', which is the complex dimension at which the real and most impactful worldwide weather patterns become apparent for the first time.

Sciences prior to the Integral levels have simply missed this crucial data. This can still be a difficult issue, especially when you consider that certain stakeholders have deliberately sought to plant the seeds of doubt by fighting science with science.[10] When we are unsure about anything, we tend to turn to the 'experts' for advice and knowledge. Powerful stakeholder groups know this and have engaged equally credentialled experts to refute or at least cast doubt on findings, and it is this deliberate obfuscation that has further exacerbated the wicked problem. The very fact that perfectly credentialled authorities can rather easily be found to argue the opposite scientific conclusion points out, yet again, that so-called 'facts' are not just lying around out there waiting for all and sundry to casually perceive. The very notion of what is a 'fact' and what is not is significantly determined by one's level of development (in the 'I') and one's cultural background (in the 'WE') along with the rest of the Integral matrix.

The failure to grasp this has been thoroughly elucidated by postmodern theorists. For example there is a postmodern enduring 'true but partial' truth called 'the myth of the given'. The myth that there is a single, pre-given world of unchanging 'facts' and universal 'truths' that exist 'out there'. Rather, individuals will recognise and actually co-create those 'facts' so that they fit with their developmental level, cultural background, and, of course, their overall Integral matrix. This is why logic, data, and 'facts' have never been enough to change a person's level of development. The level determines the 'facts' more than the 'facts' determine the level. You cannot 'argue' a person out of their present level; and if you could, if 'facts' and data and logic were enough to convince a person to change levels, we could simply and quickly 'argue' everybody to an Integral level just like that! Instead, it is like arguing level 5 science with a level 4 fundamentalist. Evolution is denied by the fundamentalist,

[10] Oreskes, N. and Conway, E. (2010) *Merchants of Doubt*, London: Bloomsbury.

and so the scientist says, 'Well, what about the fossil record, that's unarguable!' And the fundamentalist replies, 'Oh, yes, the fossil record. The Lord created that on the fifth day.' So much for 'facts'. Growth and development is more a matter of life experience, of thoroughly tasting a level, becoming drenched in it, fully experiencing its realities and learning its basic lessons, and then slowly starting to realise its limitations, its contradictions, its inadequacies and thus beginning to open oneself to the next-higher level or dimension of development, which solves many of the problems and inadequacies of the previous level. Then, of course, the new level introduces its own problems, which will only eventually be solved at the yet next higher level, and so on, as far as we can tell, indefinitely.

'Sociology' in most Anglo-Saxon cultures means the objective scientific study of the collective dimension of human beings, their systems and structures. Other quadrants (and levels and lines and states) are sometimes included in sociology, but only if reduced to an exterior, objective, 'scientific' correlate. Thus 'consciousness' is reduced to material data bits and bytes of 'information' in the brain. An Integral sociology indeed focuses on the collective dimension, but it includes both left-hand as well as right-hand factors, and in their own terms, not reduced to exterior objective terms.[11]

One of the most noticeable shifts in modern societies that are having an impact on climate change is the shift from the focus on physical, observable effort or labour to mental, knowledge-based labour. This is a shift from exterior to interior or a move from right-hand quadrants to left-hand quadrants. In the early

[11] Academia in general refers to this as 'mixed methodology', and Integral Meta-Theory refers to it as 'Integral Methodological Pluralism' (along with 'Integral Epistemological Pluralism' and 'Integral Ontological Pluralism' – the point being that the Integral 'mixed methodology' is not merely a hash eclecticism, but a coherent and integrated Framework relating each of its elements to each other.

eras of human development, economic muscle was based on human muscle. This reliance on physical exertion, which led to the whole Marxist approach to history, gave way to a reliance on machines. This shift had profound climate change repercussions. For example, with a move away from human physical labour to machinery the need to 'own' human bodies and forced labour (actual slavery) became less alluring. So within a single century (roughly 1770-1870), a blink in historical time, every single rational-industrial (level 5) society on the face of the planet actually outlawed slavery. This was the first time that had ever happened anywhere in history. Other changes followed the shift from muscle to machine. The average advantage of greater upper body strength in males made male dominance of the productive systems less imperative, and the entire feminist movement began in earnest. This level 5 shift in reliance on machines was accompanied by changes in the other quadrants. These included level 5 cultural shifts which spoke of the 'universal rights of men' and subsequently women. These societal changes heralded in the 'Age of Reason' and all that came with it, including the slew of extraordinary modern sciences. Modernity was on us and as Marx described it we created a society 'where everything solid melts into air'. The traditional mythic-literal world with its fundamental leading edge was gone forever (although it remains in all of us and in all societies as a subculture or stage of human development).

The very emergence of 'reason' and ultimately 'multi-perspectival reason' (postmodern level 6) meant that the Machine-Industrial Age rather quickly gave way to the post-industrial 'Information Age'. All of a sudden, vocations were not about using the physical body or even machines per se, but about using the mind in information systems. The 'physical worker' was supplanted by the 'knowledge worker' as the primary mover in economic systems. This shifted the balance further from the external objective world to the internal subjective world or from the right-hand quadrants to the left-hand quadrants. In most developed countries, 'manual labour' was 'outsourced' to developing countries, where it was much cheaper than in the countries of greater development where living standards were higher.

Maslow's 'needs hierarchy' can help us understand these shifts. Put very briefly, Maslow was researching the line of needs or motivation, and he found that in all people, a person's needs tend to emerge through the levels that he named: physiological needs (our levels 1 and 2), safety needs (our level 3), belongingness needs (our level 4), self-esteem needs (our level 5), self-actualisation needs (our levels 6 and 7), and self-transcendence needs (our level 8 and higher). Remember, a central finding for Maslow, which we have made considerable use of is 'prepotency' – the fact that each higher level will fully emerge only if its immediately preceding lower level has first been satisfied. An individual's need for safety will only emerge once they are no longer starving and struggling to survive. Their need for belongingness will only emerge once their safety needs are met and so on. Since all of the basic levels of development remain in a human even after the period during which they emerged, this 'prepotent' necessity for handling all of our levels becomes a crucial component of any truly comprehensive or Integral approach. The overall human eras we are briefly examining were likewise being laid down in a prepotent fashion – so even with the emergence of modern and postmodern reason, people still had to eat, and still needed safety and belongingness, and so on. As mentioned earlier, for 'Integral Coherence', prepotency tells us one crucial item: *lack of coherence on a previous level prevents the emergence of the next-higher level.*

Such evolutionary shifts also have significant effects on the climate change agenda. As labour is outsourced to emerging economies where the ecological standards of production are lower the planetary impact changes. As societies continue to evolve the climatic impact also evolves. Social theorists are now atwitter trying to prognosticate the nature of the new coming Age. Many pull out elements from the Integral matrix that have been left out or ignored up till now and put them front and centre claiming them to be the dominant factor in the coming 'New Age'. Thus the next stage has been called:

1. Gaiacentric (or Eco-centric) – focusing on the planet and climate change.
2. Trans-humanism – focusing on Artificial Intelligence and the downloading of human consciousness into computers, thus achieving a type of 'immortality'.
3. The Age of the Singularity – where technology so outpaces human development that it essentially takes over all the most important questions – and answers.
4. The Partnership Society – where all human beings, especially the sexes, reach an egalitarian or perfectly equal status.
5. The Co-evolutionary Era – where humans, and their technology, essentially take over and consciously control the overall evolutionary process itself, thus co-creating their own futures.
6. A few prescient theorists, such as one of America's greatest sociologists, Jeffrey Alexander, refer to it as 'the Integral Age'.

There are also dozens of dystopian predictions which are essentially all sort of versions of watching *Blade Runner* while on a bad acid trip.

The point here is simply that, no matter how 'high' our human development or evolution might reach, now or in the future, these higher levels will still rest on the lower levels' fundamental needs and structures being effectively addressed. All individuals, no matter how high the level of their culture's centre of gravity (level 6, level 7, level 8, level 9, level 10…) are still born at level 1 – basic physiological needs – and have to begin their overall development at that level in any and every line that develops at all. The basic elements of every single level that has emerged to date in humans (levels 1, 2, 3, 4, 5, 6, 7, 8…) are still present and still need to be accommodated in order for growth and development to occur at all.[12] This is exactly like evolution at large, where every major element that has evolved to date is still present and still has its own requirements and realities – quarks, atoms, molecules, cells, multi-cellular organisms (through the entire Tree of Life) are still present, still demanding their own fundamental requirements which, if not met, means simple extinction for that element. This is true of all existing entities, including – of course – human beings.

Most humans, especially those in 'developed' countries, are at least vaguely aware that the life they are leading rests on a whole slew of 'lower-level' activities (and needs) that the vast number of human beings no longer know how to perform. Not to mention certain higher-level activities that are so specialised virtually nobody can do them. This became glaringly obvious on a worldwide scale for the first time with 'Y2K', the fear that, since all computers prior to that time had been programmed not to be able to flip the date to 2000, then at midnight that very day every computer in the world would break down, leaving humanity face-to-face with just how much of their lives – all the way down to food, water, and shelter – depended on computer activity.

---

[12] What changes and alters – and does not remain in existence – is the 'exclusive identification' with any one of these levels. Development starts with the self, with consciousness, exclusively identified with level 1, with physiological needs – psychoanalysis's 'oral stage'. As level 2 emerges, if all goes well, the self dis-identifies with an exclusive identification with level 1 and switches that to level 2. Level 1 remains, but not the limited view from, or identification with, that level (if there is some lingering identity with that level, then the result is not just an oral need – the simple physiological needs which will remain in existence – but there is an 'oral fixation' – a pathology due to fixation to this earlier level. The same thing happens with each level in each line – there is an exclusive identification with whatever the leading-edge is, and then a dis-identification with that limited identity and a new identification with the next-higher level; the earlier level itself remains in existence, but no longer the limited view from or exclusive identification with that earlier level. Thus, development is 'transcend and include' – the limited identification with a level is transcended and let go of; the level itself is included and integrated.

The point is that the higher the level, the more fragile it is. When building the fourth floor of a high rise it is absolutely crucial that the structural integrity of the lower floors is sound and able to support the higher floors, otherwise the entire building may collapse with the addition of each new floor. Since climate destruction most immediately (but not solely) affects the physical level – *the level of physiological needs in humans* – the impact of truly severe climate destruction could potentially wreak havoc on virtually all higher levels (via 'prepotency' – or their dependence upon lower levels all the way down to physiological).

This is rarely taken into account when forecasters attempt to determine the impact that will result with things like food shortages, water shortages, dramatically inclement weather making shelter difficult, and so on. Such factors are most often judged simply for the impact of their own lack, and not by also taking into account the 'prepotent' impact those shortages could potentially have on virtually all higher levels. Alternatively, higher levels are not thought of on their own at all. It is simply assumed that the material/biological world constitutes the entire or sum total realities of a human being, and thus their destruction is utterly identical to all higher-level destruction as well. For us, a complete lower-level destruction might indeed take all higher levels with it, *not because of direct identity, but rather prepotency.* An Integral account looks carefully at all of these factors because they are significant.

Should fairly severe physical shortages start to impact higher levels, whether they be emotional, mental or spiritual, the wealthy (the owners of knowledge, things, or land) will have the first call on scarce resources; followed by the general 'knowledge workers'; then the 'physical workers'. The sociological stresses and class warfare that this could generate might even be hard for Marx to imagine. If we start to see more widespread crop failures impair food supply, the consequent sociological unrest could create a rapid escalation of dramatic challenges as the very fabric of society (and its 'higher levels') comes under pressure. According to the World Bank, rising food prices have caused 51 food riots in 37 countries since 2007 and more are expected.13 Much of the hike in food prices that is causing this social unrest is a consequence of severe weather events such as the Russian wheat crisis of 2010.

There are numerous other sociological factors that can massively impact climate change, such as population rate increase – the sheer number of people on the planet that need feeding (the pressure of physiological needs starts exactly here). If climate change is indeed being accelerated by human beings, then the fact that there are now almost 8 billion people living on the planet is clearly a cause for concern. But whatever the exact outcome of societal changes they are all just another example of an Integral maxim, which is that 'all things are connected, to one degree or another, to all other things'. An Integral approach to these issues watches 'all other things' very carefully.

Appendix 4: Technological Dimensions of Climate Change

When you unpack some of the depressing statistics on climate change, one of the main sources of counterbalancing optimism is technology. It is often argued that we are an incredibly inventive species and will come up with new ideas that will save us from disaster such as the waterless washing machine,[14] 3-D printing of

[13] Adams, M. (2014) 'World Bank warns of food riots as rising food prices push world populations toward revolt', *Natural News*, www.naturalnews.com/045369_World_Bank_food_riots_emergency_preparedness.html#

[14] Zolfagharifard, E. (2014) 'The (almost) WATERLESS washing machine: System uses plastic beads to clean clothes – and it's more effective than detergent', Daily Mail, www.dailymail.co.uk/sciencetech/article-2548677/The-washing-machine-WITHOUT-water-System-uses-tiny-plastic-beads-clean-clothes-works-better-detergent.html

everything from food[15] to body organs,[16] and the 12-volt house.

But the reality is that the technological components of climate change are so diverse and complex, we do not really know how business, markets and consumer needs will change and how innovations will impact us. Is it possible that we could get weaned off products and services that contribute to climate change? It is possible, but our willingness will depend on a variety of different factors such as price, performance and accessibility (let alone each person's ability to make changes in the dimensions of 'I' and 'WE').

The potential benefits of technology are often cited when we consider research and development in alternative fuels. But whether we capture the benefit from 'green' technology is inextricably linked to economics and the profit motives of big business. For example, in 1963 the German car company Daimler Benz invented an electric car capable of 53 miles per day, which even by today's standards would probably be enough for 80 per cent of car users. In the early 1970s, Honda invented a workable hybrid car, and in the 1980s Renault had a fully functional electric car.[17] Had we adopted those technologies back then, the wicked problem of climate change may not be as wicked as it is now. Unfortunately, most consumers were completely unaware of these developments. Although the technology was there the political, economic, and commercial will to even tell consumers about these options was not. The 'IT' was present but the 'I'

---

[15] Wong, V. (2014) 'A Guide to All the Food That's Fit to 3D Print (So Far)', *BusinessWeek*, www.businessweek.com/articles/2014-01-28/all-the-food-thats-fit-to-3d-print-from-chocolates-to-pizza

[16] Williams, R. (2014) 'The next step: 3D printing the human body', *The Telegraph*, www.telegraph.co.uk/technology/news/10629531/The-next-step-3D-printing-the-human-body.html

[17] Semler, R. (2005) Leading By Omission Lecture to Massachusetts Institute of Technology (MIT) Sloan School Of Management.

and the 'WE' were big holes. Why? Because the adoption of these technologies would have inevitably meant a move away from fossil-fuel dependent economies and impaired the profits of the global energy companies as well as vehicle manufacture and all the associated industries. In fact, many of the global energy companies have been actively suppressing alternative fuel technologies for years, often by acquiring new tech start-ups and shelving their innovations to protect their own profits.[18]

Technology is often cited as the great hope for our salvation. For those that either do not believe climate change is a real phenomena or do not think it is nearly as bad as scientists say it is, technology will be the saviour. The dream is that someone somewhere will invent some amazing technology that will pull the planet back from the brink of disaster and all will be well with the world.

Then there is, as mentioned in Part One, the whole 'singularity' argument. Put forth most visibly by Ray Kurzweil[19] this is the idea that the rate of technological growth and innovation will soon reach an almost infinite rate. This will not only make machines that are smarter than humans, but machines that will start asking – and answering – their own questions about the most urgent solutions required by the whole planet. There is no doubt that technology inherently advances and evolves; that more and more sophisticated technological inventions are constantly – and will constantly – unfold; that many intractable problems today will seem child's play to tomorrow's technology. But it is also true that, as some of the above examples made clear, that whatever 'IT' technologies may exist, the 'I' and the 'WE' will be fundamental in determining whether they are employed or

[18] Vesperman, G. (2008) *Energy Invention Suppression Cases*, www.commutefaster.com/EnergySuppressionGV.html

[19] Kurzweil, R. (2013) *How to create a mind: The secret of human thought revealed*, New York: Penguin Books.

not, and exactly how. Problematic here is the tendency to forget the interior 'I' and 'WE' dimensions, and see all advance and progress occurring in the 'it' dimensions. But advances in the 'IT' dimension do not guarantee overall advances – moral, ethical, aesthetic, developmental, or otherwise – in the 'I' and 'WE' dimensions: what good is it if the Nazis have the singularity?

The trans-humanism movement goes so far as to see human beings as obsolete, soon to be replaced by having their consciousness downloaded into computers, thus living essentially an immortal life (let's hope no one drops your computer). The biggest problem with this idea is the same problem we find with many 'solutions' – it fails to embrace all quadrants, levels, lines etc. In short, it is partial. Right now, if we downloaded the typical computer 'geek's' consciousness – somewhere around level 5 or 6 – into an unchanging frame that would preserve that consciousness indefinitely, that would in effect end the evolution of consciousness to Integral and even higher levels (which are certainly to follow Integral levels). For all eternity, humanity would be stuck at a level of consciousness that even a thousand years from now will be viewed as virtually infantile in comparison (assuming climate change does not destroy the planet before then). This would arguably be the single worst catastrophe in humanity's history – and it is billed as its great saviour. How much evidence do we need that less-than-Integral approaches can be utterly disastrous?

In the meantime, we may need to count on exterior-quadrant technology to help with climate change issues, but most effectively only if combined with increasing developments in the interior quadrants as well. Growth and development needs to be Integral across all dimensions if the greatest benefit – and least catastrophe – will ensue. Exterior sustainability requires interior sustainability to hold it in place – all four quadrants develop together, or they do not develop at all.

Appendix 5: Legal Dimensions of Climate Change

There are those that argue that the only way to tackle climate change is to drive through legal changes enforced by government. This perspective certainly has some merit, but the execution of that perspective is notoriously difficult.

So far the international agreements that have sought to limit the greenhouse gases responsible for climate change, such as the Kyoto Protocol, have been ineffective. Kyoto put the obligation to reduce current emissions on developed countries on the basis that they are historically responsible for the current levels of greenhouse gases in the atmosphere. As a result, it set binding emission reduction targets for 37 industrialised countries. Unfortunately, although the US signed the Kyoto agreement in 1998, it needed to be ratified by the Senate. The Senate had already passed the non-binding Byrd-Hagel Resolution which effectively stated that it was *not* the sense of the Senate that the United States should be a signatory to the Kyoto Protocol. The US Senate expressed disapproval of any international agreement that 1) did not require developing countries to make emission reductions and 2) 'would seriously harm the economy of the United States'. Consequently, although Kyoto was signed by President Clinton, it was never submitted for ratification.

In 2011, Canada, Japan and Russia stated that they would not take on further Kyoto targets and Canada withdrew, citing Canada's liability to 'enormous financial penalties' under the treaty unless it withdrew.

Further attempts at a global agreement, whether legally binding or not, have followed, including the Bali Climate Change Action Plan of 2007 which brought together 10 000 participants and representatives from over 180 countries to the UN Climate Change Conference in Copenhagen in 2009 to the 17th Conference of the Parties (COP 17) to the UN Framework Convention on Climate Change (UNFCCC) in Durban, South Africa in 2011. There is plenty of talking but very little agreement or resolution, which of course makes resolving climate change on a global level almost impossible.

It helps to remember that the actual legal system, the set of formal laws itself, is a network of Lower-Right structures, rules and behavioural regulations. These both express, and are driven by, particular sets of Lower-Left cultural ethical standards. That is, interior 'WE' agreements as to how we ought to exteriorly behave – not restrictions on what we inwardly, silently think. We are free, interiorly, to think whatever we want but there are restrictions on how we exteriorly act and behave. Thus, with the rise of worldcentric level 5 Reason and its universal fairness 'regardless of race, colour, sex, or creed', individuals could still think whatever they wanted in the privacy of their own home, including hating pagans, hating infidels, hating unbelievers, but people are no longer allowed to publicly burn witches! Thought is free, behaviour is governed. When laws are put into place from the leading-edge of evolution at that time, a person does not have to be able to understand those laws or why they are there; but they do have to behave as if they did. They cannot force themselves to understand, but they can control their behaviour, and that is what the law demands. Thus, at level 4, it might be law that a thief has his hand cut off; at level 5, that he pay a fine and serve a prison sentence. Neither one of those individuals has to understand exactly why this is the law, but they do have to behave accordingly – namely 'do not steal.' In short, laws govern collective behaviour in the right-hand quadrants, and not thoughts or beliefs in the left-hand although left-hand factors such as cultural beliefs and ethics drive the right-hand laws.

As that example also makes clear, the nature of the law depends in large part on the nature of the worldview or cultural belief system. A level 4, ethnocentric, authoritarian culture with fundamentalist religious beliefs tends to have fairly harsh retribution for legal infringements, from cutting off hands of thieves to stoning women to death for adultery. A level 5 worldcentric culture, which aims to treat all people fairly 'regardless of race, sex, colour, or creed', will tend to have more 'rational' and 'humane' treatments although individuals from level 6 still tend to see many of them as barbaric, especially the death penalty. The point is that it is not just the formal laws in the Lower-Right, but the collective ethics in the Lower-Left that tend to determine what laws are put into place to begin with; and as ethics evolves (which they do), so our laws evolve as well, embodying those interior views.

Keeping all of this in mind, what is required for a worldwide environmental ethics that can be embodied in laws or protocols, includes, first, presenting the scientific facts as disclosed by the highest level of evolution generally available. In today's world, that means science done at the Integral level (which indeed grasps 'systems within systems within systems') and then interpreting those facts using a more fine-tuned approach according to the values and beliefs of each major level of development.

As examples, we will focus on the four most prevalent levels in today's world, which all together account for 80–90 per cent of the world's population at this time (2015). They are from higher to lower: level 6 – postmodern, pluralistic, relativistic, multicultural, eco-centric. The Integral view from level 7/8 would be 'downwardly interpreted' in order to resonate with level 6 by putting it largely in planet-centric ethical terms, where the correct action is to honour the planet and all of its inhabitants equally and fairly. Level 5 – rational-scientific-business-progress-achievement would be 'downwardly interpreted' in terms of understanding that the switch to renewable fossil-free fuels can actually increase profit. Renewables are dropping rapidly in price, more and more investment organisations are divesting themselves of fossil-fuel companies so progress in the future will be fossil-fuel-free progress. Level 4 – traditional, mythic-literal, conformist, fundamentalist would be downwardly interpreted' into terms of the stewardship model, with humans seen as being the divinely empowered stewards of the creation given to humans to oversee. Those first three approaches are the three value sets present in the 'Culture Wars', and thus summarise the basic value arguments that humans in most places are engaged in. The fourth and last – and 'lowest' – is the egocentric, power, self-safety level which would be 'downwardly interpreted' as steps necessary to keep *you* alive.

One of the basic difficulties we have now, and an issue that directly contributes to the wickedness of this problem, is a lack of differentiation. Thus in most environmental arguments the individual argues two sets of items as if they were but one and the same thing, fusing two different items together in an indissoluble single item. They argue the scientific facts (as they see and interpret them from their level), and they argue those facts as being inherently bound to the values-level that they believe is absolutely true. Other groups, coming from other value-levels, might have a chance in agreeing on certain scientific facts, but they will never agree to the values that the other group is insisting also be agreed with. This brings the discussion to a grinding halt. And that is where it has remained to this day. That problem is the major reason why there has been no major environmental agreement protocol for political, not scientific, reasons. The politics, the mix of those four value systems, and their deep disagreements (not to mention differences in the rest of the Integral matrix), makes the facts pale in comparison and in importance. Since facts and logic are not strong enough anyway to change levels, the discussions end there.

That is why, in a strange and ironic fashion, there is actually a silver lining in allowing the situation to get this bad – it becomes harder and harder for any level to ignore for level 3 reasons (i.e., the situation is so bad it is quickly coming to a life-and-death scenario) and with it the entire debate is reduced to a level 3 argument. The data itself will increasingly become impossible for any level to deny. Under those circumstances, sometime in the relatively near future, a binding global protocol will very likely be put into place – driven by level 3, and worded in a mixture of level 5 and 6 terms (the two highest leading-edge levels dominant in today's world). Of course any level will be free to interpret that protocol in any fashion they want (as they will do so in any event).

Appendix 6: Environmental Dimensions of Climate Change

Obviously the whole issue of climate change is in large measure an environmental issue. For this particular wicked problem, this perspective is a central territory of the challenge we face. Kyoto and Bali-style agreements, the EU targets, together with carbon markets, the activities of businesses and NGOs will all be extremely important in any attempts to solve it, particularly if organisations manage to differentiate the scientific facts from their own value systems. All of those types of organisations and activities represent the full four levels largely driving today's world, so there is enough of the population represented by them to make any ensuing protocols widespread enough, if each can keep its values to itself; not get rid of them, just keep them to themselves.

Individuals also play a role in exerting pressure on politicians and businesses to push through change. They might simply argue the facts as they understand them, but more likely will be acting through and pressuring the various representatives, who they have already chosen because they have the same value systems. Thus Catholics will want the Pope to represent them; business people may have joined a right-wing political party to represent them; a 'Gaia-centric' person will have joined any number of environmental organisations – and they will exert pressure through their value systems, not outside them. This is unavoidable in the real world.

As more and more particularly destructive 'facts' come to light, then more individuals will be moved to begin to take various sorts of environmental action. Making accurate information available and ensuring the source of that information is *trusted* is critical here. Take deforestation of land to produce palm oil, for example. Palm oil is a commodity and is therefore bought and sold on the stock exchange. It is found in thousands upon thousands of products, and often the manufacturer itself does not even know where the palm oil comes from. They may not know whether the palm oil they purchase is resourced responsibly, or whether vast tracts of land are being turned over to palm oil production at the expense of the environment and local wildlife such as orang-utans. Alternatively, manufacturers may know where it is coming from and simply choose to hide behind the veil of ignorance and secrecy regarding the source of their raw materials. The value-level of their various customers is also key here. Do consumers have the desire to turn away from products they like to other, more ethical but expensive products? A level 5 person who initially acts ethically and does 'the right thing' still might end up reverting back to the original product, choosing to turn a blind eye instead, when money is tight.

An individual's interest in environmental causes will be almost totally motivated according to the overall Integral matrix as it is operating in them (including quadrants activated, levels reached, lines used, and so on). Sean EsbjornHargens and Michael Zimmerman, in a brilliant book called *Integral Ecology*,[20] which is a direct application of all elements of Integral Meta-Theory to ecological and environmental issues, point out that there are today over 200 different schools of ecology. Using the overall Integral Framework, they are able to integrate the essentials of all of those schools into an Integral overview. As for an individual's selection of which of these schools they would belong to, or simply the individual's overall environmental beliefs and viewpoints, they demonstrate that particularly influential is the developmental level the person is at. Accordingly, they offer eight levels of environmental interest and motivation which match our eight levels precisely. We are, after all, both using the same meta-model and are both focused on the four most common and prevalent levels in today's world, accounting for some 80–90 per cent of the worldwide population.

---

[20] Esbjorn-Hargens, S. and Zimmerman, M. (2011) *Integral Ecology: Uniting Multiple Perspectives on the Natural World*, Boston: Shambhala Publications.

But the point is that, again, there simply is not one environment, a single environment, a pregiven environment, which has one and only one correct representation or map or model; there are literally as many 'environments' as there are elements in the Integral Framework (at least). Esbjorn-Hargens also wrote a superb paper where he points out that, once again, there is not a single item called 'climate change', but rather as many 'climate changes' as there are methodologies used to explore climate change realities.[21] He points out that, 'No single method (e.g., level) can by itself "see" or reveal climate change in its entirety'. Only by using an Integral Framework can we get a complete handle on the full extent of the challenge that climate change presents.

We have been focusing on the subjective side of the street in individuals and in cultures, their values, needs, motivations, ethics, pointing out how each different level generates, co-creates or co-enacts a different reality. The same is true, of course, for the objective side of the street as well. Each evolutionary or developmental level or dimension brings forth a different reality, a different set of 'facts', data, existing worlds, actual entities. Nothing short of an Integral approach to both of these can begin to encompass the totality of what is actually occurring in real people in the real world. And our point in all of this is that wicked problems are wicked primarily because they are not approached from an equally wicked, complex, encompassing, multi-dimensional Integral stance.

---

[21] Esbjorn-Hargens, S. (2009) 'An Ontology of Climate Change: Integral Pluralism and the Enactment of Multiple Objects', Journal of Integral Theory and Practice, vol. 5, no. 1 [Online] http://s3.amazonaws.com/integral-life-home/Hargens-OntologyOfClimateChange.pdf [30 June 2015]

Biographies

Alan Watkins is recognized as an international expert on leadership and human performance. Over the past 18 years he has been a coach to many of Europe's top business leaders. Alan is currently the CEO of a leadership consultancy, Complete Coherence, that work to develop enlightened leaders in all walks of life. His company is particularly focused on working with leaders and executive teams in large multinational organisations and helping them to make a more positive impact on all our lives.

He is an inspiring and entertaining keynote and TEDx speaker and was the sole 'expert' in a BBC1 series, Temper your Temper, where he coached ten people with anger issues live on TV. As well as his work with global business leaders Alan advised the GB Olympic squad, coaches and athletes prior to London 2012. He continues to work with them in the run up to Rio in 2016.

Alan was originally trained as a physician at Imperial College in London and worked for 11 years in the UK's National Health

Service. He also worked for a year as a physician in Australia and a year in academic medical research in the USA. An integrationist at heart he ended up in neuroscience research before leaving medicine to work on a more global stage. In addition to his medical degree Alan also has a first class degree in Psychology from the University of London and a PhD in Immunology from Southampton University, UK. He has written numerous scientific papers in peer reviewed journals on a wide variety of subjects and many book chapters. He has written two book of his own and has three more out this year.

He lives with his wife and their four boys in Hampshire, England.

According to Jack Crittenden Ph.D., author of Beyond Individualism, “The twenty-first century literally has three choices: Aristotle, Nietzsche, or Ken Wilber.” If you haven’t already heard of him, Ken Wilber is one of the most important philosophers in the world today. He is the most widely translated academic writer in America, with 25 books translated into some 30 foreign languages. Ken Wilber currently lives in Denver, Colorado, and is in the process of writing and publishing half a dozen new books.

What makes Ken Wilber especially relevant in today’s world is that he is the originator of arguably the first truly comprehensive or integrative philosophy, aptly named “Integral Theory.” As Wilber himself puts it: “I’d like to think of it as one of the first believable world philosophies....” Incorporating cultural studies, anthropology, systems theory, developmental psychology, biology, and spirituality—it has been applied in fields as diverse as ecology, sustainability, psychotherapy, psychiatry, education, business, medicine, politics, sports and art.

In short, the Integral Approach is the coherent organization, coordination, and harmonization of all of the relevant practices, methodologies, and experiences available to human beings. Wilber states: "You can't [realistically] honor various methods and fields, without showing how they fit together. That is how to make a genuine world philosophy."

In 1997 Wilber founded the Integral Institute, which is the first organization fully dedicated to the advancement and application of the Integral Approach in relation to contemporary global issues.

In 2007 Wilber co-founded Integral Life, a social media-hub dedicated to sharing the integral vision with the world wide community.

In 2014 Wilber co-founded Source Integral and began developing the Integral Society initiative, which in collaboration with recognized global experts, will demonstrate how to develop human societies in the most comprehensive manner possible.

Ken Wilber is Ubiquity University's inaugural chancellor.

Index

Complete was founded in 2004 by Dr Alan Watkins, drawing on his background as a physician and neuroscientist.

Alan felt compelled to start his own company to expand the alleviation of suffering. By transferring his skills from the medical world to the business world, Alan found he could positively impact the lives of many, many more people.

Since it began, Alan and the Complete team have helped thousands of leaders, teams and organisations to grow with transformational coaching and development programmes.

Find out more at:
www.complete-coherence.com

Made in the USA
Las Vegas, NV
06 January 2023